America Online® FOR DUMMIES®

6TH EDITION

by John Kaufeld

IDG BOOKS WORLDWIDE

IDG Books Worldwide, Inc.
An International Data Group Company

Foster City, CA ◆ Chicago, IL ◆ Indianapolis, IN ◆ New York, NY

America Online® For Dummies®, 6th Edition

Published by
IDG Books Worldwide, Inc.
An International Data Group Company
919 E. Hillsdale Blvd.
Suite 400
Foster City, CA 94404
www.idgbooks.com (IDG Books Worldwide Web site)
www.dummies.com (Dummies Press Web site)

Library of Congress Catalog Card No.: 99-66698

ISBN: 0-7645-0670-6

Printed in the United States of America

10 9 8 7 6 5 4 3 2 1

6B/RQ/RR/ZZ/IN

Distributed in the United States by IDG Books Worldwide, Inc.

Distributed by CDG Books Canada Inc. for Canada; by Transworld Publishers Limited in the United Kingdom; by IDG Norge Books for Norway; by IDG Sweden Books for Sweden; by IDG Books Australia Publishing Corporation Pty. Ltd. for Australia and New Zealand; by TransQuest Publishers Pte Ltd. for Singapore, Malaysia, Thailand, Indonesia, and Hong Kong; by Gotop Information Inc. for Taiwan; by ICG Muse, Inc. for Japan; by Intersoft for South Africa; by Eyrolles for France; by International Thomson Publishing for Germany, Austria and Switzerland; by Distribuidora Cuspide for Argentina; by LR International for Brazil; by Galileo Libros for Chile; by Ediciones ZETA S.C.R. Ltda. for Peru; by WS Computer Publishing Corporation, Inc., for the Philippines; by Contemporanea de Ediciones for Venezuela; by Express Computer Distributors for the Caribbean and West Indies; by Micronesia Media Distributor, Inc. for Micronesia; by Chips Computadoras S.A. de C.V. for Mexico; by Editorial Norma de Panama S.A. for Panama; by American Bookshops for Finland.

For general information on IDG Books Worldwide's books in the U.S., please call our Consumer Customer Service department at 800-762-2974. For reseller information, including discounts and premium sales, please call our Reseller Customer Service department at 800-434-3422.

For information on where to purchase IDG Books Worldwide's books outside the U.S., please contact our International Sales department at 317-596-5530 or fax 317-596-5692.

For consumer information on foreign language translations, please contact our Customer Service department at 1-800-434-3422, fax 317-596-5692, or e-mail rights@idgbooks.com.

For information on licensing foreign or domestic rights, please phone +1-650-655-3109.

For sales inquiries and special prices for bulk quantities, please contact our Sales department at 650-655-3200 or write to the address above.

For information on using IDG Books Worldwide's books in the classroom or for ordering examination copies, please contact our Educational Sales department at 800-434-2086 or fax 317-596-5499.

For press review copies, author interviews, or other publicity information, please contact our Public Relations department at 650-655-3000 or fax 650-655-3299.

For authorization to photocopy items for corporate, personal, or educational use, please contact Copyright Clearance Center, 222 Rosewood Drive, Danvers, MA 01923, or fax 978-750-4470.

is a registered trademark under exclusive license to IDG Books Worldwide, Inc. from International Data Group, Inc.

America Online® For Dummies, 6th Edition

Cheat Sheet

Top Emoticons and Abbreviations for Chatting

When you use the America Online chat rooms to communicate with other members, you may want to express yourself in ways that mere words can't accomplish. Use emoticons to convey the facial expressions and body language that accompany spoken conversation but are a little hard to type. Abbreviations enable you to use familiar phrases without typing the entire phrase. (You can find more info about emoticons and abbreviations in Chapter 28.)

:-)	Smile, you're on America Online.	AFK	Away from the keyboard
:-D	Big smile. The sun shines brightly on you today.	BAK	Back at the keyboard
;-)	Wink, wink. Nudge, nudge. Just kidding.	BTW	By the way
:-(	Frown. Just got the phone bill, eh?	IMHO	In my humble opinion
:-o	Mr. Bill. Oh, no!	LOL	Laughing out loud
		ROFL	Rolling on the floor laughing

Macintosh and Windows Shortcut Keys

Group	Function	Macintosh	Windows
Editing	Cut	⌘+X	Ctrl+X
	Copy	⌘+C	Ctrl+C
	Paste	⌘+V	Ctrl+V
	Undo	⌘+Z	Ctrl+Z
Mail	Compose new mail	⌘+M	Ctrl+M
	Read new messages	⌘+R	Ctrl+R
People-related	Locate AOL member online	⌘+L	Ctrl+L
	Get info (user profile)	⌘+G	Ctrl+G
	Send an Instant Message	⌘+I	Ctrl+I
Navigation	Go to a keyword	⌘+K	Ctrl+K
	Make current window a Favorite Place	None	Ctrl++ (plus sign)
	Custom Favorites⇨My Shortcuts items	⌘+1 to ⌘+0	Ctrl+1 to Ctrl+0
Documents	Stop incoming text	⌘+. (period)	Esc
	Save a document	⌘+S	Ctrl+S
	Print a document	⌘+P	Ctrl+P

...For Dummies®: Bestselling Book Series for Beginners

FOR DUMMIES

BESTSELLING
BOOK SERIES

America Online® For Dummies,®
6th Edition

Cheat Sheet

Local America Online Access Numbers

Fill in the blanks and use this section as a handy reference guide for your AOL access numbers at home and on the road.

Location	Phone Number	Modem Speed	Network
Main local access			
Alternate local #1			
Alternate local #2			

A Few Favorite Places

Record your Favorite Places to go in America Online. Each line has room for the keyword that takes you there and a short description of the area. (Refer to Chapter 23 for details on how to modify your personal My Shortcuts menu in the Favorites toolbar button.)

Favorite Place	Keyword	Brief Description

Screen Names and Passwords

Use this space to record your America Online screen names and passwords. An AOL account can have as many as five screen names. (If you fill in the Password area, be sure to keep this card in a safe place!)

Screen Name	Password	Screen Name	Password
Primary			

IDG BOOKS WORLDWIDE

...For Dummies®: Bestselling Book Series for Beginners

About the Author

John Kaufeld got hooked on computers a long time ago. Somewhere along the way, he discovered that he *enjoyed* helping people understand how computers worked (a trait his computer science friends generally considered a character flaw but that everyone else seemed to appreciate). John finally graduated with a B.S. degree in management information systems from Ball State University and became the first PC support technician for what was then Westinghouse, outside Cincinnati, Ohio. He learned about online services in the Dark Ages of Telecommunication (the 1980s) by guessing, failing, and often doing unmentionable things to his modem.

Since then, John logged more than a decade of experience in working with normal people who, for one reason or another, were stuck using a "friendly" personal computer. Today, he runs Access Systems, Inc (a computer consulting firm) and LinguaPlay (a very fun little division of Access Systems, at www.linguaplay.com). He also conducts seminars for up-and-coming Internet entrepreneurs, and writes game reviews for InQuest Gamer magazine in his copious free moments.

John's other IDG Books titles include *Games Online For Dummies, Access 2000 For Dummies, Access 97 For Dummies,* and too many other database books to still qualify him as a normal human. He regularly uses America Online (where he's known as JKaufeld) and other online services. He loves to get e-mail and valiantly attempts to answer every message arriving in his mailbox.

John lives with his wife, two children, one marginally lovable American Eskimo dog, and (most delightfully) *no* canary in Indianapolis, Indiana.

ABOUT IDG BOOKS WORLDWIDE

Welcome to the world of IDG Books Worldwide.

IDG Books Worldwide, Inc., is a subsidiary of International Data Group, the world's largest publisher of computer-related information and the leading global provider of information services on information technology. IDG was founded more than 30 years ago by Patrick J. McGovern and now employs more than 9,000 people worldwide. IDG publishes more than 290 computer publications in over 75 countries. More than 90 million people read one or more IDG publications each month.

Launched in 1990, IDG Books Worldwide is today the #1 publisher of best-selling computer books in the United States. We are proud to have received eight awards from the Computer Press Association in recognition of editorial excellence and three from Computer Currents' First Annual Readers' Choice Awards. Our best-selling *...For Dummies®* series has more than 50 million copies in print with translations in 31 languages. IDG Books Worldwide, through a joint venture with IDG's Hi-Tech Beijing, became the first U.S. publisher to publish a computer book in the People's Republic of China. In record time, IDG Books Worldwide has become the first choice for millions of readers around the world who want to learn how to better manage their businesses.

Our mission is simple: Every one of our books is designed to bring extra value and skill-building instructions to the reader. Our books are written by experts who understand and care about our readers. The knowledge base of our editorial staff comes from years of experience in publishing, education, and journalism — experience we use to produce books to carry us into the new millennium. In short, we care about books, so we attract the best people. We devote special attention to details such as audience, interior design, use of icons, and illustrations. And because we use an efficient process of authoring, editing, and desktop publishing our books electronically, we can spend more time ensuring superior content and less time on the technicalities of making books.

You can count on our commitment to deliver high-quality books at competitive prices on topics you want to read about. At IDG Books Worldwide, we continue in the IDG tradition of delivering quality for more than 30 years. You'll find no better book on a subject than one from IDG Books Worldwide.

John Kilcullen
Chairman and CEO
IDG Books Worldwide, Inc.

Steven Berkowitz
President and Publisher
IDG Books Worldwide, Inc.

*Eighth Annual
Computer Press
Awards ≥1992*

*Ninth Annual
Computer Press
Awards ≥1993*

*Tenth Annual
Computer Press
Awards ≥1994*

*Eleventh Annual
Computer Press
Awards ≥1995*

IDG is the world's leading IT media, research and exposition company. Founded in 1964, IDG had 1997 revenues of $2.05 billion and has more than 9,000 employees worldwide. IDG offers the widest range of media options that reach IT buyers in 75 countries representing 95% of worldwide IT spending. IDG's diverse product and services portfolio spans six key areas including print publishing, online publishing, expositions and conferences, market research, education and training, and global marketing services. More than 90 million people read one or more of IDG's 290 magazines and newspapers, including IDG's leading global brands — Computerworld, PC World, Network World, Macworld and the Channel World family of publications. IDG Books Worldwide is one of the fastest-growing computer book publishers in the world, with more than 700 titles in 36 languages. The "...For Dummies®" series alone has more than 50 million copies in print. IDG offers online users the largest network of technology-specific Web sites around the world through IDG.net (http://www.idg.net), which comprises more than 225 targeted Web sites in 55 countries worldwide. International Data Corporation (IDC) is the world's largest provider of information technology data, analysis and consulting, with research centers in over 41 countries and more than 400 research analysts worldwide. IDG World Expo is a leading producer of more than 168 globally branded conferences and expositions in 35 countries including E3 (Electronic Entertainment Expo), Macworld Expo, ComNet, Windows World Expo, ICE (Internet Commerce Expo), Agenda, DEMO, and Spotlight. IDG's training subsidiary, ExecuTrain, is the world's largest computer training company, with more than 230 locations worldwide and 785 training courses. IDG Marketing Services helps industry-leading IT companies build international brand recognition by developing global integrated marketing programs via IDG's print, online and exposition products worldwide. Further information about the company can be found at www.idg.com.
1/24/99

Dedication

To Jenny, whose smile lights my days. I couldn't do this without you.

To J.B. and the Pooz, for understanding that sometimes *two* books happen at the same time. Ready for some Young Jedi action?

To my friends and compatriots at IDG Books Worldwide, Inc., for the opportunity of a lifetime.

Thank you, one and all.

Author's Acknowledgments

I think I finally figured out why book acknowledgments are always kind of philosophical. It's because the author has just spent most of the past two weeks (and particularly the preceding 72 hours) on a constant caffeine high and is now devoting a large portion of his time to preventing his brain from floating off into space.

Luckily, that's not going to happen to me. I've got a hat on (and it has a chin-strap).

First, I want to thank my project editor, Kyle Looper, without whom this book simply wouldn't be. Thanks for picking up the ball in the middle of the game, and running to the goal in the face of impending deadlines, unforeseen changes, and the peculiar brand of "fun" which surrounds every AOL beta.

Extraordinary thanks also to my technical reviewer, Matt Converse, who made extra-special-sure that the book is actually correct. Without Matt's help, I *never* could have kept the book moving in a sane, orderly fashion. Arrrrgh, matey!

Further up the Editorial Food Chain, thanks to Diane Steele for being one of the best folks to work with on the planet. Way out at the other end of the known world, thanks to Steve Hayes (my acquisitions editor) and Andy Cummings (who runs the Acquisitions Department Asylum).

At America Online, particular thanks go to Kimberly McCreery, who won the PR lottery and got me as a contact. Extra-special "You're the greatest" thanks to Adam Bartlett, Jon Brendsel, Steve Dennett, and Reggie Fairchild, who rank just below Ben & Jerry's Chocolate Chip Cookie Dough Ice Cream in my world.

Another *huge* round of kudos and chocolate goes to the great team of folks in Members Services and Technical Services who took the time to help me make this book all the better: Marc Blackwood, Ben Brown, Kristie Cunningham, Philip Fleet, Keith Jenkins, Charlier Knadler, Martha Lemondes, and Wes Turner. And, of course, a special tip of the hat to Steve Case for the original vision that spawned AOL.

Finally, my sincere appreciation to The Sunday Refugees (another round of Formua De, anyone?), who remind me a little more every day of what *community* really means. Champagne wishes and digital dreams to (in alphabetical order) Art, Barb, Cap, Jen, Lau, Myst, Nick, Ren, Rho, and all the other online friends and acquaintances who helped me maintain a few shreds of sanity while writing this book. Let's JKPARTY, y'all!

Publisher's Acknowledgments

We're proud of this book; please register your comments through our IDG Books Worldwide Online Registration Form located at `http://my2cents.dummies.com`.

Some of the people who helped bring this book to market include the following:

Acquisitions, Editorial, and Media Development

Senior Project Editor: Kyle Looper

(*Previous Edition: Rebecca Whitney*)

Acquisitions Editor: Steve Hayes

Copy Editor: Constance Carlisle

Technical Editor: Matt Converse

Associate Permissions Editor: Carmen Krikorian

Editorial Manager: Leah P. Cameron

Media Development Manager: Heather Heath Dismore

Editorial Assistant: Beth Parlon

Production

Project Coordinator: Regina Snyder

Layout and Graphics: Amy Adrian, Kate Jenkins, Barry Offringa, Jill Piscitelli, Doug Rollison, Brent Savage, Brian Torwelle, Maggie Ubertini, Dan Whetstine, Erin Zeltner

Proofreaders: John Greenough, Marianne Santy, Rebecca Senninger, Toni Settle

Indexer: Anne Leach

Special Help
Emily Perkins, Ryan Rader

General and Administrative

IDG Books Worldwide, Inc.: John Kilcullen, CEO; Steven Berkowitz, President and Publisher

IDG Books Technology Publishing Group: Richard Swadley, Senior Vice President and Publisher; Walter Bruce III, Vice President and Associate Publisher; Joseph Wikert, Associate Publisher; Mary Bednarek, Branded Product Development Director; Mary Corder, Editorial Director; Barry Pruett, Publishing Manager; Michelle Baxter, Publishing Manager

IDG Books Consumer Publishing Group: Roland Elgey, Senior Vice President and Publisher; Kathleen A. Welton, Vice President and Publisher; Kevin Thornton, Acquisitions Manager; Kristin A. Cocks, Editorial Director

IDG Books Internet Publishing Group: Brenda McLaughlin, Senior Vice President and Publisher; Diane Graves Steele, Vice President and Associate Publisher; Sofia Marchant, Online Marketing Manager

IDG Books Production for Dummies Press: Debbie Stailey, Associate Director of Production; Cindy L. Phipps, Manager of Project Coordination, Production Proofreading, and Indexing; Tony Augsburger, Manager of Prepress, Reprints, and Systems; Laura Carpenter, Production Control Manager; Shelley Lea, Supervisor of Graphics and Design; Debbie J. Gates, Production Systems Specialist; Robert Springer, Supervisor of Proofreading; Kathie Schutte, Production Supervisor

Dummies Packaging and Book Design: Patty Page, Manager, Promotions Marketing

◆

The publisher would like to give special thanks to Patrick J. McGovern, without whom this book would not have been possible.

◆

Contents at a Glance

Cartoons at a Glance

By Rich Tennant

page 283

page 71

page 259

page 233

page 163

page D-1

page 7

Fax: 978-546-7747 • E-mail: the5wave@tiac.net

Table of Contents

Part II: The Basics of Online Life *71*

Chapter 6: Doing the Screen Name Tango
(And the Parental Control Two-Step) *73*

Chapter 7: Navigating the System and
Marking Your Favorite Destinations *97*

Foreword

Several years ago, we founded America Online, Inc., with a simple objective: to make online services more accessible, more affordable, more useful, and more fun for people from all walks of life. And that formula appears to be working. America Online is now the largest consumer online service in the nation.

That success has been driven in large part by remaining faithful to our original charter: making online services accessible to everyone. In designing the service, we wanted to make it as intuitive as possible, meaning everybody from Fortune 500 executives to elementary school students could surf throughout our many departments. We wanted to make the software easy to install and use, and, as a result, new America Online customers are usually up and running in less than 15 minutes. Try doing this with your VCR.

We've also worked hard to continually add new services through strategic partnerships with content providers. If it seems as if America Online is in the business sections of major newspapers on an almost daily basis, it's because we are; we are adding new content to our service at an incredibly rapid pace and have no plans to slow down.

And still there's more: With increased interest in the Internet and the World Wide Web, we are upgrading our Internet gateway to permit AOL subscribers full access to this network of networks and all it has to offer. And it's all there at a simple, affordable price.

But as good as we've been at making the service simple to operate, the sheer volume of information available has made the online world akin to trying to tour the Smithsonian in one day. That's where this book, America Online For Dummies, 6th Edition, comes in. Although we think America Online is already "dummy-proof," John's book makes AOL just that much easier to enjoy. And enjoy you will as we continue to add unique new services, sign on more content providers, and expand AOL subscribers' access to the Internet.

As you'll discover, America Online is a living, breathing, electronic community that bridges the lives of all our members in an engaging, interactive format. Every day, tens of thousands of AOL subscribers go online and scan their stock portfolios, talk to friends, make airline reservations, read their favorite magazines and newspapers, and actively participate in discussions about hundreds of different topics. We provide the framework; beyond that, America Online is shaped by the collective imagination of its participants.

How often do you get take part in a revolution? A new interactive communications medium is emerging, and it will change the way we live, work, and play. America Online is at the forefront of this revolution, and we invite you to join us in shaping this new medium.

Steve Case, President and CEO
America Online, Inc.

Introduction

∙ ∙

*H*i — welcome to the neighborhood!

That probably wasn't the first thing you expected to hear when you joined America Online, but it's just the first of many surprises awaiting you. America Online is quite different from those *other* online services. Luckily for you, *America Online For Dummies,* 6th Edition, is equally unique.

This book is your friendly tour guide and road map to an intriguing corner of the digital world. You can find everything you need to get started with (and get the most from) the friendliest and fastest-growing online service in the United States: America Online. The best part is that you don't need to be some normalcy-challenged computer technoid to make sense of it all. *America Online For Dummies,* 6th Edition, is written in plain language — the way everyone talked back when *computers* interfaced and *people* had conversations. This book is designed to give you the information you need quickly so that you can get back to the fun stuff at hand.

Don't just take my word for it — jump on in and discover what's here for you. I think that you'll be pleasantly surprised.

Who I Think You Are

To know you is to understand you, and goodness knows, if I can't understand you, I can't help you. With that statement in mind (a challenge in itself), here's what I know about you:

- ✔ You're either interested in America Online or are now using it (and are feeling the effects).
- ✔ You use an IBM-compatible or a Macintosh computer.
- ✔ You have a modem attached to your computer, or connect to the Internet through a cable modem or other high-speed access.
- ✔ You care more about dinner than about modems and computers *combined.*
- ✔ Terms such as *bps, download,* and *Internet* nip at your heels like a pack of disturbed Chihuahuas.

If these statements sound familiar, this book is for you.

Although the book's instructions are geared primarily toward the Wonderful World of Windows, Macintosh users still benefit from the *America Online For Dummies* Channels Directory, plus all the content information in Parts III, IV, and V. When the America Online 5.0 software for the Macintosh *finally* arrives, the instructions in Parts I and II should help, too.

It's All English — Except for Parts in "Geek"

Whenever you're working with America Online, it's kind of like being in a two-way conversation: You give commands to the system, and the system displays messages back at you (so be careful what you say!). This book contains stuff about both sides of the conversation, so keep in mind the following ways to help you figure out who's talking to whom:

```
If the text looks like this, America Online is saying some-
thing clever on-screen that you don't want to miss. World Wide
Web sites and other Internet addresses also look like this.
It's the computer book version of the high-tech computer look.
```

If the text looks like this, it's something you have to tell America Online by typing it somewhere on-screen. (Remember to be nice — no yelling.) If you need to choose something from a menu or from one of the funky drop-down menus that pop out from underneath some of the toolbar buttons, the text shows some options separated by an arrow — for example, Mail Center⇨ Write Mail. It means that you should choose the menu or toolbar button marked Mail Center and then click the Write Mail option. None of the menu items and toolbar buttons share the same name, so don't fret about clicking the wrong thing.

Because you're using America Online in a Microsoft Windows environment, you also must deal with the mouse. In this book, I assume that you know the following basic mouse maneuvers:

- ✔ **Click:** Position the mouse pointer and then quickly press and release the mouse button (specifically, the *left* button, if your mouse has two to choose from).

- ✔ **Double-click:** Position the mouse pointer and then click twice — basically, two regular clicks. (Remember that the people who designed this stuff weren't hired to be clever.)

- ✔ **Click and drag:** Position the mouse pointer and then press *and hold* the mouse button as you move the mouse across the screen. As with other mouse actions, use the left button if you have more than one. After the mouse pointer gets to wherever it's going, release the button.

✔ **Right-click:** Click the right mouse button. The most popular place to use the right mouse button with America Online is in an e-mail message or Instant Message. Right-click in the area where you write the message to see a pop-up menu of cool options (see Chapter 6 for more about that).

If all this mouse stuff is news to you, I wholeheartedly recommend picking up a copy of *Windows 95 For Dummies,* 2nd Edition, or *Windows 98 For Dummies* (both by Andy Rathbone), or *Macs For Dummies,* 6th Edition, by David Pogue (all from IDG Books Worldwide, Inc.).

Frolicking (Briefly) through the Book

This book is organized into six distinct parts and a special directory. To whet your appetite, here's a peek at what each section contains. Pay special attention to the *AOL For Dummies Channels Directory.* It's your roadmap to the best content on America Online.

Part I: Driver's Ed for the Digital Traveler

This section answers the stirring questions "Just what the heck *is* America Online, and why do I care?" Part I gives you a broad overview of what the whole service is about. It explains what you generally need to know about online services, walks you through some cool ways to plug America Online into your day, points out the features and highlights of the America Online access software, and gives you some pointers for making the place a little more like home. In short, it's kinda like digital driver's education.

Part II: The Basics of Online Life

As part of their quest to join society, people learn many basic skills — things like walking, talking, ordering in a restaurant, balancing a checkbook, and julienning a potato into french fries (although I somehow skipped that particular session in the school of life).

Likewise, to take your place in the online world, you have to know how to handle the basic tools of this new realm — and that's what Part II is all about. It starts by creating your online persona, and then continues with navigating through the digital world and remembering your favorite online hot spots, and expressing yourself through the basic online communication tools (e-mail, chat rooms, Instant Messages, and message boards).

Part III: Diving into the Fun Stuff

The questions I hear most often from both new and existing America Online members are straightforward: Where's the way-cool online information? Where are the best chats? I'm getting hungry — where's the kitchen? The chapters in Part III deliver the goods by focusing on the what's-out-there side of online life. You uncover and explore the lively, topical, and up-to-date America Online content areas; hack, slash, and blast your way through the games; take a trip on the Internet; and fill your computer with new software (courtesy of the voluminous America Online file libraries).

Part IV: Going Your Own Way

This part is especially for you — well, for you, your kids, your neighbors, and various broad strata of the country's entire populace. You see, this part has a chapter for just about everyone. That's the whole point of Part IV: to give you a view of America Online from whatever unique perspective you may have, whether as a parent, a student, a small-business person — or something else. Rather than describe the broad scope of America Online, Part IV turns the telescope around and pinpoints places to go depending on *your* particular interests.

Part V: Secret Tricks of the AOL Gurus

Shhh. I don't want *everyone* to hear about this part. Well, at least I don't want *them* to hear about it just yet (you know how spurned technoweenies behave sometimes). Part V contains the collected wisdom of many America Online experts. It's filled with tips and goodies for making your America Online connection truly come alive. Customizing your member profile with new categories and tweaking the toolbar until it's uniquely yours are just two of the cool technotricks documented in this part. Enjoy!

Part VI: The Part of Tens

It just wouldn't be a *...For Dummies* book without The Part of Tens. In this section, you find tips for getting the most from your America Online experience, code charts that decipher the sometimes peculiar comments in the chat areas, ways to find help when your connection doesn't work, and places to visit when the urge to explore takes hold of your mind. It's a potpourri of things to brighten your digital day.

America Online For Dummies Channels Directory

In yet another attempt to keep you from completely shorting out when faced with all the stuff America Online has to offer, the helpful folks at America Online organize all the content areas into a series of channels. *America Online For Dummies Channels Directory* — a unique book-within-a-book — takes you for a trot through all the channels, introducing you to the goodies within each one. You find out what's available on each channel and in each channel's departments (subsections of a channel, just like departments within a large store). Plus, you uncover tips for making the most of each channel's special features or content.

Icons, Icons Everywhere

To make finding the important stuff in the book a little easier (and to help you steer clear of the technical hogwash), this book has a bunch of icons scattered throughout. Each icon marks something in the text that's particularly vital to your online existence. Here's a brief guide to what these little road signs mean:

If you see a Remember icon, get out your mental highlighter because the text is definitely worth bearing in mind, both now and in the future.

You can benefit from my experience (both good and bad) whenever you spy a Tip icon. Whether it marks a trap to avoid or a trick to make your life easier, you can't go wrong heeding a Tip.

Like it or not, I have to include some truly technical twaddle. To shield you from it as much as possible, I mark the techie stuff with this icon. If you see this turkey, flip — don't lazily turn — to the next page. Really, it's better for everyone this way.

If you need to do something that's just the tiniest bit dangerous (such as walk the trail into the Grand Canyon while blindfolded and on laughing gas), this icon tells you to proceed with caution. Pay close attention to these warnings; they mark the most dire of pitfalls. (Don't worry; they aren't too frequent on America Online.)

It's Time to Get Started!

The beauty of a ...*For Dummies* book — apart from the friendly yellow cover and the cute little Dummies guy — is how it presents information. Unlike many books on the market, you don't have to read *America Online For Dummies,* 6th Edition, in chapter-by-chapter order. Sure, you *can* do it that way (after all, it is your book), but the information in here comes out just as easily whether you march sequentially through the chapters or bound and romp from topic to topic. The choice is yours, driven by the needs of your quest for knowledge.

Either way, go on out there and have some fun — and keep this book handy, just in case you need a little help now and then.

Part I
Driver's Ed for the Digital Traveler

The 5th Wave
By Rich Tennant

"It's a free starter disk for AOL."

In this part . . .

Driver's education class is the only thing holding this country together. It's a massively shared experience. Everyone, at one time or another, learns how to drive. And we all do it with white knuckles the first time, thinking that 20 miles per hour is kinda fast and that maybe we ought to ease it down to a nice, pedestrian 10 miles per hour for a while.

The first time you face the vast plains of the online world, that old memory may rise up. Gripping the disks with white knuckles, you wonder whether 56,000 bps is just a little fast and perhaps you should just run the modem at 14,400 bps until you get the hang of it.

Hey — it's going to be okay. The truth is that you can surf the Internet, hold an interactive conversation with people all over the country, and receive files from a computer that's 7,000 miles away without knowing (or caring to know) the details of how it all works.

This part gives you an overview of what this crazy America Online thing is all about and what it can do. It also offers some tips for getting comfortable in your digital habitat and a note or two about working and playing well with others online.

Get ready for the ride of your life. Now, where did I put those car keys?

Chapter 1

What You've Gotten Yourself Into (And What You Need to Get Out)

*P*erhaps you just bought a new computer and happened across a stray icon labeled America Online. Or maybe your parent, child, or significant other decided that it was time for you to join the online revolution and endowed you with all the goodies this revolution requires. Or perhaps you don't quite know what to make of all this talk about the information superhighway and worry that you're getting left behind at a rest stop.

For a good understanding of what the term *online* means and where America Online fits into the equation, start here. This chapter explains the introductory stuff, and prepares you for that first trip into the online world. (Don't panic — the journey itself starts in the next chapter.) For now, kick back and get ready to understand what your parent, child, or significant other has been talking about all this time.

What Online Really Means

What is this "*Internet* online service" stuff, anyway? Does it have something to do with the information superhighway? Do you even care? Why or why not? Please write a detailed answer on the inside cover of a matchbook and then set the whole thing on fire, watching with pleasure as it burns to a crisp. Don't you feel better now?

If you do, you're not alone. Many people feel apprehensive about this mysterious electronic world you're entering. Take heart, though, because online services and the Internet used to be much more mysterious than they are today. Don't worry if the whole concept seems more than a little bizarre to you right now. That's okay; the reaction is normal. Those feelings prove mainly that you're not a nerd. Congratulations on passing the test!

Back to the question at hand: What is an online service? Conceptually, it's much like cable TV. With cable TV, you buy a subscription from your local cable company and hook your television into its network with a funny-looking box that freaks out sometimes. From there, a special wire connects the box to a wall socket.

If the technology does what it should, you turn on the TV and choose from among a wide variety of programming, depending on your interests. When it doesn't work, the problem may be in your TV, in the brain-dead little box, or somewhere between your wall socket and the cable company itself. At the end of the month, you get a bill that you grudgingly pay, all the while wondering whether cable TV is really worth all the time and money you spend on it.

With a few clever substitutions, the cable company example also describes America Online (and those other online services). You hook your computer to an odd little device called a modem (which, like its cable-TV counterpart, sometimes freaks out) and plug a plain phone cord from the modem to the phone jack on the wall. If you use a special high-speed connection (like things called *DSL* or *cable modems*), you get an even more esoteric device with its own cool cable (more about that in Chapter 24).

As with the cable TV example, if the technology behaves, your computer runs the special America Online software, dials a (hopefully) local phone number, and contacts the America Online computers in Virginia. (Don't worry about long-distance calls to Virginia — you just pay for the local part of the call, while the America Online communications system does the rest.) After connecting (or, in computer parlance, *going online* — more about that shortly), you choose from among a wide variety of services, depending on your interests. When things don't work, the problem may be with your computer, the America Online software, the modem (stupid modems), or somewhere from the wall jack to America Online itself. At the end of the month, you get a bill you gleefully pay, flush with the happy memory of everything you did online.

 By the way, the term *online* means "connected." If you're online with America Online, a link is set up through the phone between your computer and the America Online computers. When you get right down to it, the computers are having this swell digital conversation behind the scenes while you're busy reading the news, sending electronic mail, or doing whatever else you do on America Online.

The entire process looks much like Figure 1-1. Your computer, running the special America Online software, tells the modem to call a particular phone number. The modem dials the number and waits to hear from another modem. The two modems whistle and beep at each other for a while (the technical term for this process is *feature negotiation,* although I always thought of it as some kind of electronic flirting). After the modems settle down, they get to work completing your connection to the America Online computer system.

Figure 1-1: Going online usually means "going on phone line."

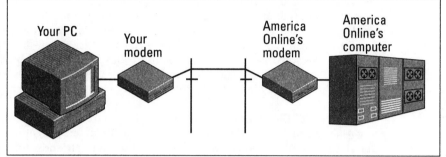

Your PC   Your modem   America Online's modem   America Online's computer

Now for the great part: That's *all* you need to know about the technology behind America Online. Really — I wouldn't kid you about something like this. All the cool things you can do, all the fun tricks, all the stuff that makes America Online a really wild and woolly place — all these require a great deal of technology, but *it doesn't matter to you.* You don't have to know any of this stuff to use America Online!

All It Takes Is a Bunch of Stuff

Now that you have a conceptual picture of how all this online business happens, you're ready to dig a little deeper and get into some specifics. You need four parts to make the online thing a reality: the America Online software, a computer, a modem, and a phone line. The following sections explore each element just enough to give you a good understanding of what you need without turning you into a computer nerd (ewww — the very thought gives me the shivers).

If you're starting from scratch and need to get *everything,* I recommend finding a computer guru to give you a hand. Depending on where you find your guru, this help may cost anywhere from a few dozen brownies to a few dozen greenbacks. If you do seek expert help, make sure that your expert understands online services (preferably America Online) and gives sound, unbiased advice. Don't get help from someone you just met whose primary experience in the field comes from working at a computer store or discount electronics place. Check with your friends for the name of a trusted and handy computer guru you can borrow for a while.

First, you need the right software

America Online is a pretty special place, not only because of its content and services but also for the look and feel of its *interface* (the buttons, menus, and windows that are on-screen). The America Online programmers decided to do things the *right* way from the start. This decision meant a break with tradition because people would need special software to join America Online. Granted, the software was free (and still is today — but more about that in a moment), but the idea itself was pretty risky for the time. Luckily, the risk paid off handsomely in better features, ease of use, and consistency.

Free software? Did somebody say *free*? Yes, by purchasing this book, you can try America Online for 100 hours, all within a 30-day period (after which regular charges apply). Just call 800-827-6364, and tell the friendly folks at AOL that your access code is 76540. (You need a major credit card or direct-debit card from a checking account to set up an America Online account. You can't go online without it!)

If the America Online software came preloaded on your computer (both Windows 95 and Windows 98 include it in the Online Services folder on the desktop), make sure that you have the latest version. Table 1-1 shows the current software version number for each kind of computer platform America Online supports and explains how to politely find out which version you have. You don't have to be (and, in fact, *shouldn't* be) signed on to America Online to find out the software version number.

Table 1-1	Version, Version, Who's Got Which Version?	
Platform	*Current Version*	*How to Find the Version Number*
Macintosh	4.0	In the Finder, click the America Online icon once and then choose File⇨Get Info from the Finder menu or press ⌘+I. The version number is in the pop-up information dialog box.
Windows	5.0	With the America Online software running, choose Help⇨About America Online from the menu bar. The version number is near the top of the screen (see Figure 1-2).

Figure 1-2:
The latest
America
Online
software for
Windows
shows off its
version
number.

Although knowing your program's version number seems a little nerdy, you have a good reason to find out what it is. This book covers the newest America Online software. If you're using an older version, you may get confused very quickly (and that's definitely not my goal).

A computer is a must

You can't get around this one: To use America Online, you must have a computer. Sorry, but that's the way these things go. Having settled that point, the next logical question is "Okay, smart guy, what *kind* of computer?" "Well," I reply, "that's up to you."

Because the America Online special access software comes in both Macintosh and Windows versions, you have some leeway in choosing your computer. (A DOS version also exists, but for now, just pretend that I didn't say that.) Choose the type of machine that makes you most comfortable. Don't worry if you use Windows at work but prefer a Macintosh for home (or vice versa). You can still share documents, spreadsheets, and many other files between your computers without any (well, *many*) problems.

If you buy a new computer for your online adventures, make sure that it has

- **A fast processor:** A Pentium, Pentium II, or Pentium III for Windows or a PowerPC, iMac, G3, or G4 for the Macintosh crowd

- **Plenty of random-access memory (RAM):** 32MB to 64MB is a good minimum for either a Macintosh or Windows machine

- **A high-quality color monitor:** 15 inches is a good minimum size

- **Plenty of hard disk space:** 1 gigabyte or more

If all this computer jargon sounds foreign to you, pick up a copy of *PCs For Dummies,* 7th Edition, by Dan Gookin, or *Macs For Dummies,* 6th Edition, by David Pogue (both published by IDG Books Worldwide, Inc.).

A modem enters the picture

The next piece of the puzzle is a *modem,* the device that converts your computer's electronic impulses into whistles, beeps, and various digital moose calls. The modem then yells these noises through the phone line to an equally disturbed modem attached to another computer.

The term *modem* is actually an acronym (and you thought you were safe, didn't you?). It stands for *mo*dulator/*dem*odulator, which is a computer nerd's way of saying that it both talks and listens. To find out more than you could possibly want to know about modems, get a copy of *Modems For Dummies,* 3rd Edition, by Tina Rathbone (IDG Books Worldwide, Inc.).

The main things you're looking for in a modem are a well-known manufacturer and blazing speed. Here are my recommendations:

- **Get a modem made by 3Com/U.S. Robotics or Creative Labs.** Although many other modems are available, these manufacturers stand behind their products better than all the rest.

- **If you buy a new modem, make sure that it's fast.** Modems that run at 56,000 bits per second (bps) are the rage these days. Manufacturers usually call them *56K modems* because "K" means roughly *1,000* in the computer world. Condemning yourself to anything slower than 28,800 bits per second just won't do. (I care about your sanity too much for that.) See the following sidebar, "A few words about modem speed," for a little more information about these extraordinarily fleet animals.

- **Watch those standards when you pick up a new modem.** If you buy a 56K modem, be sure that it supports the V.90 standard. *V.90* is the international screeching and whistling specification for 56K modems.

- **If you have a high-speed access line, you don't use a modem.** Special connections through the cable TV system or with the phone company require some equally special equipment. Chapter 24 guides you through the befuddling maze of high-speed high tech.

Many computers include a modem as part of the deal these days. If you aren't sure whether your PC includes one, glance at the back of the machine and look for a place to plug in a phone cord. Congrats — there's your modem!

What about a phone line?

All this other stuff doesn't do you a whit of good if you don't have a phone line to connect it to. The phone is your link with beautiful, metropolitan Vienna, Virginia, the home of America Online. Luckily, you don't need a special phone line — just about any phone line will work.

The key words in that last sentence are *just about* because not all phone lines are created equal. Many phone lines have been endowed by their subscribers with certain very alien services — such as call waiting — that interfere with a computer's basic rights to life, liberty, and the pursuit of a connection with America Online.

(Sorry, I've been reading American history lately and got a little carried away. If I had an "I'm so embarrassed" icon, rest assured that I'd insert it here.)

As you probably guessed, high-speed connections don't use a phone line at all. If they did, everyone could zip through America Online in a collectively quick blaze of glory.

To successfully use a modem, you need an *analog* phone line. If your home has a single phone line (or two plain, old-fashioned phone lines), you have an analog phone line. Because fax machines need the same kind of phone line, in times of emergency you can unplug the fax and use its phone line to reach America Online.

A few words about modem speed

A modem's speed is measured in *bits per second (bps).* The more bits per second, the more information the modem stuffs down the phone line in a given period.

Because America Online doesn't charge extra to use a faster modem, you save a lot of money in the long run by using the fastest modem you can. America Online uses fast 56K modems on most of its local access numbers, although support isn't available everywhere yet. For more about 56K access to America Online, check out keyword **High Speed**.

My advice: Pay a little extra and get the fastest, highest-quality modem possible because the money you spend pays you back tomorrow and many days thereafter. If you own an older 28,800 or 33,600 bps modem, check your modem maker's Web site and find out whether your modem can be upgraded to support higher speeds. Sometimes the upgrade is free — all you need to do is ask.

At work, the story is a little different. Many office telephone systems use *digital* phone lines. You shouldn't plug a normal modem directly into one of these lines. Please, for the sake of your modem, don't try. At best, the modem won't work this time. At worst, the modem won't ever work again because it's fried. If you're planning to use America Online from the office, contact your telephone folks and tell them that you have a modem and need something to connect it to. Remember to ask nicely, or else they may not give you the answer you're looking for.

Chapter 2

I Didn't Know You Could Do That Online!

*B*eep Beep Beep Beep BEEP BEEP! [whack] {yawwwwn} <<strrreeetch>
Ah, good morning! Nice to see that you're up (and looking as bright-eyed and bushy-tailed as ever, I might add). A full chapter lies ahead, so I'm glad that you slept well.

This chapter is a whirlwind tour through the cool stuff America Online offers. Think of this tour as a visual sampler, a platter of digital appetizers, each one delicious in itself but also tempting in the knowledge that still more awaits discovery. Collectively, this chapter gives you a broad idea of what you can do with America Online — and what it can do for you.

For now, kick back and read on. If something piques your interest, take a break and try it online. Each section of the chapter includes the keywords and menu instructions you need.

First, You Need to Sign On

Every online experience starts somewhere, and signing on to the service is as good a place as any. Just follow these steps to sign on to America Online:

1. **Turn on your computer, monitor, modem, stereo, food processor, and that cool cordless toothbrush/answering machine in the bathroom. Marvel at what modern technology has accomplished (and how noisy it all is), and then turn off the unimportant stuff.**

   No, you need to leave the computer *on* for now.

   If you have a Windows machine, your computer should start blissfully and leave you with a ready-to-go desktop screen. If that's you, go on to Step 2.

   If you use an older PC with Windows 3.*x,* Windows may or may not start automatically. If Windows does fire up on its own, go ahead to the next step. To manually start Windows, type **WIN** at the DOS prompt (C:\>), and then press Enter. In just a moment, the friendly Microsoft advertisement — er, the Windows logo screen — appears.

2. **Find the triangular America Online icon cowering among all your other software icons and double-click it to start the program.**

   In Windows, look on the Start button menu or on the Windows 95 or 98 desktop. After the program finishes loading, it displays the Sign On dialog box.

3. **Choose the screen name you want to use by clicking the down arrow next to the Select Screen Name list box and then clicking the name of your choice.**

   If this is the first time you've picked this particular screen name with the America Online 5.0 software, the program accosts you with another dialog box that demands to know whether you want to store your password. For now, click Cancel and ignore the dialog box. If your curiosity is piqued by this option, flip to Chapter 4 and unpique it with the details awaiting you there.

   Don't panic if the Enter Password text box disappears after you choose a screen name. It means that the password for that name is already stored in the access software.

4. **Press Tab to move down to the Enter Password text box and then type your password.**

   Your password appears as asterisks — not as words. That's a protection feature to keep that guy who's looking over your shoulder from breaking in to your account. What guy? Why, that one right there. (Yipe!)

5. **Click Sign On or press Enter to open the connection to America Online.**

   The software goes through all kinds of cool visual gymnastics while connecting. Granted, it's not a Hollywood masterpiece, but at least it's marginally entertaining.

   If the connection process doesn't work for some reason, make a note of the last thing the software did (initializing the modem, dialing, connecting, or requesting network attention, for example) and then try connecting again. If it still doesn't work, close the America Online software, restart your computer, and give your software one last chance to get things right. (Aren't you glad that your car doesn't work this way?)

   If your software *still* doesn't connect to America Online, breeze through Chapter 26 for a list of the top ten problems and how to solve them.

6. **After a moment, the Welcome window appears on-screen.**

   Congratulations — you're online and ready to get some stuff done.

Although the Welcome window sorta takes over the screen, the Channels window isn't far away. To see the Channels window, click the Channels button on the toolbar and select the channel you want to see (I recommend starting with AOL Today). Check out *AOL For Dummies Channels Directory,* your guide to channel mastery — you'll know it by the annoyingly yellow pages.

Checking the E-Mailbox

Electronic mail (or e-mail) is one of the most popular America Online services. That's why the e-mail button takes a position of pride and power on the left side of the Welcome window. If the flag is up and a letter sticks out of the mailbox, you have mail waiting (an everyday occurrence in my world, and soon to be a regular feature of yours, too). If you don't have any mail waiting, the graphic shows a closed mailbox, like the one shown in the margin of this paragraph.

To read your mail, either click the You Have Mail button or click Read on the toolbar. After the New Mail dialog box pops up, click Read to start through your mail.

- ✔ If you're writing a mail message instead of reading one, why are you logged on? Sign off from the system and click the Write toolbar button or press Ctrl+M to write your message offline. After you finish, turn to Chapter 8 and read about the myriad ways to send mail.

- ✔ If you do a lot of e-mail with America Online and want to save time, I see Automatic AOL sessions in your future. Mark your place here, and flip to Chapter 8 for more about this incredibly useful feature.

Say the magic keyword and get there fast

Keywords are the America Online answer to the *Star Trek* transporter. A *keyword* is a single code that immediately takes you to a particular forum or service on the system. A sidebar in Chapter 7 explains all the details of keywords, but for now, I want to briefly tell you how to use them. Check out that other sidebar for more detailed information.

To use a keyword, type the keyword into the big white box on the navigation bar and then press Enter. Was that fast or what?

For the keyboard-centric folks (that's me), press Ctrl+K to open the Keyword dialog box. After the box appears, type your keyword and press Enter.

As you probably figured out by now, Chapter 8 tells you everything you need to know about addressing, sending, receiving, and generally dealing with e-mail. I had to put the information somewhere, and that seemed as good a place as any.

Reading the Morning Paper

Nothing is like disappearing behind the morning newspaper while waiting for that first cup of coffee to turn you into a human being. With America Online, you have your choice of not one, not two, but — heck — a slew of newspapers and magazines. To get there, start with a channel that interests you, such as Computing, Families, Games, Interests, International, Sports, or Workplace. Each channel has its own individual newsstand area, like the Newsstand For News, as shown in Figure 2-1.

Figure 2-1: The Newsstand For News is one of several channel-specific magazine and newspaper areas.

To find out almost everything you could possibly want to know about the channels, check out the *AOL For Dummies Channels Directory,* easily identifiable by its yellow pages.

If newspapers are your thing, try the *Chicago Tribune* (keyword **Tribune**), *The New York Times* (keyword **Times**), or the *Orlando Sun-Sentinel* (keyword **Sun-Sentinel**). Are you more into magazines? Check out *George* (keyword **George**), *Premiere* (keyword **Premiere**), or *Spin* (keyword **Spin**).

To curl up with whatever publication suits your fancy, look for a link in your favorite online area (the Pictures forum offers a link to *Popular Photography* Online, for example) or turn to a likely-looking channel. If you go the channel route, find the Newsstand department in the Channel window, and click the button. After you're in the Newsstand department, scroll through the publications list to find the magazine of your desire. If no newsstand is on the channel, try using the Find system (covered in Chapter 13) to track down your reading quarry.

Eyeing the Markets

Managing your stock portfolio has never been easier. The Quotes & Portfolios service (keyword **Quotes**, or click Quotes on the toolbar) tracks the stocks closest to your heart and pocketbook.

Columbus, Eriksson, Magellan, and you

New services appear on America Online faster than facial aberrations on a teenager. Something new seems to appear every week. How do you explore it all? Leave it to those clever America Online programmers to think of a way: the QuickStart new member guide (keyword **QuickStart**).

QuickStart includes an overview of what's on AOL organized by your interests, an introduction to the myriad features of the system, and the requisite syrupy public relations stuff. Don't let that put you off, though, because QuickStart includes some genuinely useful goodies.

My personal picks in QuickStart include Match Your Interests (the interest-oriented AOL content list) and Meg's Insider Tips (a compendium of useful tips about life on AOL). Take a few minutes and check them out. It's definitely worth the trip.

To satisfy a brief curiosity, you can look up a single stock by its symbol. Figure 2-2, for example, tracks America Online stock activity by using the symbol AOL. If looking at the big picture is more to your liking, the Display Portfolio feature (keyword **Portfolio**) follows all the stocks you choose, tracking the current market price and how that translates into a gain or loss for your invested dollars.

  ✔ Don't panic, but the information in Quotes & Portfolios is delayed about 15 minutes. I guess that means you can't call it up-to-the-minute information. Hmm — how about up-until-quite-recently information?

  ✔ You can save the portfolio information to a text file by choosing File⇨Save from the menu bar.

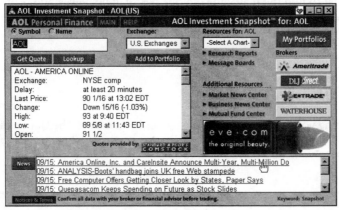

Figure 2-2:
Be a stock
spy with
Quotes &
Portfolios.

America Online charges no extra fee to use the Quotes & Portfolios service — it's just part of the service. Flip to Chapter 14 to find out more about the America Online financial offerings.

Internet On-Ramp, Next Right

At this point in your online life, you've probably heard, read, or otherwise been exposed to *something* about the Internet. If you haven't heard about the Internet yet, don't worry; you're about to.

The *Internet* is the worldwide network of networks that's all the rage these days. You can't get your hair done, shop for tires, or even play cricket without bumping into the Internet somehow. "Oh, is that a new cricket bat?" you ask. "Aye, a player in the `rec.sport.cricket` Internet newsgroup recommended it." See what I mean?

The America Online Internet Connection (keyword **Internet**) is your portal to the World Wide Web, Gopher, the Internet newsgroups, and much more. The Internet Connection makes a great starting point for your jaunts into the digital wilderness.

There's far too much to say about the Internet to do so here, so cruise to Chapter 17 and get ready for the ride of your life.

The Joys of (Nearly) Free Stuff

It seems like everywhere you turn in America Online, you find a software library. You don't have to be anywhere special; just about every service area has something to offer.

Exactly what's available depends entirely on where you are — but the range of stuff out there is utterly amazing. In Space Exploration Online (keyword **Space**), browse through images from the Hubble Space Telescope, photographs of the International Space Station, volumes of news from space programs around the world, and more model rocketry programs than any one person could use. The Food area (keyword **Food**) serves up recipes and a variety of cookbook programs (both shareware and commercial demonstrations). Try your hand at computer animation in the Animation and Video area's (keyword **A&V**) Windows libraries and resource centers (and pick up a trailers from your favorite movies, too).

Thanks to the America Online Internet links, you also have access to the infinite software libraries available through File Transfer Protocol, lovingly known in Net lingo as FTP. Troll the likes of Winsite (`ftp.winsite.com` — widely acknowledged as the world's largest Windows software library), Info-Mac (`ftp://mirror.aol.com/pub/info-mac` — the newly improved version of Stanford's old Sumex library, the home of more Macintosh software than anyone could possibly need), and the Walnut Creek Archive (`ftp.cdrom.com` — a great spot to find all kinds of programs) with ease. Filling your hard drive has never been so much fun!

Whether it's fonts and clip art, games and playing tips, or something a little more businesslike, in Chapter 16, you can find the details of getting it, unpacking it (watch out for the foam peanuts!), and making it work for you. For FTP info, check out Chapter 17.

Let the Fun and Games Begin!

Because all work and no play makes me really grumpy (and probably does the same thing to you), take a break from the Internet and indulge in some fun. The online world offers games to suit every age, style, and taste.

If you're a shoot-'em-up kinda person, work through your aggression (and sharpen your aim) in Splatterball (keyword **Splatterball**), part of a new breed of interactive online action games. For enthusiasts of more sedate games, America Online offers options like *The New York Times* crossword area (keyword **Crossword**, requires $9.95 annual subscription) and chess (keyword **Chess**). For a trip into the imagination of online theater, check out the Simming area (part of keyword **Gaming**) or the Urban Legends chat (part of keyword **Urban Legends**).

Multiplayer computer games live all over the Internet as well. Visit Yahoo! Games (games.yahoo.com) or Excite Games (go to www.excite.com; then click the Games link) for card games like Canasta, Hearts, and Spades, strategy games such as Backgammon and Go, and a cool collection of fantasy sports games. Best of all, the games are free, so play as long as you want (or until your Better Half casually suggests that you stop).

All this fun stuff and more is waiting on the Games channel. For more fun, flip to Chapter 15.

Shopping without the Crowds

Imagine shopping the malls on the day after Thanksgiving. After you regain consciousness, get a drink of water and then come back and keep reading.

Now imagine the same shopping trip with no crowds, no pushy children, and no whining adults. It's a dream, right? No, it's the America Online Shopping channel (keyword **Shopping**), your 24-hour shop-till-your-fingers-drop electronic mall.

Take a stroll through the Classifieds (keyword **Classifieds**), the America Online version of a digital flea market. Or pick up some high-tech goodies at Sharper Image (keyword **Sharper Image**). Have something a little bigger in mind? Try Netmarket (keyword **Netmarket**), with the best in just about everything you could want — and great prices.

If your credit card is already out, take a break and power-shop through the Shopping channel in *AOL For Dummies Channels Directory,* the book-within-a-book that sports those eerie yellow pages.

Enjoying a Little Chat

The People Connection (choose People⇨People Connection or use keyword **People**) is the home of the America Online *chat* areas. There, you can interactively talk live with other America Online subscribers. All this chat happens in what the technology jockeys call *real time,* which is a fancy way to say that right after you type a message, the other people in that chat area see the message on their screens, wherever they are.

The chat areas usually hold a maximum of 23 people. America Online does have some larger rooms, known as *conference rooms* or *auditoriums* — you can find out about them in Chapter 9.

When Problems Come Up

Compared to other online services, America Online offers a truly awesome level of support. You can find online chat areas, discussion boards, and even an old-fashioned, pick-up-the-phone-and-call-a-human line. Whew — they really have you covered.

Precisely where you look for answers depends on the problem you're having. Following is a two-step guide to help you find assistance fast:

✔ If you *can* sign on but don't know how to do something (for example, send an e-mail or read your Internet newsgroups), look in this book first because that information is probably in here somewhere. If I left it out, you have my apologies (goodness knows, I tried). Now that I'm done groveling, go to the Member Services help center (keyword **Help**) and click the topic that's causing you grief. Another great resource is the Members Helping Members discussion area (keyword **MHM**). Pose your question there, and fellow AOL members offer their best solutions.

✔ If you can't sign on, call the America Online Technical Guru Department, at 800-827-3338. Wade through the menu prompts, cross your fingers, and get ready to work through your problem with one of the helpful America Online technical-support folks. If you call at one of the system's peak times (like early in the evening), keep some reading material handy because you may be on hold for a while.

For general assistance and live online help, take a look at the AOL Neighborhood Watch at keyword **Neighborhood Watch**. It covers online conduct, viruses, scams, account security, and more. When you have questions, it's definitely a great place to go.

Handling the Rude, the Crude, and the Socially Maladjusted

Few things spoil a perfectly wonderful online evening quite like an annoying oddball in your favorite chat room, a persistently pestering instant message, or an obnoxious e-mail. When problems arise, you need to take action — and this section points you in the right direction.

The following list explains how to handle the various (and unfortunately *common*) annoyances of online life. If something comes up that's not on the list, check the keywords **Help, Neighborhood Watch, Notify AOL,** or **TOS** for suggestions.

- ✔ **Disrupting a chat room:** Click the Notify AOL button along the bottom of the chat window to report the problem and summon some help. Fill out the brief form and then click the Send button.

- ✔ **Someone just asked for your password in an instant message:** Click the Notify AOL button in the Instant Message window to open the I Need Help dialog box and then follow the instructions from there. If you're in a chat room, be sure to warn everyone else that someone is fishing for passwords! If you accidentally *did* give out your password, go immediately (and I mean *right-now-don't-wait-to-think*) to keyword **Password** and change your account password.

- ✔ **Annoying instant messages:** Don't close the Instant Message window just yet. Instead, click the Notify AOL button in the Instant Message window to open the Notify AOL dialog box, then follow the on-screen instructions carefully to complete your report.

- ✔ **Questionable e-mail messages:** To report e-mail problems, click the Forward button in the bothersome e-mail message and send it to screen name TOSEmail. If someone you don't know sent you an e-mail message with an attached file, *do not download the file!* Instead, forward the message directly to screen name TOSFiles. (The odds are *very* good that the file would mess up your computer or steal your America Online password!)

For help reporting other problems, like raunchy screen names, vulgar member profiles, or tasteless America Online member Web sites, go to keyword **Notify AOL** and click the appropriate button to bring up the correct reporting window.

Wait — There's More!

This chapter doesn't even begin to tell you what's available out in the wilds of America Online. Come to think of it, that's what the rest of this book does:

✔ To find out more about a specific channel, look up the area in *AOL For Dummies Channels Directory,* the super-cool yellow-paged book-within-a-book.

✔ To follow the biddings of your own interests, look in Part IV.

✔ If you feel the need to follow other interests, the bathroom is down the hall.

When It's Time to Say Good-Bye

All good things must come to an end, and so it is with America Online. But signing off from the system is quick and painless. Here's a quick list of good-bye (and good-bye–related) options in the America Online 5.0 software:

✔ To sign off from the system, choose <u>S</u>ign Off⇨<u>S</u>ign Off from the main menu. This action closes your online connection and leaves you sitting quietly in front of the main America Online software window.

✔ To switch to another screen name, choose <u>S</u>ign Off⇨Switch Screen Names from the main menu. In the Switch Screen Name dialog box (shown in Figure 2-3), double-click the name you want to use, and follow the on-screen instructions for typing your new password. In just a moment, America Online signs your other screen name on to the system — and you don't even have to redial the phone! For more about creating new screen names, see Chapter 6.

✔ To shut down the America Online software, choose <u>F</u>ile⇨E<u>x</u>it. You're done!

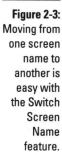
Figure 2-3:
Moving from
one screen
name to
another is
easy with
the Switch
Screen
Name
feature.

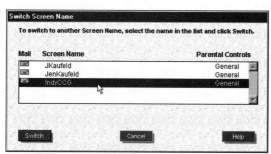

Chapter 3

Surviving the Software

• •

In This Chapter

▶ Camping on the toolbar

▶ Cruising with the navigation bar

▶ Browsing the menus

• •

*U*sing America Online is one thing. But, before you can actually use it, you must tangle with (insert scary organ music here) the user interface!

No, it's not something else you need to buy. The term *user interface* is just a fancy way of describing the menus, buttons, and goodies you use to interact with a program. It's like an automobile engineer looking at the layout of a dashboard and thinking, "Golly, that's a clever user interface." (Yes, despite the various specialties, most engineers respond to the simplest stimulus in predictably unintelligible ways — they're just that way.)

This chapter covers the three main parts of the America Online 5.0 user interface: the toolbar menus, the navigation bar, and the menu bar. It doesn't matter whether you use these tools together or separately, because they make your life a little easier either way (and that's more than you can say for most software on the market.)

Revealing the Toolbar (And Its Way-Cool Menus)

It's always there, right below the menu bar — watching you, daring you, enticing you with color buttons. However, the toolbar itself remains a mystery. What do those little pictures mean? Why are there so many of them? Why do some give you a menu and others just do their thing? (By the way, is it time for lunch yet?)

Don't worry if the toolbar looks a little, well, odd at first glance. That's because the America Online 5.0 software features a very different kind of toolbar than most programs use today (it's quite avant-garde, for whatever that's worth).

The America Online programmers endowed the 5.0 toolbar with a combination of old-fashioned click-the-button-to-do-something features and newfangled click-the-button-and-watch-the-menu-appear functionality. The new incarnation brings to life a sort of graphical menu filled with colorful possibilities. In a final burst of refined simplicity, those same developers added names below each toolbar button, indicating what each entry does. (No more guessing what the pictures mean!)

You probably also noticed the small downward-pointing triangle next to some of the toolbar buttons. The triangles aren't anything dramatic, but they *are* very helpful. A triangle next to a toolbar button indicates that when you click that particular button, a whole menu hops into view. Buttons *without* the little triangle are, well, just buttons — click 'em and they do whatever they say they do. Most buttons that contain drop-down menus also include a hot key (the little underlined letter in the name of the button). To use the hot key, just hold down the Alt key and press the underlined letter. With no further ado, that button's menu appears. Talk about speed!

To make the various functions easier to find, the America Online developers organized the toolbar items into five groups according to what the buttons do. Each group shares a background color to make it stand out from the others (and probably to enhance the group's self-confidence a bit — you know how insecure buttons get sometimes). Here's a quick overview of the various button groups, starting from the left side of the toolbar (as shown in Figure 3-1):

✔ The first group of toolbar buttons governs e-mail and printing. All the e-mail goodies live here, along with the vaguely dejected Print button, which doesn't understand why it's grouped with the e-mail tools.

✔ The second group covers a bunch of utility functions, including your Personal Filing Cabinet, chat logs, saved mail, and Favorite Places entries. As though it didn't already have enough on its plate, this group also includes My AOL, which is home to the wide range of settings that customize your America Online experience (for more about these settings, see Chapter 4).

✔ The two buttons in the third group form your gateway to all the cool content available on both the America Online channels and the world-wide Internet. One click here and you can kiss a few hours farewell as you dive into the amazing bounty of online information.

✔ Next to the toolbar's content area sits a single, lonely button, ostracized by those around it, and banished into its own little group. The People button opens the doors to chat rooms and discussion areas all over America Online. (Considering all the interaction that happens in the chat areas, it's kinda funny that the People button lives by itself on the toolbar.)

> ✔ If your screen has enough space for them, the last group of entries on
> the far right sit in the customizable area of the toolbar. Although the
> America Online software plunks down some buttons here by default, this
> toolbar section really belongs to you, the member. To find out more
> about laying claim to an area that's rightfully yours and cramming it full
> of icons for your favorites-of-favorites, flip to Chapter 23.

Figure 3-1:
The new
America
Online
toolbar.

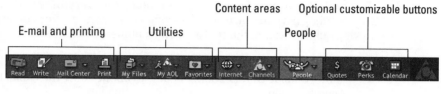

Now that you know how they're organized, it's time to dig into more of the
button details. The following sections rattle off the name and purpose of each
toolbar button. Some buttons (like Read and Print) perform one particular
task, so their descriptions are straightforward and short. However, most of
the toolbar buttons lead to drop-down menus, filled with options galore.

The description sections for these toolbar buttons start with a quick
overview of that button's overall goal in life and then follow with details on
all the button's menu selections. By the way, the sections are in the same
order as they appear on the toolbar, so don't blame me for the fact that (as
my young daughter would say) Muh-Muh-Mail Center comes before Fuh-Fuh-
Favorites.

Read

Clicking this button displays the New Mail section of your e-mail box, just like
clicking the You Have Mail button on the Welcome window or choosing Mail
Center⇨Read Mail elsewhere from the toolbar. This button works only when
you're signed on to America Online.

To read mail you downloaded through an Automatic AOL session (what used
to be known as a FlashSession), choose Mail Center⇨Read Offline Mail.

Write

The toolbar's Write button is a single-purpose button that opens up a blank
e-mail window, ready and waiting for your next digital missive. This button
does the same thing as pressing Ctrl+M or choosing Mail Center⇨Write Mail.

Write works both online and offline, although you can't send your new mail message until you sign on to America Online. For the details about all things e-mail, check out Chapter 8.

Mail Center

This toolbar button offers one-stop shopping for everything to do with e-mail, from reading new messages to managing your online address book. The following bullets explore the button menu's numerous choices:

- **Mail Center⇨Mail Center:** Pop in to the Mail Center, home of all you can know (outside of this book, of course) about doing the e-mail thing with America Online.

- **Mail Center⇨Read Mail:** Read your incoming mail; same as Ctrl+R or clicking the Read toolbar button.

- **Mail Center⇨Write Mail:** Write a new e-mail message; same as Ctrl+M or clicking the Write toolbar button.

- **Mail Center⇨Old Mail:** Revisit mail you've already read at some point or another. Mail remains here for seven days or fewer, so don't be surprised if something you want to see is gone.

- **Mail Center⇨Sent Mail:** Take another look at the outbound missives (and other types of notes) you sent within the last 30 days or so.

- **Mail Center⇨Recently Deleted Mail:** Retrieve mail that you deleted (either on purpose or on *Whoops!*) within the last 24 hours with the Recently Deleted Mail window.

- **Mail Center⇨Address Book:** Open up the built-in Address Book and manage your ever-growing collection of online friends.

- **Mail Center⇨Mail Preferences:** Display the Mail Preferences window and adjust the details of how America Online handles your incoming and outgoing e-mail.

- **Mail Center⇨Mail Controls:** Adjust the e-mail restrictions for your account.

- **Mail Center⇨Set up Mail Signatures:** Make, modify, or maul your e-mail signatures.

- **Mail Center⇨Mail Extras:** Check out all the cool things you can do with e-mail, like sending electronic cards and such.

- **Mail Center⇨Set Up Automatic AOL (FlashSessions):** Automate the process of sending and receiving e-mail with a few well-chosen settings.

✔ **Mail Center⇨Run Automatic AOL (FlashSessions) Now:** Send your America Online software out to carry on an Automatic AOL session (what used to be called a FlashSession until the folks at the America Online Department of Renaming Things got hold of it).

✔ **Mail Center⇨Read Offline Mail:** Display messages that arrived during an Automatic AOL session.

✔ **Mail Center⇨Mail Waiting to be Sent:** Review and send mail you wrote offline (without signing on to America Online).

Print

Click the Print button to make a paper copy of an online article, graphic, or Web page that tickles your fancy. The Print button sends the contents of the current window (whatever you happen to be looking at right then) over to your printer. It works the same as choosing File⇨Print from the menu bar. Print works both online and offline.

My Files

Whether you want to browse or add something to your Personal Filing Cabinet, log the conversation in a chat room, adjust your America Online-based Web page, or cruise through your offline newsgroup information, this button takes care of you. Here's a look at the menu items it offers:

✔ **My Files⇨Personal Filing Cabinet:** Open the Personal Filing Cabinet window, your very own digital attic for storing your digital, um, stuff.

✔ **My Files⇨Save to Personal Filing Cabinet:** Save a copy of the content of the current window on your computer, by carefully tucking it away in a file folder within your Personal Filing Cabinet.

✔ **My Files⇨Offline Mail:** Open a window containing the Incoming/Saved Mail, Mail Waiting to Be Sent, and Mail You've Sent file folders.

✔ **My Files⇨Download Manager:** Fire up the Download Manager, your always-willing accomplice in the task of filling up your hard drive.

✔ **My Files⇨You've Got Pictures:** Whisks you away to the colorful You've Got Pictures area for a visit with your online photographic efforts.

✔ **My Files⇨Offline Newsgroups:** Open a window with the Incoming/Saved Postings, Postings Waiting to Be Sent, and Postings You've Sent file folders. It works only if you have set up newsgroups to read offline (see keyword **Newsgroups** for more about that — it's kinda advanced).

✔ **My Files⇨Log Manager:** Call forth the Chat and Session Log dialog box. For more about chat logging, see Chapter 7. Session log details are in Chapter 12.

My AOL

Thanks to the programmers' hard work, you have lots of ways to customize just about *anything* about both your America Online software and your online experience. Your online profile, screen names, access passwords, Parental Controls — the list of customizable goodies goes on and on. The My AOL toolbar button serves up all these items on its drop-down menu, outlined in this list:

- **My AOL⇨My AOL:** Take a lush tour of the many things you can do to make your corner of the America Online world as cool as can be; same as keyword **My AOL.**

- **My AOL⇨Preferences:** Go straight into the America Online Preferences window, the nerve center of your America Online customization opportunities; same as keyword **Preferences.**

- **My AOL⇨AOL Access Numbers:** Find a new AOL access the quick and menu-driven way; same as the Search button in keyword **Access.**

- **My AOL⇨My Member Profile:** Create, adjust, or simply blow away your online member profile. (See Chapter 23 for tips about building a *very* cool profile, complete with custom subject headings.)

- **My AOL⇨Screen Names:** Open the screen name management window, where you can create, delete, recover, and generally annoy the screen names on your account (works only if you're signed on with the master screen name — see Chapter 4 for details).

- **My AOL⇨Passwords:** Choose this option to change your America Online password, which, of course, you should do every month or two, just for good measure (and to test your memory, too).

- **My AOL⇨Parental Controls:** Bring up the Parental Controls window, which explores and explains everything you ever wanted to know about the Parental Controls feature. Check Chapter 4 for the lowdown on the Parental Control options.

- **My AOL⇨My Calendar:** Keep your busy schedule in the one place that you won't lose it — on America Online!

- **My AOL⇨AOL Quick Checkout:** Shopping doesn't get much easier than this. AOL Quick Checkout stores your shipping address and credit card information so you don't have to retype (and risk mistyping) it when you shop.

- **My AOL⇨Online Clock:** If your kitchen clock suddenly poops out, choose this option to see the current time.

- **My AOL⇨Buddy List:** Open the Buddy List window for viewing, editing, and otherwise working with your Buddy List.

✔ **My AOL⇨My Web Page:** Go to the My Place area to create, edit, and marvel at a Web page of your very own.

✔ **My AOL⇨Stock Portfolios:** Track your investment dollars in the portfolio system, delightfully delivered by this menu option.

✔ **My AOL⇨Reminder Service:** Never forget a date again (unless you forget to read your e-mail, that is!) by using the Reminder service on America Online.

✔ **My AOL⇨News Profiles:** Tell the News Profiles system what kind of news, sports, business, or feature information you like and then watch in amazement as stories from the wire services start filling your e-mail box.

✔ **My AOL⇨Interest Profiles:** List the things that interest and intrigue you and let America Online point out online matches.

Favorites

As you browse through America Online, developing a list of online areas you enjoy doesn't take long. The more time you spend using the system, the more areas you find (trust me on this one — it's a truism of digital life), so at some point you need a way to keep track of everything. Of course, a couple of helpful navigation tools don't hurt, either.

That's where the Favorites button comes into play. Use the items on this menu to cruise through your Favorite Places and for easy navigation anywhere inside and *outside* of America Online. Chapter 7 explains the details of the whole Favorite Places system, but for now, here's an overview of the Favorites menu:

✔ **Favorites⇨Favorite Places:** Open the Favorite Places window for a few quick trips around either America Online or the Internet.

✔ **Favorites⇨Add Top Window to Favorite Places:** Add a Favorite Places item for the cool content area you happen to be in right now.

✔ **Favorites⇨Go To Keyword:** Bring up the Keyword dialog box for quick navigation around both America Online and the Internet.

✔ **Favorites⇨My Shortcuts:** This corner of the menu system belongs to you — fill it with up to ten of your favorite keyword areas. Check out Chapter 24 to find out how.

✔ **Everything at the bottom of the Favorites list:** When you mark something as a Favorite Place (more about that in Chapter 7), it lands here, at the bottom of the Favorites menu.

Internet

Click here for easy access to the World Wide Web, Internet newsgroups, and all the other goodies the international network of networks has to offer. The toolbar menu gives you specific menu choices for different Internet-based information tools, like the World Wide Web, newsgroups, and FTP (File Transfer Protocol), plus links to the system's main Internet site. Here's the quick list of what's waiting for you:

- ✔ **Internet➪Internet Connection:** Open the AOL Internet Connection window, your doorway to the Web, the world, and beyond.

- ✔ **Internet➪Go to the Web:** Fire up the America Online built-in Web browser and load the `www.aol.com` Web site.

- ✔ **Internet➪Search the Web:** Start the built-in Web browser and then direct your attention to the helpful and fact-filled NetFind search system.

- ✔ **Internet➪Visit AOL Hometown:** Amble down the digital boulevards of AOL Hometown, a great little neighborhood to build a Web site; same as keyword **Hometown**.

- ✔ **Internet➪AOL Instant Messenger:** Opens the Web-based Instant Messenger information site, with, well, plenty of information about Instant Messenger (and why it's a wonderful thing).

- ✔ **Internet➪My News:** Customize a whole page of news you can use with America Online's My News system; same as keyword **My News**.

- ✔ **Internet➪Shortcuts:** Leads you to a preset page of presumably interesting links, plus a handy Web Search box.

- ✔ **Internet➪White Pages:** Run the America Online built-in Web browser and display the White Pages section of the `www.aol.com` Web site. Search for long-lost friends and acquaintances by entering a name, city, and state.

- ✔ **Internet➪Yellow Pages:** Like its pigmented neighbor, the Internet Yellow Pages option helps you to find businesses by category (hotel, restaurant, plumber, astrophysicist, and such) or by business name.

- ✔ **Internet➪Maps and Directions:** Make your own maps and get driving directions for any destination in the United States and Canada. (Note to fellow men: It's not like stopping to ask for directions, so go ahead and give it a try.)

- ✔ **Internet➪Newsgroups:** Go straight to the Usenet Newsgroups window, where a sometimes strange (but always interesting) world of information awaits.

- ✔ **Internet➪FTP (File Transfer):** Get a head start on filling your hard disk to overflowing with a trip to the Internet's voluminous file libraries, all available directly through the America Online FTP (short for File Transfer Protocol) window.

To find out more about the America Online connection to the Internet and what you can do out there, check out Chapter 14.

Channels

A *lot* of great stuff is on America Online — so much, in fact, that you need a map of some kind to ensure that you don't accidentally get lost. The America Online *channels* perform that task for you by organizing all the online content areas into a much smaller collection of subject-oriented channel windows.

After signing on to the system, the Channels toolbar button offers a drop-down list of America Online content channels. To see a channel, click the Channels button and then click your particular choice from these options:

- **Channels⇨Welcome:** Take a look at what's timely and cool all over the system (and see if you have mail).

- **Channels⇨Computing:** Turn here when you need the latest troubleshooting tips, software notes, or file downloads.

- **Channels⇨Entertainment:** News, reviews, discussion, and more about the wild world of movies, music, books, and TV await you here.

- **Channels⇨Families:** Worried about your kids? Concerned about your parents? Wrestling with a relationship? This channel delivers information and discussion you can use to keep the home fires burning bright without torching the house in the process.

- **Channels⇨Games:** Relax here for a while (or a whole night, if you aren't careful) with online games, game shows, and game information.

- **Channels⇨Health:** Keep a sharp eye on health concerns for both you and your family with this channel's information areas.

- **Channels⇨Interests:** Explore your hobbies and interests in this digital potpourri of magazines, discussion areas, chats, and more.

- **Channels⇨International:** Click here to enjoy a peek at online life from other perspectives (and in other time zones).

- **Channels⇨Kids Only:** Finally — an area that's just for kids! Explore, play, meet, and chat here with kids from all walks of life.

- **Channels⇨Lifestyles:** When you long for a good discussion about the ebb and flow of life, try the message boards, information areas, and chat rooms in here.

- **Channels⇨Local:** Drop in here to explore online links and information areas about your particular corner of the world.

- **Channels⇨News:** Keep up on the latest in news, sports, features, and weather.

- **Channels⇨Personal Finance:** Manage your money with the news, information, and discussion that's awaiting you here.

- **Channels⇨Research & Learn:** When your mind reels with questions, turn to this channel for answers. The resources are organized by both topic (history, science, and so on) and type (dictionary, encyclopedia, and others).

- **Channels⇨Shopping:** Shop, shop, shop, shop. (What else can I say?)

- **Channels⇨Sports:** Thrill the sports fanatic in you with scores, schedules, and more from events all over the world.

- **Channels⇨Teens:** Check out the best in teen life with the polls, lifestyle discussions, style debates, and more in the Teens channel.

- **Channels⇨Travel:** Plan a trip, arrange a trip, or just dream about a trip in this warehouse of globe-trotting information.

- **Channels⇨Workplace:** No matter what your job, this channel covers you with business news, research sources, lunch chats, and discussion areas for everything from accounting to vending. (Okay, technically it's from accounting to veterinarians, but that just doesn't ring.)

For all the details about the channels, flip to the *America Online For Dummies Channels Directory* — the very cool yellow pages to AOL channels — you can't miss it!

People

This friendly-looking toolbar button links you to the wonderful world of the People Connection and AOL Live, home to more great conversation than a convention of talk-show hosts. The People toolbar button takes you directly to chats and presentations all over the system and includes other people-related things, like locating members online and searching the member database. By the way, this button works only when you are attached to America Online.

Here's the lowdown on what's available under People:

- **People⇨People Connection:** Drop in to the People Connection main window, the America Online home for 24-hour conversation.

- **People⇨Chat Now:** Dive straight in to a randomly selected lobby of the People Connection.

- **People⇨Find a Chat:** Seek out a particular chat room by searching for its name.

- **People⇨Start Your Own Chat:** Click to create a new member chat room.

✔ **People⇨AOL Live:** Hear celebrities, scientists, singers, and, yes, even authors as they hold forth on all kinds of fascinating topics; same as keyword **AOL Live**.

✔ **People⇨Instant Message:** Drop an Instant Message on a friend's desktop with this menu item; just like pressing Ctrl+I.

✔ **People⇨View Buddy List:** Display your Buddy List and find out which of your friends are spending a few relaxing hours on the system.

✔ **People⇨Send Message to Pager:** If someone you know subscribes to the right pager service, send that person a full text-and-numbers page directly from AOL! (Check the information in this area for details about which pagers and services the system covers.)

✔ **People⇨Sign On a Friend:** Invite your friends to join the world of America Online (and pick up some free online time for yourself).

✔ **People⇨Visit AOL Hometown:** Head off to America Online's hopping Web page neighborhood.

✔ **People⇨Search AOL Member Directory:** Discover that special someone by sifting through the millions of profile entries in the America Online member directory.

✔ **People⇨Locate AOL Member Online:** Find out whether a particular screen name is signed on to America Online. If the person is signed on, the system tells you whether that person is in a chat room, a private chat room, or just wandering around the service somewhere; same as pressing Ctrl+L.

✔ **People⇨Get AOL Member Profile:** Discover more about the person you just bonked on the head with an Instant Message or bumped into in a chat room; same as pressing Ctrl+G.

✔ **People⇨Internet White Pages:** Search the Internet for people and businesses with this powerful online tool.

For all the best information on the ins, outs, ups, downs, and all-around-the-towns of the People Connection, flip to Chapter 7.

The customizable buttons

Depending on an odd technical detail about your computer, your America Online toolbar may or may not include these last three buttons. Even though it seems a bit odd, one of your computer's screen settings decides the fate of these poor, innocent buttons.

Your monitor displays information by using a certain number of dots on the screen. Because the word *dots,* of course, is far too simple and obvious to qualify as Official Computer Lingo, the technology people invented the high-tech term *pixel.* The number of pixels on the screen tells you the screen's *resolution.* To see the customizable buttons, your screen must have at least an 800 x 600 resolution (a common setting on today's computers). Older computers may use a 640 x 480 resolution, which unfortunately cuts the customizable buttons off the screen.

For a complete discussion of the whole screen-resolution thing, plus step-by-step instructions for changing the settings on your computer, check out *Windows 95 For Dummies,* 2nd Edition, or *Windows 98 For Dummies,* both written by Andy Rathbone and published by IDG Books Worldwide, Inc.

Quotes

Open the America Online stock quoting system to track your market investments (and, depending on the day, to send you into blissful ecstasy or hair-ripping wails of angst). This button does the same thing as keyword **Quotes** and works only while you're signed on to America Online.

Perks

Take a quick look at what's new, exciting, and generally fun on America Online by clicking the Perks button. If you don't feel like clicking the button, try using keyword **Exclusives** instead. Like the other buttons on this lonely end of the toolbar, Perks works only while you're attached to America Online.

Calendar

The online Calendar (keyword **Calendar**) stores your schedule, appointment book, and goodness only knows what else, putting all the important information in your world right where you need it — just a mouse-click away.

Sailing around the Navigation Bar

Just below the toolbar is a thin little group of controls, known as the *navigation bar.* Even though the navigation bar is small, it plays a vital role in your time on America Online by acting as both your native guide and skillful scribe.

The navigation bar includes only a few controls, but what they lack in number, these controls make up for in power. Here's a quick breakdown, from left to right, of the cool things awaiting you (for a complete multimedia experience, follow along in Figure 3-2 as you read these bullets out loud — but don't let anybody see you do it, okay?):

✔ **Browser buttons:** The five buttons on the left side of the navigation bar provide the basic features you need to steer through the Web. (The buttons work with America Online-based information areas, too, although it takes some practice before you get the hang of it.) The right- and left-pointing triangle buttons are Back and Forward. Back takes you to the Web site or information area you last saw, and Forward returns you to the page you were on when you clicked Back. The X-in-a-circle button is Stop, which whacks your America Online software over the head, making it lose its concentration for a moment and stop whatever it's doing. The curly arrow is Reload, which tells your Web browser to reload the current page (it doesn't work with America Online areas). Finally, the little house button is Home. Click the button, tap your heels, and sing "Somewhere Over the Rainbow" to display the America Online Web site (or whatever site you have configured as your home page).

✔ **Find button:** Opens a menu with options to find just about anything (short of your car keys, that is) and anyone on America Online and the Internet.

✔ **Address window:** This handy box saves you time and energy by accepting both America Online keywords and World Wide Web addresses. This always-present box does the same thing as the Keyword dialog box (the one that comes up when you press Ctrl+K in Windows or ⌘+K on the Macintosh). Just type a keyword or Web address in the box and then either press Enter or click Go. America Online immediately whisks you away to the appointed online destination.

✔ **Go button:** After you've typed a keyword or Web address in the Address box or chosen an item you already saw from the Address box's pull-down menu, click this button to go there.

✔ **Search button:** One click brings up the AOL Search dialog box; same as keyword **Search**.

✔ **Keyword button:** Click to open the Keyword dialog box; same as pressing Ctrl+L.

Figure 3-2:
The navigation bar: small, but jam-packed.

Browser buttons   Address window   Search button ⌐
                                                  Go button ⌐   Keyword button

Running through the Menus

Beauty, as the cyberbard says, is only button deep — and there's more to the America Online interface than mere pretty buttons. How about that menu bar up there? What does it do? Actually, quite a bit. I can't *imagine* trying to figure out America Online without the menu bar.

This section looks at the menu areas one by one, giving you a brief description of both the whole menu area and the individual items that populate it. If you're an old hand with America Online, remember that *most* of the menu items you know and love have moved to the new toolbar, covered earlier in this chapter.

File

The File menu governs everything dealing with documents (such as magazine articles, bulletin board postings, and forum announcements), files, and other trivialities such as exiting the America Online access program (but who'd ever want to do that?). Here are the most interesting File menu commands:

- **File⇨New:** Start the built-in text editor and get ready to create a new plain-text document. I often keep a blank document window open when I'm browsing through the system and use it like a notepad for keywords, screen names, and anything else I want to remember. It works really well!

- **File⇨Open:** Open a document (a plain-text file — not a WordPerfect or Microsoft Word .doc file), graphic, or sound file you downloaded or saved to your computer's disk drive.

- **File⇨Open Picture Gallery:** Display the Open Image Gallery window, which offers a quick way to view, change and use the graphics files in any folder on your computer. Pick a folder and then click Open Gallery to view a nice thumbnail display of the graphics files there. Click a particular picture to see it full-size.

- **File⇨Save:** Save the current document (article or discussion board posting, for example) as a plain-text file on your computer's disk drive. If a graphic is in the window (a photo accompanying a news story, for example), then the America Online software automatically offers to save a copy of it, too.

- **File⇨Save As:** Save the current document under a new filename. If the current document is an article, discussion board posting, or something else in an online area, this command behaves just like File⇨Save.

✔ **File⇨Save to Personal Filing Cabinet:** Save the current document (article, discussion board entry, or other text item) in a folder within your America Online software's Personal Filing Cabinet. For the whole scoop on the Personal Filing Cabinet, yank open Chapter 8 and check out the section about organizing your e-mail mess(ages), which explains this electronic organizational wonder.

✔ **File⇨Print Setup:** Open the Printer Setup dialog box, where you can change the options for the default printer or temporarily select a different printer.

✔ **File⇨Print:** Print the current document. If you choose this option and don't have a printer connected to the computer, your computer may seem to lock up for a minute or two. Be patient — the machine should come back to life, probably complaining that your nonexistent printer is either turned off or out of paper. (Silly computer.)

✔ **File⇨Exit:** Close the America Online access software.

Edit

Just about every Windows program has an Edit menu. It contains your basic text-editing tools; apart from that, the Edit menu is nothing to write (or rewrite, for that matter) home about. Here are your main choices on this menu:

✔ **Edit⇨Undo:** Undo the last change you made. I use this command often when I'm writing e-mail messages. Because my fingers enjoy playing tricks on my brain, they take charge of the mouse and randomly delete text. After my brain goes spastic for a moment, it brings the hand digits back under control and uses Undo to recover the nearly lost text.

✔ **Edit⇨Cut:** Remove highlighted text from the screen and put it on the Clipboard.

✔ **Edit⇨Copy:** Copy the highlighted text from the screen to the Clipboard, leaving the original text in place.

✔ **Edit⇨Paste:** Insert text from the Clipboard into the current document.

✔ **Edit⇨Select All:** Highlight all the text in the current document.

✔ **Edit⇨Find in Top Window:** Search the current window for a given piece of text. Open a Web page, an article in the News section, or a discussion board posting and give this menu choice a try.

✔ **Edit⇨Spell Check:** Scour the e-mail message, newsgroup posting, bulletin board entry, or other text document you're creating.

✔ **Edit⇨Dictionary:** Open a search screen that scours the online Merriam-Webster dictionary (keyword **Collegiate**) for whatever *correctly* spelled word you enter.

✔ **Edit➪Thesaurus:** Bring up the online version of the Merriam-Webster Thesaurus (keyword **Thesaurus**) to help you track down synonyms for your favorite word.

✔ **Edit➪Capture Picture:** If your computer includes a video camera (like the Connectix QuickCam, for example), this item enables you to shoot pictures on the fly, right from your America Online software. If you don't have a camera, well, it doesn't do a whole lot.

If none of these menu items sounds familiar to you, get a copy of *Windows 95 For Dummies,* 2nd Edition, or *Windows 98 For Dummies;* both written by Andy Rathbone and available from IDG Books Worldwide, Inc. You can thank me later.

Window

This menu is a whoa-I-have-too-many-windows-open navigational lifesaver. If you misplace an Instant Message window or lose track of your Web browser, head to the Window menu and find it right away. Best of all, tracking the errant window is merely a two-step process:

1. **Choose <u>W</u>indow from the main menu.**

   The Window menu drops down, displaying some marvelously technical options near the top and a numbered list of your open windows at the bottom. On the Macintosh, the windows aren't numbered, but they're still listed at the bottom of the menu.

2. **Click the name of the window you want to display.**

   The until-so-recently-lost window immediately pops to the top of the heap. Is this a great country or what?

Two menu items deserve a quick mention:

✔ **Window➪Close <u>A</u>ll Except Front:** If you're completely fed up with all those open windows (or if it unexpectedly starts raining), close them all with a quick visit to the <u>W</u>indow➪Close <u>A</u>ll Except Front menu choice. Like it says, choosing this option makes all the open service windows go away, except for the window you're currently looking at. It also helpfully minimizes the Welcome window.

✔ **Window➪A<u>d</u>d Top Window to Favorite Places:** If you want a way to add things to your Favorite Places without using your mouse, look here. This, as the name implies, adds a link to your Favorite Places for the site in the top window of your screen. You can also use the handy shortcut key Ctrl++ (that's the Ctrl key and the Plus sign key).

As for the other items on the Window menu, don't worry about them. They're for people who *care* about the difference between tiling and cascading windows — definitely folks with too much time on their hands.

Sign Off

When it's time to hit the trail and mosey off to other matters, the Sign Off menu is the place to go. This menu is not big, but you couldn't get through online life without its two options:

- ✔ **Sign Off⇨Switch Screen Name:** Want to change screen names without signing off from the system completely? This menu option does the trick. Choose it, pick your preferred screen name from the pop-up list, type the password, and (thanks to some cool technical magic) sign on with the new moniker.

- ✔ **Sign Off⇨Sign Off:** Yes, it's redundant, but it's better than the Windows Start⇨Shut Down combination. Choose this option to close your America Online connection. The software bids a fond farewell to the online world by clipping the link between your computer and the rest of the system.

Help

If you have trouble getting on America Online, check the Help menu for assistance. This menu isn't particularly good at helping you with problems *after* signing on to the system, but it does a great job with the *before* sign on problems. Help menu options include

- ✔ **Help⇨Offline Help:** Display the Help system's Contents page.

- ✔ **Help⇨About America Online:** Show the version information for your America Online software. (Sometimes the America Online technical-support folks may ask you to open up this window — it's a techie thing.)

For help *after* you sign on to the system, check out these Help menu goodies:

- ✔ **Help⇨Member Services Online Help:** Go directly to the free Member Services window. Same as using keyword **Help**.

- ✔ **Help⇨Parental Controls:** Bring up the Parental Controls window to adjust the controls for your various screen names. You must sign on from the master screen name (the one you created when you signed up for America Online) to use these controls. Same as using keyword **Parental Controls.**

✔ **Help▷Help with Keywords:** When keywords get you down, try this Help menu for tips and tricks for making the little animals behave.

✔ **Help▷Accounts and Billing:** View and change your account billing information with this helpful window. Same as using keyword **Billing.**

✔ **Help▷AOL Access Phone Numbers:** Search the world (literally!) for local America Online access phone numbers. Also includes notes about international access and the surcharged 800 numbers (still cheaper than long distance). Same as using keyword **Access.**

✔ **Help▷What's New in AOL 5.0:** Displays an online slideshow overview of a few cool new features of America Online's version 5.0 software. It covers the big things (like the new Welcome window, and the You've Got Pictures and Calendar buttons), plus a few of the smaller things (like e-mail signatures).

Chapter 4

Making Your Preferences Known

In This Chapter

▶ What the preferences do

▶ Finding the elusive little things

▶ A romp through the various settings

A new America Online account is like a college dorm room on the first day of school: completely bare — devoid of anything beyond the institutional necessities of lime-green cinder blocks and gray linoleum. As the new residents move in, they put a distinct face on the nondescript space and make it uniquely their own.

Making yourself at home on America Online means setting things up just the way you want them — and that's what this chapter is all about. It covers the extensive America Online Preferences area, exploring the useful, helpful, and valuable settings, while steering you clear of the odd, esoteric, and nerdy ones.

If you're completely new to America Online, spend some time messing around with the service before digging deeply into this chapter. Several of the preferences (particularly the Mail and Web settings) make a lot more sense after you use America Online for a while. If you want details about creating screen names and online profiles or if you need guidance setting the parental controls, flip ahead to Chapter 6. If you're hungry, go get something to eat (and order me a vanilla malt, would you?).

What They Do, Where They Live, and Why You Care

The Preference settings tweak the special America Online software so that it behaves exactly the way you want. (No, you can't install preference settings in your kids — I tried, but it didn't work.) The options cover every aspect of your time with America Online, from sign-on to sign-off, plus a bunch of stuff in between.

Although America Online remembers your Preference settings from session to session, you can change them whenever you want. For example, if I'm working late and want to keep the sound level down, I hop into the Preferences window (explained in the next section), click the General button, and turn off the Enable Event Sounds option. Later, when I'm ready for some noise, I turn it back on (and then crank up the speakers).

Finding the Preference settings takes only a couple of mouse clicks. Dive straight into them by choosing My AOL⇨Preferences from the toolbar. The Preferences window (shown in Figure 4-1) immediately hops into action.

Figure 4-1:
The
Preferences
dialog box,
in its option-
filled glory.

For an online walk though your Preference settings, use the Preferences Guide that's built into the My AOL area. To get there, either choose the quaintly redundant My AOL⇨My AOL from the toolbar or use keyword **My AOL**. When the My AOL window appears, click the Preferences Guide button. For an easy trot through some other common account adjustments, check out the sidebar "Hitting the highlights in one easy step," later in this chapter.

Setting Your Preferences

The following sections dive into the preference settings one at a time, offering a quick explanation of the various options available and pointing out the items that truly enhance your online world.

To make the information easier to find, this section lists the Preference settings in alphabetical order. Of course, that kind of easy-to-follow organization is far too straightforward and useable for a computer program. Instead, America Online cleverly arranges the buttons in the Preferences window by some highly advanced method that apparently involves a wall-sized target shaped like a dialog box, lots of Velcro, and a big pile of low-flying stuffed animals.

Associations

This preference makes its first appearance in America Online's Version 5.0 software. The Associations preference only does one thing: It tells your computer to use the America Online software any time another program wants to send e-mail, visit a Web site, or perform any other Internet-related task. In geek-speak, this setting *associates* the America Online software with all Internet tasks, which is how the programmers came up with its odd-sounding name.

If you use America Online as your one and only connection to the online world, click the OK button in this setting's dialog box. If you connect to the Internet through a local or national Internet Service Provider, leave this preference alone.

Auto AOL

Although the America Online software includes a number of tools to make your online life easier, none of them holds a candle to Automatic AOL and Automatic AOL sessions (the new name for FlashSessions). Automatic AOL sends and receives e-mail, Internet newsgroup postings, and America Online message board postings with incredible ease, saving you both time and effort (and phone time, in case your household includes teenagers).

Automatic AOL helps you manage time by downloading all your e-mail and Internet newsgroup postings to your computer and then signing you off from America Online. From there, you can work offline, reading and responding to your incoming messages and postings. All your replies are saved on your computer. When your replies (and whatever new messages you feel like writing) are ready to go, the Automatic AOL session signs you onto the system and sends them all out in a nice big batch.

Clicking the Auto AOL button in the Preferences window takes you directly to the Automatic AOL setup window. You end up with the same window by choosing Mail Center⇨Set Up Automatic AOL.

For all the details about Automatic AOL sessions and the joys and mysteries of setting these preferences, flip to Chapter 8.

Chat

The most interesting settings in the Chat Preferences dialog box are the notification options and the capability to alphabetize the chat group member list.

The notification options tell America Online to let you know when new people join the chat area or when current attendees leave. After hours and hours of personal testing, I loved seeing who just joined the chat room (Notify Me When Members Arrive), but seeing when people left (Notify Me When Members Leave) got on my nerves. Try turning on one or both notifications for yourself and determine how the results strike you. You can turn on these settings by clicking the appropriate check boxes.

The Alphabetize the Member List option is genuinely handy — I recommend turning it on. If you turn off this setting, the chat area member list transforms into an absolute morass of mixed-up names. Don't let that happen to you. Run — don't walk — to turn on this setting.

As for the Double-Space Incoming Messages setting, I honestly can't think of a reason to turn this on (and believe me, I tried). Most chat rooms scroll by pretty quickly on their own, but this setting makes them fly. Unless you feel like practicing speed reading, leave this one alone.

Download

These settings govern some trivial (and not so trivial) details about downloading files. The most useful of the bunch is the impressive-sounding Automatically Decompress Files at Sign-Off setting. This setting tells your America Online software to automatically unpack any compressed files (commonly called ZIP files) so that you don't need to do it yourself.

Turn off the Delete ZIP Files after Decompression option until you feel comfortable moving files here and there on your computer's hard drive. That way, if you accidentally delete something, you can pull out a replacement from the original compressed ZIP file.

You may as well leave everything else in the dialog box turned on (with a check mark in the box next to the setting). If you do a lot of downloading, turn off the Confirm Additions to My Download List option, because it may drive you nuts in short order.

Font

In the past, no matter where you typed on America Online — e-mail, instant messages, or chat rooms, for example — you had a choice of, to paraphrase Henry Ford, any font you wanted, as long as it was Arial. Thankfully, those days are gone. Now, thanks to the Font preferences, the curtain rises on a brave new world of fontographic choice. Dress up your e-mail, instant message, and chat text with any font installed on your computer!

Hitting the highlights in one easy step

When you're new to America Online, the options get a bit overwhelming. You have so many things to choose from — where should you begin? What should you change first?

In an effort to reduce your stress and make the settling-in process slightly simpler, America Online collected the most-used goodies together in the cool Set Up AOL Now dialog box. With a clear menu and descriptive instructions, this dialog box leads you through the most popular account changes. You can change your screen names, member profile, and parental controls (see Chapter 6 for details about all of those), as well as Buddy Lists (more about that in Chapter 10) and news and stock portfolios (hiding in Chapter 14).

To open the Set Up AOL Now window, choose AOL⇨My AOL from the toolbar and click the big Set Up AOL Now button on the left side of the My AOL window.

Use the Font preferences setting to choose the default typeface (Century Gothic, Mistral, or Times New Roman, for example), size, style (bold, italic, or underlined), and color for your e-mail, instant messages, chat room text, and message boards.

E-mail messages and chat windows include their own font controls; so if you decide on something a little different, changing your settings on the fly is easy. This setting also covers the default font for your signatures in e-mail and discussion boards. Unfortunately, if you already made some signatures, it won't automatically update them to your newly chosen font. (You need to do that yourself.)

General

The next stop on the preferences tour is the General area. Although this area is nothing to jump up and down about, a couple of settings in here earn a quick mention.

The most useful item in here governs event sounds — the various dings and voices that accompany your time on America Online. If it's late in the evening and you want to keep the noise level down (or if someone in your chat room won't stop playing sounds), turn off the Enable Event Sounds setting and the Enable Chat Room Sounds setting.

Graphics

Almost every time you wander into a new area within America Online, the system sends all kinds of art files to your computer. They're the artsy buttons, background graphics, and other stuff that make America Online look so cool. However, all that downloaded art hangs out on your hard drive and takes up space. The most important setting in the Graphics preferences gives you control over how much space the artwork occupies on your hard disk.

The setting in question is labeled `Maximum disk space to use for online art` — the first one in the window, as Figure 4-2 shows. The default size is 20MB (or megabytes, short for millions of characters), which is a little small if you use America Online often. If you have plenty of hard drive space available (which most current machines do — after all, it's tough to fill a multigigabyte hard disk), bump this setting up to 40MB or 50MB.

Figure 4-2:
The
Graphics
Viewing
Preferences
dialog box,
looking
very, um,
graphical.

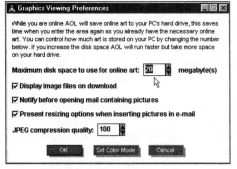

If you can't afford the disk space, nudge the maximum size down to 15MB, but do this *only* as a last resort. The America Online software gets a little irked if you don't give it plenty of space for its graphics — and it doesn't take America Online much time to outgrow that little space.

What happens when the art database grows bigger than the maximum size you set? An electronic version of the old-fashioned spring cleaning, that's what. The America Online software throws out art you haven't used for a while to make room for the new stuff. It happens automatically, although it makes you wait a minute or two while it throws things out. (I think it wants you there for moral support.)

You can find out how big your art database is by using Windows Explorer. Check the size of a file named MAIN.IDX in the IDB subdirectory of the America Online software. That file contains the art database, plus a few other digital odds and ends.

Language

Unless you travel the world extensively and enjoy fluency in several languages (or if you have a wicked practical-joke streak in you), there's no need to change the Language Preferences setting. On the other hand, if you suddenly get an urge to add support for another language to your America Online software, this area is the place to do it.

Mail

E-mail is one of the most useful features of America Online. But keeping track of your e-mail is one of the most hair-reducing features. Thankfully, help is waiting in the Mail Preferences dialog box, as shown in Figure 4-3.

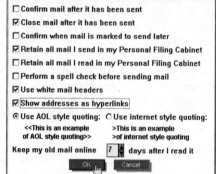

Figure 4-3:
Here's how I like to set the mail preferences.

Want to get rid of the Your Mail Has Been Sent dialog box (the one that appears automatically every time you send an e-mail message)? To make that annoying little window go away forever, select the check box next to `Confirm mail after it has been sent`. Presto — no more mail-confirmation windows!

On the other side of the scale, you simply *must* turn on the Retain All Mail I Send in My Personal Filing Cabinet option. This one is a winner, particularly if you use America Online with your business. Turn this puppy on, and the America Online software automatically drops a copy of all outgoing e-mail into the Mail You've Sent folder (which is available by choosing <u>M</u>ail Center⇨ Read <u>O</u>ffline Mail⇨Copies of Mail You've Sent).

Imagine: No more worrying about whether you replied to someone's message or wondering what you said. Life just doesn't get much better than that, now does it?

The mate to this setting, Retain All Mail I Read in My Personal Filing Cabinet, isn't quite as excellent as its counterpart but still deserves consideration. Like its sibling, this option is *great* for the times that you need to account for all your correspondence.

One word of caution: All this filing uses space on your computer's hard disk, so regularly go through the messages and delete the useless ones. For more about the Personal Filing Cabinet, see Chapter 8.

Marketing

I'm not particularly big on junk mail, pop-up sales windows, and "I'm taking a moment of your time right now" telephone calls. Frankly, I don't like them. My feelings are born from a combination of personal privacy issues, environmentalism, and the desire to enjoy dinner without the phone ringing off the hook.

If you feel the same way, here's your chance to strike back. By the same token, if you *like* junk mail, telemarketing phone calls, and their various ilk, here's an opportunity to get more of exactly that.

The Marketing Preferences dialog box isn't like the other preference settings. Rather than offering a few distinct options, it brings up a smorgasbord of preference settings that cover e-mail, postal mail, online pop-ups, telephone solicitations, and more. Invest a few minutes in browsing the various preference settings — it can only make your life better.

If you're a direct-mail hermit like me, take special note of the Additional Information button in the Marketing Preferences dialog box. This button leads to some great information about the Direct Marketing Association's Telephone and Mail services. Briefly, the document explains how to obliterate all traces of your earthly existence (at least as far as the direct-mail merchants are concerned). I highly recommend reading the information and following the instructions therein.

Passwords

Clicking the Passwords button opens a dialog box for storing your screen name passwords. Storing your password offers two distinct (and separate) benefits. First, you can tell the America Online software to automatically enter your password every time you sign on to the system. That makes signing on a quicker process because your computer never mistypes your password.

The second benefit lets you lock your Personal Filing Cabinet. By storing your America Online account password, you can *password protect* your Personal Filing Cabinet. This feature keeps prying eyes (like parents, roommates, and siblings) out of your stored e-mail and newsgroup messages.

As far as I'm concerned, the jury is still out on the whole *store your password* feature. It's nice for someone who doesn't really care about passwords (and who might otherwise write the password on a note taped to the monitor). The flip side is that after you store the password, anyone with access to that computer can sign on to America Online with that screen name. *Anyone.*

Password protecting your Personal Filing Cabinet may be a boon in some cases — particularly when you share a single computer among several people (or simply between one teenage big sister and one 12-year-old little brother).

With all that in mind, here's how to store a password and choose how it's used:

1. **Sign on with the screen name you want to use with the stored password.**

2. **Get into the Preferences dialog box by choosing My A̲OL⇨Preferences from the toolbar.**

3. **From the Preferences dialog box, click Passwords.**

4. **Type the password.**

   As you may expect, stars appear in place of the actual password. If you mistype something, press Backspace to delete the whole entry and start again.

5. **To use the password during sign-on, click the Sign-On check box. To use it to protect your Personal Filing Cabinet's contents, click the Personal Filing Cabinet check box. Click OK to save your changes.**

   After you have everything checked (and perhaps double-checked), go on with the next step.

6. **Repeat the process for any other screen names whose passwords you want to store.**

   If you change a password in the future, you must return here and change it as well.

Personal Filing Cabinet

The Personal Filing Cabinet, that collector of Automatic AOL mail, Favorite Places, and all kinds of other stuff, is a useful tool. The options in the Personal Filing Cabinet Preferences dialog box make it even better.

The two warning preferences instruct the America Online software to let you know when space is dwindling in the Personal Filing Cabinet and when the cabinet is trying to single-handedly take over your hard drive. You don't need to change these options — the default settings should be fine.

For safety's sake, I recommend leaving both the Confirm check boxes turned on. However, if all the "Are you sure?" messages annoy you too much while cleaning out the Personal Filing Cabinet, feel free to turn them off (at least temporarily).

Privacy

Buddy Lists, the cool feature that lets you see when your friends pop online, make America Online all the more fun. After all, friends make everything better. But sometimes you just want to be alone. Maybe you need to finish some research, update some advertisements in the online classifieds, or spend some quality time with one of the online games. Whatever your reasons, the Privacy preferences help you hide from the rest of the online world.

The Privacy button opens up the somewhat complex Privacy Preferences window. This is exactly the same window that hops up if you click the Privacy Preferences button in the Buddy List Setup window. Chapter 12, which covers the Buddy List system, explains the Privacy Preference settings in depth. Flip over there for the short course in online anonymity. (Don't worry — I won't tell anyone where you went.)

Spelling

It's official — the America Online software knows its spelling words and grammar rules. To celebrate this achievement, it's only logical that a few new preferences would arrive on the scene. Lo and behold, they have, in the form of the Spelling Preferences settings.

As with several of the other preference settings in this dialog box, you don't particularly have to adjust anything — the default settings are fine for almost everyone. In fact, the only reason you may want to change some of the settings is if your computer isn't very fast and performs spell-checks with all the speed of a drugged snail. In that case, try turning off some of the grammar checking options under the Advanced button because they demand serious processing power.

Toolbar

The toolbar looks bolder, brighter, and better than ever these days. Sporting a cool look (and those funky click-to-show-the-menu buttons), the toolbar still harbors a few tricks up its sleeve. Those tricks live in the Toolbar Preferences dialog box.

From the top, the Appearance option lets you pick between the normal toolbar, complete with text and button pictures, and a "lite" toolbar, which contains only the button text. By turning off the pictures, you regain some screen real estate, which means a great deal if your computer has a small monitor.

The Location setting flips the toolbar (and the navigation bar) back and forth between the top and bottom of the window. Which location is better is entirely up to your personal preference, although I must say that it looks really funny along the bottom of the screen.

Navigation and History Trail, the last two settings in the window, probably won't tweak your interest much — although the History Trail item may, if you share your computer with someone else. Turning on the Clear History Trail setting erases all the entries in the drop-down location box on the navigation bar (try saying that three times fast). Basically, it keeps someone else from finding out where you went while you were online. Turn it on and watch your siblings, roommates, or coworkers whine.

WWW (World Wide Web)

Although most of the stuff in the WWW area borders on technoweenie, I want to mention one thing: the Delete Files button.

Although Delete Files isn't really a preference setting, you should hit this button every now and then if you enjoy surfing the Web. Every time you view a Web page, the America Online Web browser keeps a local copy of what you see in a *cache*, a temporary storage area for use by the program, within a particular folder on your computer.

Storing information in a cache isn't a nefarious plot to use up your hard disk space — all the popular Web browsers do it. On the plus side, the cache makes your Web browser respond faster when you're bouncing back and forth between a couple of Web pages. The downside, though, is that the cache fills up after awhile. Unfortunately, a full cache slows down your Web browser a bit (which is precisely the kind of help the World Wide *Wait* doesn't exactly need).

Luckily, emptying the cache is easy. Just follow these steps:

1. **Click the WWW button in the Preferences window.**

   The AOL Internet Properties dialog box appears, as shown in Figure 4-4.

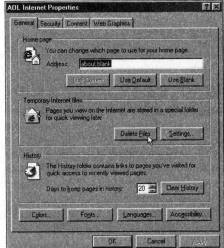

Figure 4-4:
One click
removes
those pesky
temporary
Internet
files.

2. **Click the Delete Files button in the middle of the window.**

   At this point, your hard drive probably sounds like it's going crazy. Believe it or not, that's a good sign. After a few moments (perhaps a minute or more, depending on how long ago you last emptied the cache and how large your hard drive is), everything quiets down.

3. **Click OK to finish the task.**

Chapter 5

Dealing with Spams, Scams, Viruses, and Hoaxes

· ·

In This Chapter

▶ Help — I gave my password to a scammer!

▶ Avoiding password scams

▶ Protecting your mailbox from the junk mail tsunami

▶ Keeping your computer healthy and virus-free

▶ Recognizing an online hoax when you see one

· ·

ear AOL member, you have seventeen unread NetMail messages . . . Hello! I'm Bill Gates. I need your help to test my new e-mail tracking system . . . Walt Disney, Jr., wants to send you $5,000 . . . This really works! Don't break the chain! Send this to everyone you know and the love you want will come to you . . . Due to technical difficulties with our membership system, you must re-verify your account password . . . Hi! We met in the chat room yesterday. Here are the pix I promised to send you . . .

Just when you thought it was safe to visit your e-mail box, out come the spams, scams, hoaxes, and other annoyances of online life. Like their snail mail counterparts, junk e-mail comes in all shapes and sizes, with varying degrees of officiality and believability. Worse yet, some of the messages mask outright scams designed to steal your account password, cost you money, or generally mess up your tidy online world.

Protect yourself from these mailbox perils with the tips and information in this chapter. The following pages cover the seamy realms of junk e-mail, online hoaxes, common password scams, and virus infection schemes. Forewarned is forearmed (as opposed to being four-footed or something), so read these pages carefully. Do your part to make the online world safe!

America Online *never* sends e-mails or instant messages about password problems. The customer service folks don't know your password now (it's encrypted and stored in one of their computers), they don't want to know your password if you change it, and they certainly don't want your credit card number (well, they may *want* it, but they won't ask).

What If You Just Gave Your Password to Someone?

First, don't panic — these things happen. Change your password to something new and different at keyword **Password**. It only takes a moment.

The best passwords include a combination letters and numbers, so try things like *blue17hat* or *trainfun47*. Don't make your password obvious (even if it's easy to remember). Never use things like your name, the word *password,* or simple number sequences like *123456* or *000000*.

If Someone Asks for Your Password, Just Say "No"

This ranks as one of the oldest scams in the online world, but it catches people every day. The password scam comes in a variety of flavors, but the bottom line remains the same: The scammer wants your account password and will lie, cheat, and use any trick he can to get it.

Regardless of the scam's details, they always ask for your password (some variants ask for your credit card number, but the thought remains the same). If you get an instant message or e-mail asking for either your password or credit card number, do not fall for the trap — *don't give out your information.* The message is a scam.

Defeating instant message scams

Instant message scams are the easiest to recognize and avoid. No company in the world — not America Online, American Express, AT&T, MasterCard, Visa, nor anyone else — will send you an instant message asking for account information, credit card numbers, or passwords. They just don't do business that way. Ever. (That kinda simplifies sorting out the real messages from the scams.)

If you get an instant message that asks for your America Online password, credit card number, or any other personal information, click the Notify AOL button on the message window. When the Notify AOL window pops up, briefly explain that you think the attached message is a scam and click the Send Report button. Congratulations — you just turned in the scammer!

When a scam appears on your screen while you're in a chat room, take a moment to warn the chat room that a scammer is trying to get passwords. After spreading the warning, use the Notify AOL button to ruin the scammer's day.

Unmasking e-mail scams

Although some e-mail scams look pretty authentic, they're still just a variation on the *give me your password* theme. If you stick with the basic knowledge that no company in the world will ask you to send them your America Online account password, then you're on pretty safe ground.

Some scammers try the high-tech approach to getting your password by building imposter Web sites using America Online's Web graphics. Because they still have to trick you into coughing up your screen name and password, the scammers most often create a fake page mimicking America Online's NetMail system (the real one lives at keyword **NetMail,** which the scammers *can't* fake) or they invent a fictional contest allegedly sponsored by America Online, which requires a screen name and password for entry.

No matter how genuine something looks, remember the basics: America Online won't ask for your password or any other account information. If they *do* throw a contest, you *never* have to give your account password to submit an entry.

Take a look at Figures 5-1 and 5-2. Take a *close* look, because one of them is a clever fake designed to steal your password.

Figure 5-1:
Is this a
clever fake
of the
America
Online
NetMail
window . . .

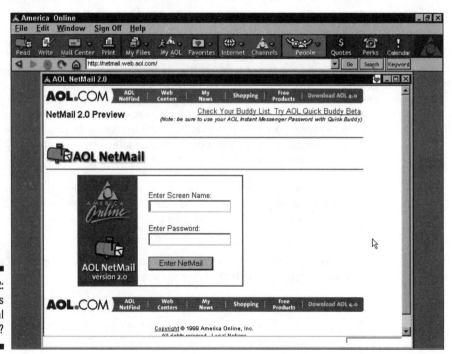

Figure 5-2:
. . . or is this
one the real
thing?

How did they find my screen name?

You can run, but you can't hide — no matter how you try, *they* seem to always find your screen name. The next thing you know, the e-mailbox bulges from all the junk. But how did *they* get your address in the first place?

Actually, they went looking for it. Every time you visit a chat room or post your thoughts to an America Online message board or an Internet newsgroup, your screen name gets posted, too. (If it didn't, other folks wouldn't know that those clever sayings belonged to you.)

That's where the online *ne'er do wells* come in. Using programs written by people with too much free time (and too little life to fill it with), these folks harvest screen names from anywhere and everywhere, including chat room lists, message boards — heck, they even pull names from the online classified advertisements! With the names in hand, they start the box-filling flow of messages which you and I struggle with today.

Here's how to tell the real thing from the *wrong* thing every time:

- To visit a real America Online-based area, you use a keyword (in the case of these figures, it's keyword **NetMail**). You can't accidentally go to a fake area by using a keyword, because scammers can't fake a keyword. But anyone can put a fake link in an e-mail message. The moral of the story: If you don't know who sent a message, don't click any links in it.

- Look carefully at the address displayed in the navigation bar. America Online *never* uses free Web hosting services like Angelfire (www.angelfire.com), Fortune City (www.fortunecity.com), Freeservers.com (www.freeservers.com), HyperMart (www.hypermart.com), Tripod (www.tripod.com), or Xoom (www.xoom.com) for its information areas. Instead, it uses the aol.com servers, or servers belonging to its partners, such as CNet (www.cnet.com), J.C. Penney (shopping.jcpenney.com), Parent Soup (www.parentsoup.com), the New York Times (www.nytimes.com), and the Time Warner companies (www.pathfinder.com).Okay, now the quiz. Which figure is the fake? (Insert appropriate game show theme music here.) And the answer is . . . Figure 5-1. It's pretty sad that the fake looks better than the real thing, isn't it?

 When you receive an e-mail scam, forward the message to screen name TOSEmail (that's TOSEMAIL with the number 1 attached to the end). The friendly folks at America Online's Community Action Team love getting e-mail like that.

Spam, Spam Everywhere (And None of It to Eat)

When it comes to bulk e-mail, I feel sorry for the Hormel company. Granted, I feel sorry for everyone who deals with junk e-mail, but Hormel gets particular sympathy. Somewhere in the Internet's past, unsolicited commercial e-mail (or *UCE,* as it's officially known these days) earned the nickname *spam.* Thus, Hormel's unstoppable juggernaut of canned cuisine innocently became the mascot of e-mail frustration.

No matter what you call it — spam, bulk e-mail, UCE, or digital trash — the stuff pops unbidden into your mailbox. The advertisements run the gamut from questionable penny stocks tips to discount long distance phone cards, plus everything you can imagine in between.

The worst thing about bulk e-mail is the simple fact that you can't stop it without blocking your mailbox from most of the digital world. Traditional postal bulk mailers, who pay to send their messages through the postal system, long ago formed groups dedicated to helping people *stop* the junk mail flood. Why? Because postal mail costs money, and the advertising companies don't like throwing their profits away on people who aren't interested.

In the online world, junk mailers don't pay any costs whatsoever (beyond their basic Internet access, that is) to send their messages. Because sending a million e-mail ads costs the same as sending 10,000, the junk e-mailers have no incentive to target their advertising at a particular audience. All a prospective spammer needs to set up shop is a computer, an e-mail account, bulk mailing software, and a fundamental lack of morals (spamming violates the Terms of Service for every major Internet Service Provider in the world), so new spammers are joining the fun in a never-ending supply.

Despite the fact that spammers want you to *think* that their activities are legal and above-board (as Figure 5-3 shows), as I write this book, *no* national laws regulate bulk e-mail. Although Congress took a few tentative steps toward those controls, in the end they just talked a lot and stopped far short of any real action (a typical Washington maneuver).

You aren't completely powerless against the rising bulk-mail tide. Here are a few ways to fight back:

> ✔ If the message includes removal instructions (like the one in Figure 5-3), give them a try. Don't expect success. Spammers are notorious for ignoring removal requests and faking removal e-mail addresses.

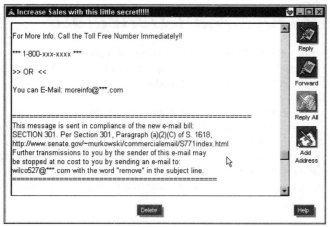

Figure 5-3:
It sounds great, but this bill never became law (the Senate passed it, but the House balked).

- ✔ Although we can't stop bulk e-mail altogether (the Internet is, after all, an international thing), we *can* outlaw its use by United States–based companies. Contact your representatives in Washington and let them know how you feel. The My Government area (keyword **My Government**) helps you find your congressional representatives, send e-mail to them, and track their voting records.

- ✔ Congress responds best when besieged by large numbers of people, so the folks at the Spam Recycling Center (www.chooseyourmail.com/spamindex.cfm) collect unsolicited commercial e-mail and forward it all to your elected officials in Washington. Check the Web site for Spam Recycling Center's forwarding address and other special instructions. (By the way, the service is free — they hate spam, too).

- ✔ Involve yourself in the fight. Visit sites like Safe E-mail Preference Service (www.safeeps.com), Fight Spam (spam.abuse.net), Coalition Against Unsolicited Commercial Email (CAUCE, www.cauce.org), Junk Email (www.junkemail.org). For a more proactive approach, try the calmly-named Death to Spam page at www.mindworkshop.com/alchemy/nospam.htm.

- ✔ If you receive junk e-mail that advertises a pyramid scheme, an illegal product, a lottery, or other such things and that uses a good, old-fashioned postal address for replies, forward the message to the United States Postal Inspection Service (www.usps.gov/websites/depart/inspect), the law enforcement branch of the Postal Service.

- ✔ Living in Canada already has its plusses (it's one heckuva beautiful country, eh?), but when it comes to spam, they're really ahead of the game. Spam is illegal in Canada, so if you live on the northern end of the continent, send your spam complaints to the Royal Canadian Mounted Police (www.rcmp-grc.gc.ca).

Fooling the Bulk Mail Behemoth

Unless you move into the online equivalent of a cave in the hills, you can't completely stop bulk e-mail from dumping into your mailbox. But you *can* cut down the flow from a torrent to a trickle.

The following sections provide two hands-on ways to protect your mailbox. The first focuses on safeguarding your accounts while chatting away in America Online's People Connection. The other tip centers on the popular Internet newsgroups, where the world swaps ideas, insights, and fanciful conspiracy theories. Since they protect different parts of your online experience, feel free to apply them both to your America Online screen names.

Make a screen name especially for chatting

Chatting adds community to the often cold online world. Unfortunately, chatting also leads to a jam-packed e-mail inbox, because spammers spend a lot of time gathering screen names from chat room lists (even though it's against America Online's rules). Protect yourself with a simple technique — make a "chat room" screen name.

Now that America Online gives you seven screen names per account (and 16 characters in each screen name), you have plenty of space for an extra identity or two. Granted, you need to tell your friends about *the new you,* but it's a small price to pay for less junk mail in your mailbox. Here's what to do:

1. **First, pick a new name for your chat identity and create the screen name.**

   If people already know you in the chat rooms, use a variation of your current name with *chat, chats,* or something like that attached to the end (such as `JKaufeldChats`).

   For help creating a new screen name, flip ahead to Chapter 6.

2. **Set the mail preferences for the new screen name to block all e-mail.**

   This step holds the big key for mailbox protection, because it kills the spammer's main tool. Your chat screen name isn't any good to them, because all the incoming mail bounces off the closed mailbox door. (Don't worry — both your friends and folks you meet in chat rooms can still send you mail. Read on to find the secret!)

   Chapter 6 also offers the low-down on settings like the mail controls. Look in the Parental Controls area of the chapter for the specifics.

3. **Build a member profile for the chat screen name. In the profile, tell people to send e-mail to your regular screen name.**

   Since the spammer's name gathering software doesn't intelligently read profiles, your other screen name is protected while you chat the night away.

Protect your e-mail address in Internet newsgroups postings

Use the Newsgroup preferences to add some extra text to the end of your e-mail address, turning it from an innocent address such as jkaufeld@aol.com into jkaufeld@aol.comkillallspam (which is both an incorrect e-mail address and heart-felt personal expression concerning unsolicited commercial e-mail). Putting this protection in place only takes a moment:

1. **Open the Newsgroups window with keyword** Newsgroups.

   If all is well with the online world, the Newsgroups window appears. (If not, then America Online's computers don't feel well right now.)

2. **Click the Set Preferences button near the bottom of the window.**

   This brings up the Global Newsgroup Preferences, a somewhat imposing window with three tabbed pages.

3. **Click the Posting tab.**

   A whole new set of preferences hops onto the screen, including the one you want.

4. **Click in the text area next to the Junk Block heading and then type something like** nospam **or** nojunk. **After you finish, click the Save button.**

   With that setting in place, every time you create an Internet newsgroup message, America Online automatically adds whatever text you typed (the *nospam* or *nojunk* thing) to the end of your e-mail address (because every message includes your address automatically).

Viruses Come in the Darnedest Packages

Despite their best efforts, healthy people sometimes come down with a common cold. They drink the right fluids, eat the best foods, and get plenty of sleep, but the cold still sneaks up and bites them. I guess it's just life's way of saying *it's time to read those new ...For Dummies books.*

Computer viruses behave the same way, but taking the right precautions dramatically improves the odds of keeping your computer healthy. And what precautions might those be? I'm glad you asked:

- *Don't download files attached to e-mails from people you don't know.* This is Cardinal Rule #1 of safe computing. Hackers often distribute password-stealing programs in e-mails with a friendly message like *Had fun chatting with you in the room last night. Here are the pictures I promised!* It seems innocent on the surface, but it hides a nefarious plot. If you don't readily recognize the screen name sending the file to you, don't download the file.

- *Don't trust file names.* Anyone can name a destructive file "fungame.exe," "screensav.exe," or "coolpic.exe" to camouflage its purpose. (After all, they sure aren't going to name it `killdisk.exe`.) If you receive a file like that attached to an e-mail message, refer to the previous bullet. Do you know the sender? If not, don't download the file.

- *Watch out for suspicious file extensions.* The file extension is the last part of a filename (the part after the period). Never, never, *never* download a file with the extension `.shs` (99 times out of 50 it's a virus). Unless you know what you're doing, don't download files ending in `.reg` (those files tweak a very important part of Windows known as the Registry). Normal files have extensions like `.exe`, `.com`, `.zip`, `.jpg`, and `.bmp` (although program files — the .exe and .com files — often harbor viruses, too). If you get a file that you don't recognize, go back to the first bullet in this section: If you don't know the sender, then it's probably a virus or hacker program.

What if you think the computer already caught a virus? In that case, you need some digital medicine. Visit keyword **Virus** for virus-killing steps and anti-virus software. If you don't want to tangle with the virus by yourself, coax one of your local computer-savvy friends into helping you (free food makes a great bribe, by the way).

Recognizing Hoaxes: No, Bill Gates Won't Give You $5,000

The Internet hosts more hoaxes than the Candid Camera show crossed with the National Enquirer. Free money. Stolen kidneys. Expensive cookie recipes. Modem taxes. Worldwide Internet cleanup day. Free beer. Dying children atop mountains of greeting cards. They all sound *soooooo* good, but despite a tiny grounding in reality (or simply a plausible concept), they're all classic Internet hoaxes.

When it comes to hoaxes, P.T. Barnum probably said it best: "Get that mule cart off my foot!" (Oh drat — wrong quote.) Mr. Barnum's correct quote has to do with the way that a good story encourages people to suspend their disbelief and join in the fun, which is precisely what happens when an Internet hoax wanders into your mailbox. (Ol' P.T. phrased it a bit differently, but the concept remains the same.)

Rather than getting blindly sucked into a hoax, take a moment to test the information in the message for yourself. Like the various scams discussed earlier in the chapter, Internet hoaxes follow a distinct pattern. After you know the pattern, picking out the hoaxes is easy. Here goes:

- ✔ **Free money or products thanks to an e-mail tracking system:** This one shows up quite a lot, promising thousands of dollars or free goodies to everyone who forwards the message to their friends. The message guarantees the reward thanks to an "e-mail tracking system," which monitors every move the message makes. *Reality check:* There's no such thing as an e-mail tracking system, and if there were one, the privacy advocates would have collective heart failure over it. Besides, neither Bill Gates nor Walt Disney, Jr., really *wants* to give you $5,000.

- ✔ **Strong statements from vague sources:** Many popular hoaxes rely on official-sounding statements attributed to police ("The Denver police report that . . .") or highly placed government officials. Unfortunately, you can't check on the details of the message because, well, it's not detailed enough. *Reality check:* Look at the Web site of any groups mentioned in the message. Sometimes, the groups in question offer pages of information debunking various hoaxes.

- ✔ **Send this to all of your friends:** Whether the hoax is spooky or sane, timely or timeless, they all request the same Pavlovian behavior: Send the message immediately to everyone you know. The message's accuracy isn't the point — quick movement of this "important information" obviously outweighs little trivialities like whether the whole thing is correct. *Reality check:* Little if any information really *needs* immediate delivery. Hoaxes count on immediacy, because it interferes with research. When hoaxes hit your mailbox, sit on them for a few days before shooting a message back (er, replying to the sender).

For some great hoax debunking resources, visit the America Online Anti-Virus Center (keyword **Virus**); then double-click the Is It a Hoax option. This sends you to a great collection of Internet hoax resources, including my personal favorite, the CIAC hoax page (ciac.llnl.gov/ciac/CIACHoaxes.html).

When debunking a hoax, be kind. Reply to both the person who sent the message to you and everyone who received it from your friend. Give a quick explanation that the hoax is, in fact, false, and that they shouldn't bother forwarding it to anyone else. Use the Favorite Places tool to put clickable links into your e-mail message so that people can read the truth for themselves. (For more about adding links to e-mail, see Chapter 8.)

Part II
The Basics of
Online Life

The 5th Wave By Rich Tennant

"OH YEAH, AND TRY NOT TO ENTER THE WRONG PASSWORD."

In this part . . .

The only thing standing between you and a brain-numbing quantity of mundane details is the America Online access software. You and this program are a team — you'll probably be amazed at what you can accomplish together.

This part shows you how to put the software into action by exploring the fine art of creating screen names, setting the Parental Controls, navigating through America Online, sending e-mail to the world at large, enjoying an online chat, and using the Download Manager to grab programs from the system's online libraries. Part II even includes a section filled with places to find help, if you ever need more than you have right here in your hand. In short, this part covers the basic stuff you need to get your citizenship papers in the Great Online World.

Best of all, I've made *sure* that it isn't the least bit boring. Really.

Chapter 6

Doing the Screen Name Tango (And the Parental Control Two-Step)

In This Chapter

▶ Figuring out the whole screen name thing

▶ Managing screen names

▶ Filling out your profile

▶ Applying some parental controls

*O*ne of my favorite Internet-related cartoons shows a dog camped happily in front of a computer, talking to another dog that just wandered into the room. (I always thought it would be funnier with ocelots, but it probably loses something in foreign translations.) The cartoon caption plays on the anonymous nature of the online world through its pithy caption, "On the Internet, nobody knows you're a dog."

The same idea carries directly into America Online. (The anonymity, that is, not the dog/ocelot thing.) Everybody on America Online knows you by the screen name you create and the information that you put into your profile. That's why choosing the right screen name and filling out your online profile are such big parts of your online experience.

Screen names are more than your online identity. They also play directly into the America Online Parental Controls system, which helps concerned and involved parents take charge of their children's online activities. Without the right screen-name setup, the Parental Controls won't do a bit of good.

This chapter guides you through the ins and outs of the whole *who you are and what you can do online* thing. It starts with screen names, carries on through the Member Profile, and closes with Parental Controls. It's a must-see chapter for your online world. (Heck, tell your friends about it, too!)

What's in a (Screen) Name?

When you joined an online service in the Days of Online Past, you received an account name mechanically generated by a computer. And this computer was quite proud of itself for calling you 71303,3713. After all, the computer had no problem remembering it — why should you?

America Online was created *by* humans and designed *for* humans. As a direct result, *you* (a human) get to choose the name you use on America Online. You can be yourself if you want: Annie, Paul, or Svengali. Of course, you can also be a little more daring and become Homeschooler, Elfcognito, or Mungojerrie. Within the bounds of good taste, the choice is up to you (but more about that later).

Every America Online account has space for seven screen names: one primary name plus six others. The *primary name* is the one you choose when you sign on to the service for the first time. This name is special — kind of like your permanent file in school (the mysterious record always spoken of in dark, terrifying phrases such as "You realize, of course, that this incident will go into your *permanent file*."). The primary name is *permanent* — you can't ever change it. However, the other six names can come and go as you please.

America Online only places a couple of limits on screen names. Screen names must be between 3 and 16 characters long and must start with a letter. After the required first letter, you can use letters, numbers, and spaces to create your online identity. Also, the assembled numbers and letters can't cross the line into what Miss Manners might call "poor taste." (For more about that, see the "Now be nice!" sidebar in this chapter.)

Here's a quick overview of the technical rules covering America Online screen names:

✔ You can have seven screen names in your account — one primary screen name and six others.

✔ The primary screen name is *permanent;* you can't ever change it. But you can create and delete the other six screen names at your whim.

✔ By default, only the primary screen name can make new screen names and adjust Parental Controls. If you want to give that ability to other screen names in your account, you can do so by making the new name a *master screen name.* See the section "Creating a new screen name" later in this chapter to find out how to create a master screen name.

✔ Choose your primary name carefully; it's yours forever.

✔ Screen names are 3 to 16 characters long, start with a letter, and contain any combination of letters, numbers, and spaces your imagination can dream up (within the bounds of good taste, that is).

Now be nice!

A creative screen name is your tool for carving out a unique identity in the world of America Online. You're *supposed* to be creative — that's the whole point. However, a subtle line separates *creative* and *obnoxious*.

Here's a simple guideline for creating a good screen name: Make it as creative as you want, but if you blush at the idea of explaining it to your children, parents, spouse, or significant other, your screen name is probably beyond the bounds of good taste.

One final thought about choosing a screen name: Make it appropriate. A screen name for official business e-mail is quite different from one for a character in the Free Form Role Playing area. If you want to be BoogerDigger, that's your choice, but your new e-mail address (boogerdigger@aol.com) may look a little funny on a business card.

Dealing with Screen Names

Managing the screen names in your account isn't just a job — it's a creative adventure. The following sections go through everything you need to know to keep your screen names in order.

These instructions *don't* apply to your account's primary name. Short of quitting AOL and signing up again, you can't change that. Never. So there.

Creating a new screen name

I think the people who started America Online read too much Shakespeare, because the whole screen name system is outlined in *Romeo and Juliet*. In the play, Romeo can't decide on a screen name. Juliet tries to calm him with the observation, "What's in a name? That which we call a rose by any other name would smell as sweet." His confidence thus buoyed by this botanic observation, he sets off to create a new screen name.

Kids — *don't* try this at home alone. Romeo and Juliet did, and look what happened to them. (If you don't know what happened to Romeo and Juliet, you can find out on the Internet. For a stroll through the classics, turn ahead to the section about the OCF Online Library in Chapter 27.)

Making a new screen name only takes a few moments. Just follow these steps:

1. **Sign on to America Online under your account's primary name or any master screen name.**

The primary name can create new screen names, as can any other screen name that has master screen name status (more about that later in this chapter).

2. **After safely connecting to the service, choose My AOL⇨Screen Names from the toolbar (or use keyword: Names).**

   The Create or Delete Screen Names dialog box opens. If you haven't read the screen names sidebar "Now be nice!" earlier in this chapter, now is an excellent time to do so.

3. **Click the Create a Screen Name option in the dialog box. After the Create a Screen Name information box appears, click the Create a Screen name button.**

   After a small bout of digital redundancy, the Create a Screen Name dialog box appears on-screen.

   If America Online protests that `Your account already has the maximum of 7 screen names,` you must delete an existing name before creating a new one. For more about that, see the section "Deleting an old screen name," later in this chapter.

4. **Type your proposed new screen name in the text box and then click the Create a Screen Name button.**

   If the screen name you typed is available, America Online creates it and asks for a password. In that case, skip ahead to Step 6. If someone else thought of the screen name before you, the system suggests that you choose something else, as shown in Figure 6-1.

5. **If America Online tells you that the screen name you want is not available, click OK to make the information dialog box leave you alone, and go back to Step 3 and try again.**

   The big computers at America Online sometimes feel creative and attempt to help you create a valid screen name. The outcome is much like having your 3-year-old "help" you make a cake from scratch. Figure 6-2 shows the computer's suggestion for poor Romeo. If you reach this point, heed Juliet's wise and earnest advice: "O, be some other name!"

   After you and America Online agree on a screen name (which may take several tries), the Choose a Password dialog box appears, asking you to set a password for the new screen name.

Figure 6-1:
Drat — you
have to
choose
something
else.

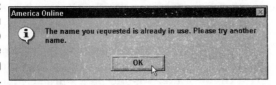

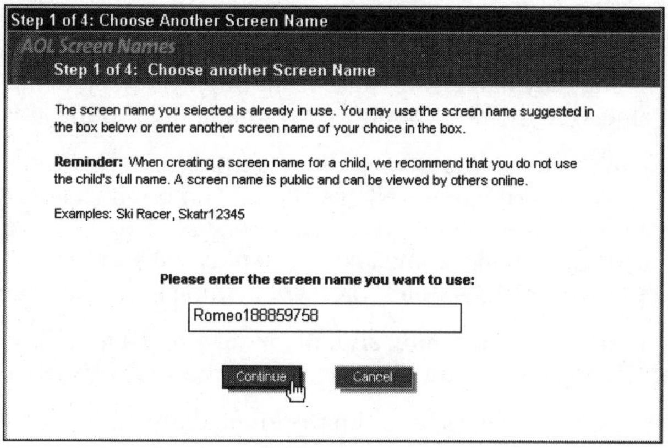

Figure 6-2:
Don't let the
computer
"help" you
make
screen
names.
Baaaad
idea.

Step 1 of 4: Choose Another Screen Name

AOL Screen Names

Step 1 of 4: Choose another Screen Name

The screen name you selected is already in use. You may use the screen name suggested in the box below or enter another screen name of your choice in the box.

Reminder: When creating a screen name for a child, we recommend that you do not use the child's full name. A screen name is public and can be viewed by others online.

Examples: Ski Racer, Skatr12345

Please enter the screen name you want to use:

Romeo188859758

Continue   Cancel

6. **Type the password twice and then click the Continue button.**

America Online passwords have to be between six and eight characters long. As you type a password, little stars (asterisks) appear onscreen. Yes, it's *supposed* to happen that way — it's a security thing.

Because you can't see what you're typing, America Online makes you enter the password twice so that you're sure you didn't make a typing mistake. Type the password in the box on the left and again in the box on the right. If the two entries don't agree, the software warns you and makes you try again.

After the password is accepted, the Parental Control dialog box appears. See the sidebar "Psst — what's the password?" later in this chapter, for some important thoughts and warnings about passwords.

7. **Select an access level for your new screen name by clicking the appropriate radio button in the Parental Control dialog box. Click OK to finish creating the screen name.**

If you choose the 18+ setting, America Online then asks you whether this screen name should be a master screen name. For more about that, continue with the next step. For all other types of screen names, skip ahead to Step 9.

Although the Parental Controls dialog box offers some guidelines for picking the right access level, the actual decision is up to you as a parent. America Online doesn't require kids to have a particular access level — it's not their job. You, the parent, have the full and final say in the matter.

You can always change the access level for a screen name if you find that it's too restrictive or too loose. For more information about the other parental controls, see the section "Parental Controls: Taking Away the Online Car Keys," later in this chapter.

8. **To designate the new screen name as a master screen name, click Yes. Otherwise, click No.**

Master screen names can create and delete screen names in your account, change parental controls, and generally do anything the primary screen name can. You may make your significant other's screen name a master screen name, but you don't want to give that ability to the kids.

After choosing the master screen name setting, America Online congratulates you on a screen name well created. It also outlines what the screen name can do with the access you selected back in Step 7, and gives you the opportunity to make some last-moment tweaks to the screen name's Parental Control settings. Click OK if everything looks just fine.

9. **To use the new screen name, sign off from America Online by choosing Sign Off⇨Sign Off and clicking Yes in the dialog box that appears.**

   The sign-on screen clears, and the Goodbye dialog box bids you a fond farewell.

10. **Click the down arrow next to the Screen Name list box and choose your new screen name from the list.**

11. **Press Tab to move to the Password box and type the new password you created.**

12. **Click Sign On.**

   Poof — it's the new you!

America Online automatically sends a "welcome aboard" e-mail message to the new screen name, describing cool sites to visit, offering some thoughts about good online citizenship, and mentioning other topics. The system also sends a reminder e-mail to your primary screen name saying that a new screen name just joined your account.

If you ever find one of those "Thanks for making a new screen name" messages in your mailbox when you *haven't* made a new screen name, immediately call the America Online Customer Service department, at 800-827-6364. Although it may be nothing more than a computer glitch, calling America Online to find out what's going on is a good precaution.

Deleting an old screen name

Even screen names reach the end of their usefulness. When that time comes for the screen names in your account, delete them and go on about your business. Just follow these steps to delete a screen name:

1. **Sign on to America Online with your primary screen name or a master screen name.**

   If you aren't familiar with master screen names, see the brief description in Step 8 of the preceding section.

2. **After connecting, choose My A̲OL⇨Scree̲n Names from the toolbar (or use keyword Names).**

   The Create or Delete Screen Names dialog box appears.

3. **Click the Delete a Screen Name option in the dialog box.**

   The Delete a Screen Name dialog box pops up.

4. **When America Online displays the aptly named Are You Sure? dialog box, take a deep breath, and click Continue.**

   The Delete a Screen Name dialog box appears, looking just the tiniest bit somber in its fateful duties.

5. **Click the screen name you want to delete and then click Delete.**

   Be *darn sure* that you want to delete this screen name before clicking the Delete button. Although you can theoretically restore deleted screen names, it's an inexact science. Translated into English, restoring a deleted screen name is up to the impish whims of the America Online computers. Maybe they'll let you restore the name, and then again, maybe they won't. Who knows how these machines think?

6. **After doing the dirty deed, America Online issues the brief, generic obituary shown in Figure 6-3.**

Figure 6-3:
He's history
(so to
speak).

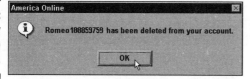

You can't delete the primary screen name. Also, any master screen name on your account can delete other screen names.

Changing a screen name

What if you have a screen name and decide that you want to change it a little? Well, you're out of luck. To paraphrase the wisdom of Yoda, the Jedi master from *Star Wars,* "There is no *change,* only *delete.*"

Your only option is to delete the existing screen name and create a new one from scratch. Sorry to break the news to you like this, but that's just life in the online service world.

Psst — what's the password?

Just like music and cooking, making a good password is an art. Here, in two sentences, is my accumulated knowledge on the subject.

The best passwords string together two common but unrelated words (such as GRAIN-FUN) or add a number to the end of a word (TRAIN577, for example). Your password should not be your name, birth date, spouse's name, dog's breed, shoe size, or anything else that someone can find out about you.

By the way, if you're setting up a screen name for a child or a password-phobic adult, you can configure the America Online software to automatically enter that screen name's password.

Restoring a deleted screen name

Having second thoughts about deleting your favorite screen name, eh? Who could blame you? (After all, that really *was* a great screen name!) Thank goodness America Online offers the Restore a Screen Name option. If all goes well, after a couple of quick clicks, your old screen name (complete with its online profile) will be back, as good as new.

Notice that I said "if all goes well." As you may suspect, things *can* go wrong with the restoration process — like the simple problem of the America Online computers saying "No, you can't have that name back." Precisely why they do this, I don't understand. It probably has something to do with zebra migrations, cat hairballs, and the number of lawyers worldwide telling the truth at any given moment.

Now that you've had fair warning that the process may not work, here are the steps to restoring a deleted screen name:

1. **Sign on to America Online with your primary screen name.**

2. **After you connect, choose My A̲OL⇨Scree̲n Names (or use keyword Names).**

   The Create or Delete Screen Names dialog box appears.

3. **Click the Restore a Screen Name option in the dialog box.**

   The Restore a Screen Name dialog box pops up.

4. **Look through the listed screen names and click the one you want to restore and then click Recover.**

   Assuming that the America Online computers feel cooperative, the system restores your screen name and gleefully pats you on the back to celebrate.

If the name you want isn't on the list or if the America Online computers decide that you can't recover it, you have my condolences (I lost a few screen names this way myself). See the section "Creating a new screen name," earlier in this chapter, because that's your next stop.

Turn a Bit and Let Me See Your Profile

When you see people on the street or in the office, the first thing you notice about them is how they look. Beyond that, they're mysteries until you meet them, talk with them, and invest some time getting to know them.

In the world of America Online, your screen name determines how you "look" to the outside world. But America Online has something else, too — something really neat that I personally wish existed in real life: the member profile.

A *member profile* is a collection of tidbits and trivia about the owner of a particular screen name. For example, my member profile appears in Figure 6-4. Despite what you may think, I'm an average, all-American game player, computer jockey, musician, husband, and father of two. (I also write books, but you already knew that.) If I'm chatting with someone online and the other person wants to know a little more about me, all he has to do is choose People⇨Get AOL Member Profile from the toolbar (or press Ctrl+G), type my screen name in the Get a Member's Profile dialog box, and click OK. Presto! My member profile appears onscreen.

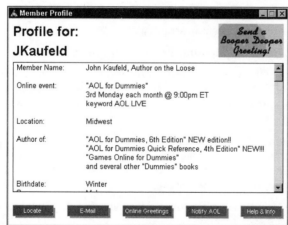

Figure 6-4:
Now you know all about me.

So where does all this profile information come from? From you — that's where (mine came from Cleveland, but that's another story). It's up to *you* to create a member profile for your screen name. If you don't create a profile, other members can't find out about your likes, interests, and hobbies. In short, you'll barely exist on Planet AOL.

- ✔ Please, oh please, fill out your member profile. Leaving it blank is like moving into a new neighborhood because you heard that it had lots of fun people and then acting like a hermit.

- ✔ There's another reason to fill out your member profile: so that people who share your hobbies and interests can find you by searching the Member Directory. Chapter 13 explains the details.

- ✔ Although this falls under the heading of *plain old common sense,* I want to drive home a point. *Do not* put your phone number, address, or other truly personal information in your profile. On a scale of good to bad, this is reeeeaaaaaally bad. Parents, check your kids' profiles every now and then just to make sure that they didn't put anything too personal or (too) weird in there.

- ✔ If you use more than one screen name, you need to fill out a member profile for each one. Every screen name has its own member profile.

- ✔ Some parts of the service (such as the online simulation and role-playing games at keyword **Gaming**) rely on information in your member profile as part of the game. For more about these cool entertainment options, see Chapter 15.

To create (or update) your member profile, follow these steps:

1. **Make sure that you signed on to America Online with the correct screen name.**

   Because every screen name has its own member profile, pairing the right name and profile is important.

2. **Choose My AOL⇨My Member Profile from the toolbar.**

   The Edit Your Online Profile dialog box appears. If you're *creating* a member profile, the dialog box is blank. If you're *changing* the member profile, your current information appears in the spaces (just like mine, as shown in Figure 6-5).

   My profile window looks like a mess because I customized it — added new categories and things like that. It's dangerously close to nerd territory, but if having a profile that's truly your own sounds intriguing, check out Chapter 22 for the scoop.

3. **Fill out the Member Profile form. After you finish, click Update.**

   Don't worry if you seem to type past the end of the boxes for Hobbies, Occupation, and Personal Quote. You have plenty of room to type — the text scrolls through the box until you can't enter any more text. At that point, the box is full. Use your directional arrow, Backspace, and Delete keys to correct any typing or editorial errors.

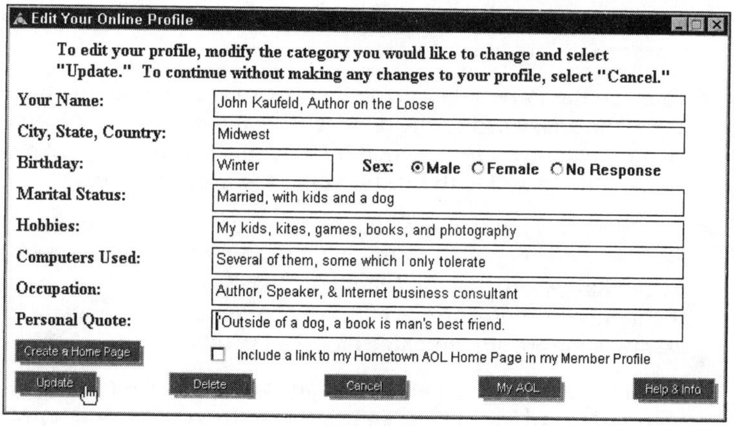

Figure 6-5:
Here's my member profile "under construction." The strange boxes are part of the secrets to creating a custom profile (see Chapter 22).

After you click the Update button, America Online replies with a little dialog box telling you that your profile is being updated. Although the update process usually happens immediately, it occasionally takes a little while (usually ten minutes or so, but *much* longer if the system is busy).

Parental Controls: Taking Away the Online Car Keys

Like any major city or tourist destination, America Online has much to see and do. Unfortunately, the similarities don't end there. Every big city also has a section that the tourist guide suggests avoiding, as well as a small, eerie population of less-than-moral people. If I said that America Online was immune to this concept, I'd be a fool (no editorial comments from readers who know me personally, please).

Whether you like the thought or not, the online world contains some places (and some people) that your kids really don't need to visit. That's what the Parental Controls are all about. They offer you, the parents, control over what your kids can and can't do with America Online.

Before going into the details, here are a few thoughts to set the stage:

✔ Different people have different views about what kids should and shouldn't do (just look around your neighborhood for proof). Please understand that I'm not hopping onto a moral high horse and proclaiming what's right and wrong for your kids and that I'm not passing judgment about what's available out there (although the thought *is* tempting sometimes). I'm just explaining the tools available and giving some very general advice for parents whose kids know the Internet better than they do.

✔ To make the Parental Controls really work, only you, the parent, should know the password to the master screen names (the screen name you created when you first signed up for America Online, plus any screen name you created with master screen name privileges).

✔ Create a screen name specifically for your child to use. Remember that each America Online account can have up to seven screen names at no extra charge — one primary name plus six others. To give each child in the family a different level of access to America Online and the Internet, create separate screen names for everybody.

✔ If you're curious why I'm making such a big cloak-and-dagger deal out of who's using which screen name, here's the reason: Master screen names are special. *Only* a master screen name can set parental controls and create new screen names on your account. If your child uses a master screen name for online access, she can simply turn off whatever parental controls you turn on. (Whoops!) Instead, create a screen name especially for her, place the controls on it, and keep the master screen name for yourself.

Starting the Controls (And Backing Safely Down Your Digital Driveway)

Open the Parental Controls screen by either choosing My AOL⇨Parental Controls from the toolbar or using keyword **Parental Controls.** Either way, the Parental Controls information screen appears. It offers general thoughts about the whole Parental Control thing, plus tosses out some cool tips and suggestions concerning online safety and the America Online premium services (the ones that cost extra to use). When you're ready to do the Parental Control thing, click the Set Parental Controls Now button at the bottom of the screen.

America Online provides two levels of parental control, depending on how much you want to tweak the digital knobs and levers. The basic level offers four general options (Kids Only, Young Teen, Mature Teen, and 18+). When you choose one of these, America Online sets a bunch of default restrictions governing what that screen name can access both within America Online and outside on the Internet (when accessing the Internet with the America Online built-in Web browser and other Internet tools).

The more advanced level is *Custom Controls*. This à la carte approach to the Parental Controls helps you pick and choose specific limitations for chatting, instant messages, downloading, Web use, e-mail, and Internet newsgroups.

Although using these settings takes a bit more knowledge of America Online, you create an online experience tuned exactly to your child's needs.

How do you choose the right controls for your kid? It depends. Consider the age and maturity of your child. Granted, our kids are all above average in intelligence and everything else, but for this one moment try to be especially objective. How responsible is your child? How naive? How trustworthy? Yes, these are tough questions, but this decision is very important. Here are a few general guidelines:

- ✔ For children 12 or younger, I recommend using the Kids Only default option. That lets them get into Kids Only, the area within America Online that's specifically designed for that age group, plus kid-friendly Web and Internet sites. You can feel comfortable that your little one won't run across anything incredibly weird (except, of course, other kids).

- ✔ The teen years are more challenging. (Stating the obvious is one of my strengths.) If you use any controls at all, start with the appropriate teen-access setting. If your online child finds that setting too restrictive, try relaxing things by using some specific Custom Control options (discussed in the following section). If you use the Custom Controls feature, I recommend blocking member rooms in the Chat control, FTP in the Download control, and any Internet newsgroup containing the magic words *sex* or *erotic* in the Newsgroup control. That combination maximizes the widely acceptable stuff while blocking off the Internet's most (ahem) *colorful* content.

- ✔ If you feel comfortable giving your kids free run of the world, that's cool. In that case, use the 18+ option, which gives them full access to both America Online and the Internet. Nothing says that you *must* use the controls — they're just available tools.

You can change the settings at any time, so don't worry about ruining your children forever by making the wrong choice. Pick the settings, talk to your children, and see how everything works. If you need to make adjustments, do so. Most of all, work with your children and let them know that you're interested in their online world. That makes a bigger impact than any control ever can.

Tailoring Online Life with the Custom Controls

Sometimes (well, *frequently,* in my case) the one-size-fits-all solutions just don't fit. If your child needs more access here and less access there than the Kids Only or teen access controls allow, try customizing the Parental Controls. From the main Parental Controls window (keyword **Parental Controls**), click the Set Parental Controls option near the bottom of the window. This leads you to the do-it-yourself side of the parental controls (as shown in Figure 6-6), where you, the parent, take complete control over what your kids can and can't do online.

The options in this window govern the most important interactive parts of America Online. Each option is described in its own section later in this chapter.

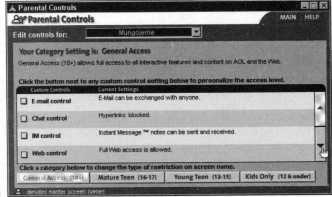

Figure 6-6: The custom controls give you incredible flexibility to tailor your child's online access.

None of these controls protects a child who has access to a master screen name on your America Online account (master screen names *always* have permission to change the Parental Controls for any screen name in your account). To take advantage of the Parental Controls, you *must* create a separate, non–master screen name for your child.

E-mail control

E-mail is a powerful communications tool, although it can also be powerfully annoying.With the new America Online Mail controls, however, you can take command of your e-mail box and, more importantly, protect your kids from mail they shouldn't get.

The Mail controls fall into two distinct groups: general limitations on all mail and specific restrictions based on a set of e-mail addresses. Here's a look at your options by group:

✔ **General limitation controls:** These options establish simple, wide-ranging limits on all mail sent to a particular screen name. The three options are:

  • **Allow All E-Mail:** Anyone on AOL or the Internet can send e-mail to this screen name.

  • **Allow E-Mail Only from AOL Members:** This option blocks all Internet-based e-mail.

- **Block All E-Mail:** So much for the e-mail thing — it was nice while it lasted.

✔ **Specific address-based controls:** Unlike the blanket controls, the address-based controls filter mail based on a list of e-mail addresses that you, the parent, enter into the system. The options on this side of the fence are

  - **Allow E-Mail from AOL Members and Only from Selected Internet Domains and Addresses:** Any AOL member can write to the screen name, but only listed Internet addresses can do so.

  - **Allow E-Mail Only from Selected AOL Members, Internet Domains and Addresses:** You can receive mail from any AOL or Internet e-mail address, as long as you put the address on the list in the dialog box.

  - **Block E-Mail from Selected AOL Members, Internet Domains and Addresses:** This option allows all mail except items from the listed addresses.

These six controls have a great deal of flexibility — hopefully, enough for everyone. My favorites on the list are Allow Mail from AOL Members Only (great for easily blocking Internet junk mail) and Allow Mail from AOL Members and Addresses Listed (because it's a slightly looser version of the preceding option). Although at certain moments the hermit-like Block All Mail option is interesting, I think defining who *is* acceptable is more powerful than blocking those who aren't.

To put up some e-mail controls, follow these steps:

1. **Sign on with your master screen name and then choose My A̲OL⇨ Parental C̲ontrols.**

   The general Parental Controls window opens.

2. **To fire up the screen you need, click the Set Parental Controls option, near the bottom of the window.**

   The detailed Parental Controls settings window appears.

3. **In the Edit Controls For box at the top of the screen, click the down-arrow to list your account's screen names. Click your child's screen name in the list.**

   The window resets itself to display the current parental control settings for the selected screen name.

4. **Click the button next to the E-mail Control entry in the Custom Controls area at the bottom of the dialog box.**

   The Mail Controls window appears, ready to help protect your kids.

5. **Click the radio button for the proper level of mail control. If necessary, enter any America Online screen names or Internet e-mail addresses in the Type Mail Address Here box and then click the Add button.**

Because these are radio buttons, you can choose only *one* mail control setting at a time (even if you really want a combination of two).

6. After you're done, click Save and then close the Parental Controls window.

Your mail controls are now in place and running.

Chat controls

The People Connection chat rooms are a popular attraction on America Online. Unfortunately, the word *popular* often translates into *time-consuming*, because it's so easy to completely lose track of time while chatting the night away.

To keep your kids (or even yourself) out of the chat rooms, follow these instructions:

1. Sign on with a master screen name and choose My AOL⇨Parental Controls.

The general Parental Controls information window appears.

2. Click the Set Parental Controls item near the bottom of the window.

The detailed Parental Controls setting window hops energetically to the screen.

3. In the Edit Controls For box at the top of the screen, click the down-arrow to see a list of the screen names on your account. Click the child's screen name in the list.

The window resets itself, displaying the current parental control settings for the screen name you chose.

4. Click the button next to the Chat Control entry in the Custom Controls area at the bottom of the dialog box.

The Chat Controls window appears, filled to the brim with detailed information about the chat controls (as shown in Figure 6-7).

5. Click in the check boxes next to your child's screen name for each chat control you want to turn on.

Table 6-1 explains each of the four options, including a Severity option that offers an opinion of how draconian that particular setting is.

6. After you're done, click Save.

America Online responds with a brief note that your changes are saved.

7. Click OK and then close all the Parental Control windows.

Another one's done!

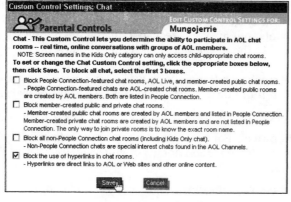

Figure 6-7:
Keep
younger
kids out of
chat rooms
with a
couple of
well-chosen
controls.

Turning off the chat options is as easy as turning them on. Just repeat the preceding steps and click in each check box again, removing the mark for it.

Table 6-1		Parental Control Options
Control	**Severity**	**Description**
Block People Connection-featured chat rooms	10	Blocks all general AOL chat areas, including AOL Live and the People Connection, but still gives access to conference rooms
Block Member-created public and private chat rooms	2	Prevents access to member-created and private chat areas, but allows the use of the regular People Connection areas
Block all non-People Connection chat rooms	9	Blocks conference rooms throughout America Online, including the discussion rooms in Research & Learn and the Kids Only chat areas
Block the use of hyperlinks in chat rooms	4	Prevents the screen name user from clicking a hyperlink that someone types in a chat room

Instant message controls

Instant messages are the immediate communication windows that appear out of nowhere (sometimes scaring the living daylights out of you, depending on the hour of the day and how hard you were concentrating at that moment). Instant messages let you carry on a private, one-on-one chat with someone else on America Online or on the Internet (through the America Online Instant Messenger software — see keyword **Instant Messenger** to find out the scoop about that).

Depending on the age and maturity of your child, you may or may not want him using instant messages. (I turned the whole instant-message thing *off* on my kid's accounts, but my kids are also in the under-10 bracket.) To limit your child's access to the instant message system, follow these steps:

1. **Sign on to America Online with your master screen name and choose My AOL⇨Parental Controls and click Set Parental Controls Now.**

   The Parental Control settings window appears, eager to help.

2. **In the Edit Controls For box near the top of the window, click the down-arrow to list of screen names in your account. Select the child's screen name.**

   The window displays the current parental control settings for the screen name you selected.

3. **Click the button next to the IM Control entry in the Custom Controls area at the bottom of the dialog box.**

   The Instant Messages control window hops to the screen, just like the one shown in Figure 6-8.

4. **Select the Block Instant Message Notes check box for this screen name if you want to disallow instant messages to your youngster.**

   The choice is clear: Let them use instant messages or not. This isn't a shades-of-gray kind of decision.

5. **After you're satisfied with the control settings, click Save to save them. Close the Custom Controls window (click the X button in the upper-right corner of the window) when you're done.**

   The instant message controls are in place (and you can breathe a little easier).

Figure 6-8:
Keep instant messages off your child's screen with the Block Instant Message Notes option.

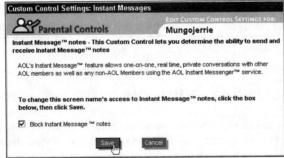

Web controls

Few things in the world change faster than the World Wide Web (although the flux-filled policy statements of many career politicians do come close). Although the Web is filled with thousands of clever and informative sites, it's also the home of many pages best left unseen by little eyes. To keep curious youngsters pointed toward the truly educational things rather than the woo-hoo-hubba-hubba educational ones, try applying some Web controls.

These controls limit the sites the America Online built-in Web browser can connect to. The decisions about which sites are in and which are out come from the Learning Company, which rates the sites by the type of content they contain. The Web controls include Kids Only (a limited list of sites for ages 6 to 12), Young Teen (another limited list for ages 13 to 15), and the Mature Teen block list (which allows full Web access but blocks specific inappropriate sites). The system's other option grants full access to the Web.

For younger kids, stick with the Kids Only approved site listing. After your child blossoms into the terrible teens, give her either the appropriate teen setting or full access (as long as she can handle the responsibility). Because so much of the America Online content is Web-based, I can't recommend completely shutting down Web access for any account.

To apply the Web controls, follow these steps:

1. **Sign on to America Online with a master screen name and then choose My AOL⇨Parental Controls. Click the Set Parental Controls button to continue.**

   The detailed Parental Controls window soundlessly enters the room.

2. **In the Edit Controls For box at the top of the window, click the down-arrow to see a list of screen names in your account. Click on the child's screen name.**

   The window updates itself and displays the current parental control settings for the screen name you chose.

3. **Click the button next to the Web control entry in the Custom Controls area at the bottom of the dialog box.**

   The Web Controls window pops onto the screen.

4. **Click the radio button next to the level of Web control you want.**

   Because the settings are radio buttons, you can pick only one setting per screen name.

5. **Click Save to store the settings; then close the Parental Controls window.**

   The Web controls are ready to serve and protect.

Additional Master (screen name)

In the world of screen names, only a few are masters — the rest, simply subordinates. That's a good way to keep things as a parent with online kids. By default, only your primary screen name (the one you created when you first signed on to America Online) is a master screen name. If adding another master screen name would simplify your life, open the Screen Names parental control and get to work.

The Screen Names window accomplishes only one thing: It turns normal screen names into master screen names. It doesn't _create_ screen names (for that, choose My AOL⇨Screen Names from the toolbar), change screen names, or even smirk at screen names. This is one seriously focused window.

Do _not_ give your child a master screen name! That's the digital equivalent of loaning your beloved teenager the keys to your 1966 Corvette, signing over the vehicle's title, handing him your gold credit card, and casually mentioning that you're on the way out the door for a two-year-long world cruise. In short, it's free rein for the child to do whatever he wants in the online world. Because master screen names can set parental controls, only parents should use the master screen names.

With that warning ringing in your ears, here's a run through the process of changing the master screen name settings:

1. **Sign on with the master screen name and then choose My AOL⇨ Parental Controls from the toolbar. After the general Parental Controls window appears, click Set Parental Controls.**

   The Parental Controls settings window finally appears, ready to work.

2. **In the Edit Controls For box at the top of the window, click the down-arrow to see a list of screen names in your account. Click on the child's screen name.**

   The window updates itself and displays the current parental control settings for the screen name you chose.

3. **Using the down-arrows on the side of the Custom Controls area, scroll down to the additional master setting and click the button next to setting's entry.**

   After that little romp, you land in the Additional Master Screen Names window.

4. **Click the check box at the bottom of the window to bestow master-screen-name status on this lowly screen name.**

   Only three of your seven screen names can be master screen names. Your primary screen name automatically has master status, so you can assign as many as two more masters on your account.

5. **After you finish setting the Master check box, click OK.**

America Online stores your preferences and updates the online records for your screen names. As a security precaution, America Online automatically sends to the primary screen name a notification e-mail that gives the time and date each screen name received master status.

If you open your e-mail box one day and find a letter saying that one of your screen names recently received master status but *you* didn't do it, immediately call the America Online customer service department at 800-827-6364 and enlist its help to find out what's happening with your account.

Download controls

Of all the parental controls, the Download controls are probably the least important. Granted, there are some things in the world that I don't want my kids downloading from America Online or the Internet, but that's hardly my biggest concern about online life.

If it's a bigger worry in your life than in mine, follow these steps to limit your child's access to downloadable files:

1. **Sign on to America Online with your master screen name and then choose My A̲OL⇨Parental C̲ontrols. After the window appears, click the Set Parental Controls option at the bottom of the window.**

If everything works just right, the Parental Controls settings window appears.

2. **In the Edit Controls For box at the top of the window, click the down-arrow to list the screen names for your account. Click the screen name for your child.**

The window updates itself and displays the current parental control settings for the screen name you chose.

3. **Using the arrows on the side of the Custom Controls area, scroll until the Download Control item appears and then click the button next to its entry.**

The vaguely impressive Downloading Control dialog box leaps into view.

4. **To turn on the download controls, click one or both of the check boxes in the window. After you're done, click Save.**

An energetic dialog box pops up, letting you know that your changes are saved.

I wouldn't bother with Block AOL Software Library Downloads, but turning on the Block FTP Software Downloads option is a good idea. FTP (File Transfer Protocol) copies files through the Internet, and there's no telling what your inquisitive kiddo may find out there.

5. **Click OK and then close the Parental Control windows.**

   Download controls are now in place!

As you may have guessed by now, to undo the download controls, you simply repeat the steps to create them. The big difference is that this time you click the check boxes *off* rather than turn them on.

Newsgroup controls

Of all the custom parental controls, Newsgroup is the most valuable. Internet newsgroups are an incredible resource, filled with discussions about almost every topic imaginable. However, not all the conversations out there are designed for eyes under age 18.

To block out the most (I'm being kind here) *exotic* material the newsgroups offer, follow these steps:

1. **Sign on with the master screen name and then choose My AOL⇨ Parental Controls. Finish your trip by clicking the Set Parental Controls button.**

   The Parental Control settings window appears.

2. **In the** `Edit controls for` **box at the top of the screen, click the down-arrow to list your account's screen names. Find your child's screen name in the list, then click it.**

   The window resets itself so you can see the current parental control settings for the selected screen name.

3. **Using the arrows on the right side of the window, find the Newsgroup controls entry. Click the button next to the Newsgroup option.**

   The Newsgroup control window pops into view.

4. **For most kids, I recommend setting the controls as shown in Figure 6-9. When you finish the settings, click Save.**

   The example setting blocks your child from any Internet newsgroup with, shall we say, stimulating words in its name. This one setting quickly blocks off most of the content that many parents are concerned about.

   This setting does *nothing* to keep your kids out of the more explicit areas of the World Wide Web — it just takes care of the newsgroups (which *really* need taken care of, by the way). For that, see the section "Web controls," earlier in this chapter.

5. **Close all the various open windows and continue with your regularly scheduled day.**

   Your child is now mostly safe from the Internet newsgroups.

To undo these restrictions, work back through the preceding steps. In Step 4, delete the entries in the Block Newsgroups text area. Remember to click OK after you're done!

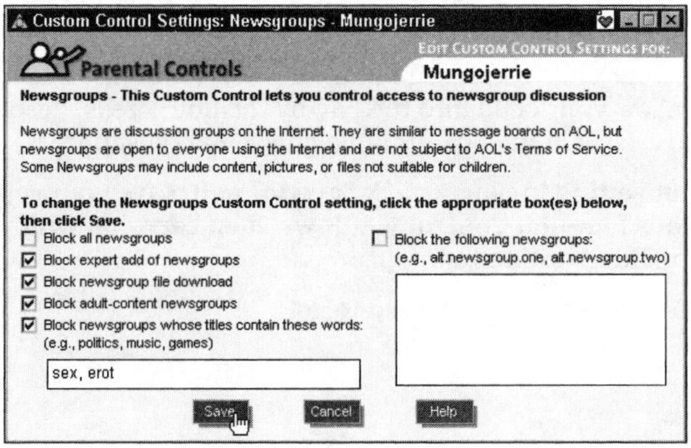

Figure 6-9:
These two little words keep your kids out of so much trouble that it's amazing.

Premium Services
================

Premium Services

Your monthly America Online fee covers an awful lot of ground. It provides e-mail access, Internet access, plus chat rooms, message boards, and lots of other goodies that America Online offers. Even so, some areas of the service (notably, some of the cool multiplayer games) bring an extra hourly fee. If your kids enjoy computer games as much as mine, then keeping junior (or juniorette) out of the for-pay games could spell the difference between fiscal responsibility and financial disaster.

There must be some parents at America Online, because all of the generic age restriction settings (Kids Only, Young Teen, and Mature Teen) automatically block access to premium service areas.

If you *want* to give your children access to the pay-by-the-hour games and other premium fee areas, follow these steps:

1. **Sign on with the master screen name, then choose My AOL⇨Parental Controls from the toolbar. Complete the journey by clicking the Set Parental Controls item at the bottom of the screen.**

   The Parental Control settings window appears on-screen.

2. **In the Edit Controls For box at the top of the screen, click the down-arrow for a list of your account's screen names. Click on your child's screen name in the list.**

   The window resets itself so you can see the current parental control settings for screen name you clicked.

3. **Using the arrows on the right side of the window, find the Premium Services entry. Click the button next to the item.**

   The Premium Services window hops into view.

4. **Click the Block Premium Services check box to pick your premium services settings.**

   To block your child's access to premium service areas, select the check box. To allow your child into the pay-by-the-hour areas, deselect the check box (click in the box until the check mark disappears).

5. **With your setting in place, click Save to, well, save your settings. Close the various Parental Control windows, then carry on with your regularly scheduled online time.**

   That's it — the settings are good to go!

Chapter 7

Navigating the System and Marking Your Favorite Destinations

*Y*ou don't need to travel much before you start collecting a mental list of places you enjoy, locales you dislike, and restaurants you never quite found, despite splendid directions from the hotel concierge. It's human nature — we know what we like, and, when in doubt, we usually choose the known rather than the unknown (particularly because we can go there without getting lost).

Human nature being what it is, by now you probably wandered the online highways and byways, got lost among the windows a few times, and discovered several (perhaps many) likable haunts on both America Online and the Internet. But, remembering your favorite spots and finding your way back to them is a problem sometimes — after all, computer monitors have only so much physical space for little sticky notes before you can't see the screen anymore.

That's where this chapter fits into your life. The chapter looks at the main windows of your online world, explores the gentle art of navigating the system, and then explains how to rid your monitor of sticky notes, thanks to the built-in Favorite Places and My Places options. If you're tired of stumbling across something cool and then losing the note that got you there (or if you're just tired of getting lost), kick back, put your feet up, and flip through this chapter. It's here to help.

Your Windows on the World

Everywhere you go on America Online, you find windows. Welcome windows, channel windows, information area windows — sheesh, spring cleaning around here must be a *total* nightmare.

Although the windows are a little confusing at first, they make America Online the special place that it is. Unlike other online services, America Online was designed with the Macintosh and Microsoft Windows graphical way of life in mind. And it shows.

This section introduces and explains the basic America Online navigation windows. The details of the content areas (the stuff *in* the windows) come later in this book. For everything you ever wanted to know about the channels, turn to *AOL For Dummies Channels Directory,* in the yellow pages in this book. For now, though, sit back, grab a bottle of spray cleaner, and head for the windows of your digital world.

The Channels window: Road map, cheerleader, and Wal-Mart greeter rolled into one

If you're looking for the right place to start your online expedition, try the Channels window, as shown in Figure 7-1 with the Welcome page open and alive. From here, your news, e-mail, calendar, and any of the 19 America Online channels are a quick jump away. Life just doesn't get better than this.

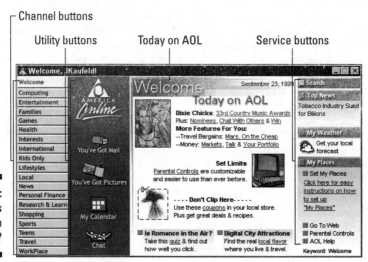

Figure 7-1:
How's this
for a warm
welcome?

Every time you sign on to America Online, the Welcome page hops right up and offers a great big "Hi there — welcome to the system!" This window is like an electronic version of the Wal-Mart door greeter, only better. This greeter doesn't just wish you well; it says hi, tells you the top news headlines, keeps tabs on your e-mail box, and never hits you with a shopping cart. Not even Californians have it this good.

Figure 7-1 shows the Welcome page on an average day. It's a straightforward affair, organized into several specific information areas: Channel buttons, utility buttons (mail, calendar, and such), Today on AOL goodies, and service areas.

Occupying the left side of the window are the *channel buttons,* offering single-click connections to the 19 content channels on America Online. Each button displays the menu of services and content available in that channel area. To make things ever more consistent and easier to understand, the 19 channels look very similar (boy, is that a welcome change!). Each channel window includes buttons for its various departments, plus some links to featured areas within the channel. The featured area buttons change periodically, but unless something groundbreaking happens, the departments remain the same.

The *utility buttons* sit to the right of the channel buttons. These handy fellows tell you if e-mail awaits your attention and if your pictures are available from the You've Got Pictures service. The utility buttons also provide quick access to an online calendar and the ever-popular People Connection (keyword **People Connection**). Just click the button, and you're off!

Next on the agenda is the *Today on AOL* area. This serves up brief descriptions of a few highlighted areas on America Online, along with links that take you to each one. These entries change all the time, so don't worry if your screen doesn't show exactly the same items as Figure 7-1.

The final column displays the *service buttons.* These useful items include the AOL search system, news headlines, weather, the cool My Places area (more about that later in this chapter). The remaining services (Go to Web, Parental Controls, and AOL Help, and others) sit at the bottom of the column.

In the lower-right corner of the channels window is the *keyword* for this particular area. See the sidebar "Psst — what's the keyword?" later in this chapter, for more about these useful little thingies. As you flip through the channels (with the previously mentioned channel buttons along the left side of the window), each channel's keyword shows up here.

For a special treat, click the America Online logo in the upper-left corner of the Welcome page. Who knows what may happen? (Okay, so it leads to the What's New area, but keep it to yourself. We don't want *everyone* to know.)

While I have your attention, here's some more stuff you should know about handling the channels:

✔ Getting back to the Channels window is never hard. Just click the Channels button on the toolbar, select the channel you want to see, and {poof!} you're there.

✔ To pick up more information about what each channel contains, flip to the *AOL Channels Directory* — a special section on yellow paper near the middle of the book.

Individual content windows: The heart of America Online

The digital foot soldiers of America Online are the individual content areas. Hundreds, if not thousands, of content areas are out there, and each has its own unique interface window. Some of the windows have lots of artwork and feature buttons (like Figure 7-2). Others are plain to the point of being utilitarian (see Figure 7-3 for a to-the-point example). Both kinds of interfaces do basically the same things, except that the fancy ones do it with more panache.

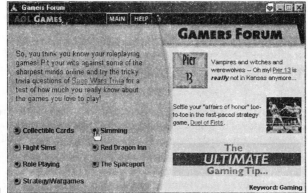

Figure 7-2:
A truly fancy service window.

A fancy service window always contains some *feature and function buttons*. These graphical buttons lead you to special parts of the service, help you search the service's archives, or otherwise do something truly fun for you. Read the button descriptions carefully — don't rely too much on the picture to tell you what the button does.

Figure 7-3:
The
essence of
simply
presented
content.

Somewhere on the window is the service's keyword. It usually sits in the lower-right corner, but not always — it migrates all over the place, depending on the service. If you're not familiar with keywords, you should be. Look in the sidebar titled "Psst — what's the keyword?" for more information.

Last on the tour is the list of *service areas* — see Table 7-1. Most of the time, both kinds of content windows contain this list, but not always (fancy content areas sometimes replace the list with a series of buttons). The list is in whatever order the service feels like using (in other words, don't bank on things coming up in alphabetical order). To get into an area on the list, double-click its entry.

Don't expect every service to look just like every other service. Some are very plain; others are quite fancy. Just relax and go with the flow — you're doing fine.

Psst — what's the keyword?

Almost every service in America Online has a *keyword*. It's like a magic carpet that whisks you wherever you want to go. Using keywords saves you time, and makes the system all the easier to use, too.

To use a keyword, click in the big white text area on the navigation bar, along the top of the screen. (Keyboard lovers in the audience should press Ctrl+K to bring up the Keyword dialog box.) Type the keyword and press Enter. If everything works as it should, you immediately jump to that keyword's window.

Jot down the keywords for your favorite services on the Cheat Sheet in the front of this book and use that list as a memory jogger or to plan your online sessions.

Table 7-1		Service Areas
Icon	*Name*	*Meaning*
🗁	File Folder	Leads to an individual service window, which in turn contains more icons
🎦	Chat	Takes you into a conference chat room within a content area
🗋	Document	Shows a document explaining something about the service
📖	Open Book	Displays a searchable database (found mostly in the various Research sections)
🗇	Disks	Opens a library of downloadable software
⊕	Globe	Usually points to an item on the World Wide Web
🗂	Bulletin Board	Opens a window of discussion boards
↷	Special	Often a Web page but may be just about anything

Adding Your Picks to My Places

As part of their ongoing effort to help you find the coolest online places (and to herd everyone in roughly the same direction — toward the ads), the America Online folks added a new tool to your navigational arsenal: the quasi-customizable My Places links (as shown in Figure 7-4). They camp in the lower-right corner of the Welcome window, ready to send you wherever — well, *mostly* wherever — you want to go.

"Wait a minute," I hear you cry in navigational confusion. "What do you mean *quasi-customizable?* And what's with the *mostly wherever* crack?"

Unfortunately, I meant just what I said. The My Places area, unlike the what-ever-you-want-to-put-there Favorite Places system and the My Shortcuts do-it-yourself menu, is *quasi-customizable.* Yes, you choose where the buttons take you, but you can only pick from a preset list of links that America Online (in their infinite wisdom) provides. If you love the online game shows, the AOL.COM customizable news page, or the online Yellow Pages, then My Places completes your life. If your tastes run toward more unique things (like the Web graphics or homeschooling forums), you're out of luck with My Places. Instead, use either the Favorite Places or My Shortcuts for quick access to those areas.

Figure 7-4:
Customize
your
Welcome
window a
bit with My
Places.

The America Online programmers (secreted away in those massive Dulles, Virginia offices) assure me that they included the "most popular" online areas in the My Places options. Still, I wish it included an "other" entry to add your favorite keyword or Web site. But alas, it doesn't. (At least not yet.)

The first time you sign on with new America Online Version 5.0 software, the Welcome window displays an uncustomized My Places area, emblazoned with the suggestion that you should nip right over and pick some places of your own. The setup process only takes a moment:

1. **With your computer signed on to America Online, click the Set My Places button in the lower-right corner of the Welcome window.**

   The somewhat simple Change My Places window pops onto the screen.

   The settings for My Places are unique to each screen name, so you need to repeat the setup process for each screen name in your stable.

2. **Pick a slot for the new My Places link; then click the Choose New Place button next to it.**

   A drop-down menu slides into view.

3. **Run your mouse through the drop-down menu until you find an interesting topic. When you find the right topic area, click it once.**

   The topic takes its position in the chosen slot.

4. **Repeat Steps 2 and 3 until you fill the five possible My Places slots.**

5. **Click Save My Changes after you finish.**

   America Online saves the My Places for this screen name (not for all screen names in your account).

Check the New Place menus every now and then to see if America Online wised up and either added more places or gave us an "Other Location or Web Site" option. (But for now, all we can do is hope. That, and write to **stevecase@aol.com** to register your demand for the setting!)

Organizing the Places of Your Heart

There's a new button in town — and it's appearing on a toolbar near you. Say hello to Favorites and its sidekick, the Favorite Places window — both of them riding hard to organize the online areas you know and love.

The Favorite Places system doesn't bring any law into your digital life (hopefully, Congress won't either), but it promises a *lot* of order. Rather than limit yourself to just ten favorite places socked away on the My Shortcuts menu (see Chapter 23 for the details about that), you can store as many favorites as you want! Is that just too cool or what?

Figure 7-5 shows a hard-working Favorite Places window in action. The heart entries link to services within America Online or to Web pages and gophers on the Internet. For example, the item highlighted in Figure 7-5 is the Collectible Cards forum on America Online. Manila folders (such as Support Areas, Gaming, and Fun Spots) apply some order to the impending chaos.

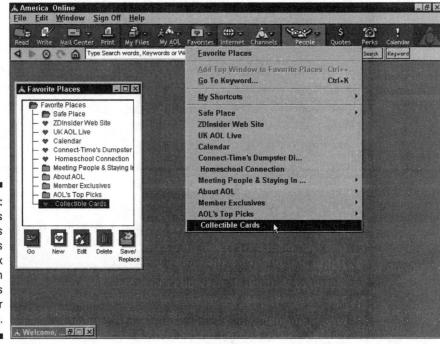

Figure 7-5: The famous Favorites Places dialog box and its twin Favorites toolbar menu.

Figure 7-5 also shows another cool feature of the America Online software: The Favorite Places *menu item list* that automatically appears beneath the Favorites button on the toolbar. When you add an online area to your Favorite Places, it automatically appears in both the Favorite Places window and on the menu list under the Favorites toolbar button. (Life's getting better all the time, isn't it?) Items in both places work the same way, so I end up in the Collectible Cards forum whether I double-click its heart entry in the Favorite Places window or just choose it from the Favorites drop-down menu.

Here are some other random musings about the Favorite Places system that wandered out of my brain at the last moment:

✔ To use the new Favorite Places system, you must have Version 4.0 or later of the America Online access software for Windows. Any older America Online software just isn't this cool.

✔ Even though all the items in your Favorite Places window are also displayed on the Favorites drop-down menu, you can make changes to the entries only in the Favorite Places window. The Favorites drop-down menu notices the changes on its own, so don't worry about that.

✔ You're not limited to the folders shown in Figure 7-5. I created those to meet my exceedingly peculiar needs. You have the freedom — yes, even the right and responsibility — to create equally peculiar folders for yourself.

Using folders in the Favorite Places window

I almost forgot to mention this, but, luckily, two of my brain cells, spurred into action by the caloric heat of a half-digested Oreo, reminded me that double-clicking is the key to using the Favorite Places window:

✔ To open a folder, double-click it.

✔ To close the folder after you're done with it, double-click the folder again.

✔ To take off for a favorite place, double-click it.

Flip back into single-clicking mode when you're using the drop-down menu under the Favorites toolbar. Because it's a menu and not a list of items in a window, you click once to choose destinations there.

Adding a favorite place

Including a new favorite place is a cinch. You can do so in two ways: the Easy Way and the Other Way. This section tells you how to handle them both.

The Easy Way is for areas inside America Online or Internet-based Web pages and gophers you've browsed your way into:

1. **Display an area you're fond of, either inside America Online or on the Internet.**

 2. **Click the heart-on-a-document icon in the window's upper-right corner.**

   A little dialog box appears (see Figure 7-6), demanding to know what you intend to do with the link to this online area.

   Not every window in America Online has one of those cute little heart document icons. It's unfortunate but true. If the window you're looking at doesn't have one, you can't add it to the Favorite Places list.

Figure 7-6:
America
Online helps
you collect
favorite
locations
and share
them in
e-mail and
instant
messages.

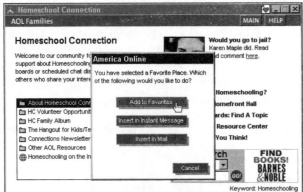

3. **In the little You Have Selected a Favorite Place dialog box, click the Add to Favorites button to include an entry for this online area on your Favorite Places list.**

   Your new entry takes up residence at either the top or bottom of both the Favorite Places window and the drop-down menu under Favorites, just like Figure 7-7 shows. (Which end of the list it lands on seems to depend entirely on how your America Online software feels at the moment. Strange, isn't it?)

   If you click the Insert in Instant Message button, a new Instant Message window appears, complete with a ready-to-use link to this favorite place. Clicking Insert in Mail does much the same thing, except that a blank e-mail message pops up, with the link in the body and a friendly Check This Out notice on the Subject line.

Use the Other Way when someone dashes up and says, "I just found the neatest Web page — you've *gotta* check it out!" The Other Way assumes that you have the address of a Web page and want to include it manually in your list of favorite places:

Figure 7-7:
The new entry lands at the top of the list.

1. **Choose Favorites⇨Favorite Places from the toolbar.**

   The Favorite Places window appears.

2. **Click the folder in which you want to store the new item.**

   If you don't know where to put the item, click the Favorite Places folder at the top of the window. That's as good a place as any — and you can always move the entry somewhere else later.

3. **Click New at the bottom of the Favorite Places window.**

   The Add New Folder/Favorite Place dialog box (designed by the Use No Articles Programming Team) appears.

4. **Type a name for this entry in the Enter the Place's Description box, press Tab, and then type the entry's address in the Enter the Internet Address box.**

   Figure 7-8 displays a finished entry, ready to be saved for posterity.

5. **Click OK to add the entry to your Favorite Places window.**

Figure 7-8:
The digital Dumpster Diver gift site is ready to join my favorite places.

Add New Folder/Favorite Place

● New Favorite Place ○ New Folder

Enter the Place's Description:

Connect-Time's Dumpster Diver digital gift

Enter the Internet Address:

http://cgi.connect-time.com/cgi-bin/dumpdive

OK   Cancel

Adding a folder

Adding all kinds of favorite places to your system is great, but you need some organization to keep everything in order. That's why those clever America Online programmers included folders.

Folders can live in the Favorite Places area or inside other folders (see Figure 7-9). Either way, creating a folder is easy. Here's how (assuming that you already have the Favorite Places window open):

1. **Click the Favorite Places button on the toolbar.**

    The Favorite Places window pops to attention.

2. **Click the Favorite Places folder at the top of the window.**

    The Favorite Places folder is highlighted (this is a good sign).

3. **Click New.**

    The Add New Folder/Favorite Place dialog box appears on your screen (another good sign).

4. **Select the New Folder radio button.**

    The dialog box suddenly shrinks to half its previous size, shedding those unwanted pounds and inches in no time at all.

5. **Click in the text box under** `Enter the New Folder's Name` **and then type the name of your new folder. Click OK after you're done (see Figure 7-10).**

    Your new folder appears at the bottom of the Favorite Places list.

6. **Move the folder wherever you want it on the list.**

    If you're not sure how to move the folder, look in the next section.

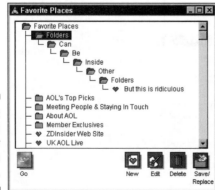

Figure 7-9:
An example
of folder
creation run
amok.

Figure 7-10:
Now there's
a safe place
for my stuff.

Moving folders and favorite places

Creating folders and favorite places is one thing, but organizing them is another. The little buggers tend to land wherever the America Online software feels like putting them. But, moving them around is easy after you get the hang of it.

The technique is the same for both folders and favorite places. After you open the Favorite Places window, follow these steps:

1. **Decide which item you want to move and where it's headed.**

2. **Put the mouse pointer on the chosen item and press and hold the mouse button.**

   The technical term for this maneuver is *click and drag,* but there's no reason to mention it, so I won't.

3. **While holding down the mouse button, move the item to its destination (see Figure 7-11) and then release the mouse button.**

   The item settles down, safe and sound in its new home (see Figure 7-12).

Figure 7-11:
The Safe
Place folder
on the
move.

Figure 7-12:
Coming in
for a perfect
landing!

Modifying folders and favorite places

A point comes in every life when it's time to make some changes. When *that time* in the life of your Favorite Places window arrives, have no fear. Although change is never fun, at least it's easy in the Favorite Places window. Open the Favorite Places window and then follow these steps:

1. **Click the folder or favorite place and then click Edit.**

   For a folder, the Rename dialog box appears. For a favorite place, the description and Internet address dialog box appear.

2. **Make your changes (usually to the name of the item) and then click OK.**

   If you change your mind and don't want to make any changes, double-click in the upper-left corner of the box.

Deleting folders and favorite places

Favorite Places entries, like other impetuous flashes in the dark sky of fading youth, have a limited life span. When it's time to delete an entry, just do the deed and go on as best you can. Solemnly open the Favorite Places window, and then morosely proceed through the following steps:

1. **Click the item you want to delete.**

2. **Click Delete and then OK in the pop-up dialog box.**

The entry is no more. Remember; ask not for whom the Delete button clicks — it clicks for thy once-favorite place.

Chapter 8

E-Mailing the World, One Mailbox at a Time

. . . .

In This Chapter

▶ E-mailing other America Online members

▶ Slinging your e-mail through the Internet

▶ Giving your messages some *oomph*

▶ Sharing links with your friends

▶ Reading your incoming mail

▶ Organizing the mailbox

▶ Tracking everyone with the online address book

▶ Speeding things up with Automatic AOL

. . . .

*I*n my humble opinion, e-mail is *the* communications medium of the millennium. It seems like everybody has an e-mail account at the office, at home, or both. Messages travel quickly, arrive safely, and rarely get delayed by any of the obscure national holidays that shut down the post office so frequently.

Through America Online, you can send e-mail to virtually anyone on the planet. (No, I'm not kidding — I'm not even exaggerating.) One way or another, your e-mail message flies on the wings of technology from your online mailbox to its destination, whether the message is headed to another America Online e-mail box or to an Internet e-mail address.

This section tells you how to join in the fun, from sending Internet mail to organizing your incoming messages. No matter what you want to know about e-mail and America Online, this chapter is the place to look.

Sending E-Mail to an America Online Subscriber

You're surrounded by other America Online subscribers every time you sign on. So, the odds are good that you'll send at least a few messages to one of these people. That's what the e-mail system was designed for in the first place, so trading messages with other members is pretty easy. The mail system also has some special features, like *unsend,* that work only when you're writing to another America Online person. (If unsending a message sounds interesting, check out the "Stupid mail tricks" sidebar, later in this chapter.)

Before sending e-mail to someone, you must know the person's screen name. Upper- and lowercase don't matter, but spelling *does.* For example, you could enter my screen name as **JKaufeld** or **jkaufeld** and the mail would still go through. But if you try **JKaufield**, don't expect a reply — at least not from me — because the name is misspelled.

Before sending your first few messages, take a second to look through these tips and suggestions for making your e-mail stand head and shoulders above the crowd:

- ✔ Writing e-mail messages is a little different from any other kind of communication. Good e-mail takes a bit of care, the right words, and a willingness to type until the message is clear. If you're new to e-mail, don't panic — I was new once, too (and look what happened to me!).

- ✔ Please don't type your messages in one huge paragraph. That makes them *really* hard to read. Press Enter (or Return) a couple of times every now and then to break the behemoth into smaller, more digestible chunks.

- ✔ According to the America Online official Rules of the Road (also known as the *Terms of Service* agreement by lawyers and other people who create official-sounding language because they enjoy it; keyword **TOS**), you can't send unsolicited advertisements through the e-mail system. If someone specifically asks to receive information from you, that's perfectly okay, but blanketing everyone in a chat room with e-mail about your company's new Web site falls on the Not Okay side of the chart.

Enough of this talk — it's time to hit the keyboard and start e-mailing! To send an e-mail message, follow these steps:

1. **If you use either the Light Usage or Limited pricing plans and you signed on to America Online to compose an e-mail message, sign off now.**

   Unless you're an excellent typist, need to send a very short message, or just don't care how high your America Online bill goes this month, don't compose messages online if you pay for access by the minute. Instead, write your message offline (unconnected from America Online) by continuing with Step 2 below. (Your credit card bill will thank me next month.)

2. **Create a new mail message by clicking the Compose Mail button on the toolbar or pressing Ctrl+M.**

A blank e-mail window mystically appears on-screen.

3. **Type the recipient's America Online screen name in the Send To box.**

To send the same message to more than one screen name, keep typing screen names in the To box and separate them with commas.

If the screen name is in your address book, click the Address Book button and then double-click the entry for that person or group. After you're done choosing addresses, click OK to make the address book go away.

You can freely mix America Online screen names and Internet e-mail addresses when sending a message. Just separate each entry with a comma, and the America Online e-mail system makes sure that the message goes to the right place. When you include a group of recipients from the Address Book window, the America Online software automatically adds commas for you. Isn't that helpful?

4. **Press the Tab key to move the blinking cursor into the CC box. Enter the screen names of people who should get a copy of the message but should not be listed as a main recipient.**

Odds are, you won't ever use the CC feature, but I had to mention it anyway. It's just the kind of guy I am.

Don't bother putting your own screen name in the CC area. You automatically get a copy of every message you send. Choose Mail⇨Check Mail You've Sent to see them. Copies only stick around for only about 30 days, so if the message is *really* important, print it and keep the paper. To save your messages *and* a few trees, try storing vital messages in your Personal Filing Cabinet. See Chapter 4 for more about that cool feature.

5. **Press Tab again to put the cursor in the Subject box. Type a brief (50 characters or fewer) description of the message.**

Write your message subject so that the other person can tell right away what it's about. If the message is *really* important, write something like *URGENT* at the beginning of the subject and be sure to include some details after that. Because your reader may have 35 other messages to look at, making the subject descriptive helps her figure out which message to check first.

6. **Press Tab once more to get into the message area at the bottom of the screen. Type your message text there.**

Enter the text as though you're using a word processor; for example, don't press the Enter (or Return) key at the end of every line. Press Enter (or Return) a couple times every now and then to break the message into easy-to-read paragraphs (see Figure 8-1).

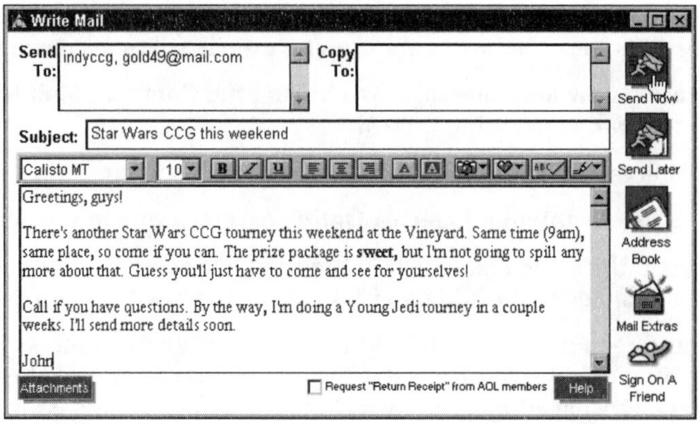

Figure 8-1:
Leave some
white space
in messages
to make
them easy
to read.

To jazz up your messages, add some cool formatting or live links to your favorite Web sites. For all the details, flip ahead to the section "E-Mailing with Panache," later in this chapter.

7. **If you're sending a file, click Attach. In the Attachments dialog box, click Attach one more time. Finally, in the Attach dialog box, find the file you want to send and double-click it (or highlight it and click the oddly named Open button).**

   After picking the file (whichever way you do it), the Attach dialog box vanishes, leaving you in the Attachments dialog box. The name of the attached file appears in the middle of the window. Click OK to make the Attachments dialog box go away and leave you alone.

   To attach another file to the same message, click Attach again. In fact, you can attach as many files as you want, and the America Online software automatically compresses them into a ZIP file for you. Isn't technology wonderful (at least when it works)?

   If you change your mind about attaching the file, click the Detach button (it's right next to Attach in the Attachments window — what a strange coincidence).

   What if you want to see just a list of the files you attached to the message? Just click the Attachments button again. After perusing the list, click Cancel to make the little window go away.

8. **If you're signed on to America Online, click Send to mail the message. If you aren't signed on right now (which is important if you still pay by the hour!), minimize the mail window and then sign on. After you're on, double-click the Mail Message window's title bar (it's probably in the lower-left corner of the screen) and then click Send.**

America Online automatically reassures you with a little message, Your mail has been sent, but that reassurance gets old if you send a great deal of mail. To stop the annoying little dialog box from popping up, turn off the Confirm Mail after It Has Been Sent option in the Mail Preferences window. (See Chapter 4 for everything you never — er, ever — wanted to know about preference settings.)

The section "Doing E-Mail the Automatic AOL Way," later in this chapter, explains the Send Later button and why it's the coolest thing since, um, well, they started tracking cool stuff.

America Online automatically keeps copies of all your outgoing mail for about 30 days. To review these old messages, choose Mail⇨Check Mail You've Sent. If you're truly attached to your correspondence, tell your America Online software to squirrel away copies of all outbound messages in your Personal Filing Cabinet. To find out more about this setting, along with the many other fascinating and tweakable items that control your America Online experience, flip to Chapter 4 and look in the "Mail" section.

Stupid mail tricks

As though it weren't enough that you can send e-mail to anyone on America Online, those zany programmers threw in some extra features designed to make your mind do loops. Look for these options along the bottom of the Mailbox window or on the right-click pop-up menu. (Right-click a mail message's entry in the Online Mailbox to see the menu.)

✔ **Status (button):** Want to see whether your buddy hasn't read the mail lately or is just ignoring you? Click the mail message you sent and click Show Status. America Online returns a dialog box with the screen name of the person who read the letter and the time and date it was read. If it's still in unread limbo, the time and date are replaced with (not yet read).

✔ **Unsend (button):** If you send a message that you quickly regret, America Online lets you reach through the system and pretend that the message never happened — as long as the other person hasn't read it yet. To

unsend a message, open your mailbox and click the Sent Mail tab. Find the message you're embarrassed about, click it, and then click Unsend. If the message hasn't been read yet, America Online yanks it from the other person's e-mail basket and throws the message away. If the person has read the message, it's truly too late — Unsend won't work now. Unsend *also* doesn't work for mail sent to Internet addresses.

✔ **Ignore (pop-up menu):** When junk mail (or any other mail you don't want to see) fills up your box, this option makes a great antidote. As its name implies, the Ignore option disregards the current message, automatically consigning it to the Old Mail page of the Online Mailbox without actually opening it. If you get a great deal of junk e-mail, the Ignore option promises to warm your heart. To ignore a message, right-click the message's entry in the Online Mailbox and choose Ignore from the pop-up menu.

Writing to the @'s: Sending Internet E-Mail

Using America Online as your e-mail link to the Internet is easy. In fact, you can pretend that you're just sending mail to another America Online user, except that the person has a very weird screen name.

To send mail through the Internet, you go through exactly the same steps as you do to send e-mail to another America Online user. The only difference with Internet e-mail is in how you address the message.

The key to sending Internet e-mail is getting the address right. Most Internet mail addresses look a little bizarre to uninitiated eyes, but that's not an issue — in a moment, you'll be initiated. Rather than simple, straightforward things like JKaufeld, Internet mail addresses look like this: imrappaport@ stagetheatre.com. The part to the left of the @ is the person's ID (the Internet term for screen name). The other half is the address of the computer the person uses for e-mail (in this case, it's one of those other online services). Put the whole thing together and you get an Internet e-mail address.

These addresses get complicated sometimes (the one for a friend of mine in France contains about 50 letters, numbers, and various punctuation symbols). An easy way to get the address exactly right is by asking your friend to send you a message first. When it arrives, carefully copy the address into your address book with the Add Address button (on the right side of the mail window, as you read the friend's message). Now you don't have to worry about the gory, technical address stuff anymore — just pick the entry from your address book and you're done.

Because you're on America Online, you have an Internet e-mail address too; it's your screen name with @aol.com glued to the end. If your screen name is Mungojerrie, your Internet e-mail address is mungojerrie@aol.com. The Internet address doesn't use the space or the capital letters in the screen name — it just ignores them.

By the way, remember to use the person's *screen name* or *Internet address* rather than her *real name* when you're sending an e-mail message. Although both America Online and the Internet use advanced technology, the computers still don't know people by their given names (and I, for one, hope that they never get to that point!).

E-Mailing with Panache

In these image-conscious times, looking good is almost as important as sounding good. Thanks to advances in the America Online software, e-mail messages are more powerful and flexible than ever. The formatting buttons put you in charge of the text size, style, alignment, and even color while you're creating e-mail. The possibilities for font size, color, and alignment are endless (for your message's sake, I hope that your design skills are better than mine).

Most of these formatting tips work with Instant Messages too. Don't let your e-mail have *all* the fun — add some formatting and dress up your instant messages.

The buttons just above the message area control the formatting magic. They're grouped into sets by what they do. Here's a quick rundown of the sets, from left to right:

✔ **Font and text size:** Pick any of your installed TrueType fonts and select the size that meets your purpose. If the person receiving the message has that same font installed and uses the America Online 4.0 software, he sees your message in the font you chose.

✔ **Text formatting:** These are the bold, italic, and underline buttons, as their labels demonstrate.

✔ **Text alignment:** Like any good word processor, the America Online e-mail system understands left, center, and right justification, plus *newspaper* justification, which is even on both sides. This final option isn't available in Instant Messages. (I guess they aren't smart enough to handle it.)

✔ **Text color:** Change the color of the text with the first button. Use the second button to change the background color of the entire message (not just a small portion of it). Remember that blue text on a blue background doesn't show up very well!

✔ **Insert picture:** The camera button inserts a graphical image into your e-mail, so you can tell Aunt Sarah about the holiday party *and* show off the digital pictures. To insert a graphic, click the camera button, select an image file, and {poof!} the graphic appears in your message.

✔ **Favorite Places:** You loved them as a Toolbar button, and now they're back in the e-mail window. The Heart button opens your Favorite Places window, making it easy to drag-and-drop Favorite Places links into your e-mail messages (see the next section for more about that).

✔ **Spell check:** Clicking the ABC button checks your spelling (yes!) to prevent embarrassing speeling misteaks.

✔ **Select signature:** The last button on the list is new to America Online 5.0. The Pencil button stands for *Signatures* (don't ask how you start with "pencil" and end up with "signature" — I don't make 'em up, I just report 'em). In e-mail terms, a *signature* is a little bit of text, usually no more than 4 lines, that your e-mail software adds to the end of all your e-mail messages. It usually includes your name, e-mail address, and some pithy quote or brief advertising message. Click the Pencil button to build a new signatures, set your default signature, or an use existing signature in your current message. (It's one of the coolest features in the new software!)

The font, formatting, color, and alignment buttons all work the same way. To use them with new text, click the buttons for your choices and start typing. The software applies the fonts, formatting, and whatever else you choose to the text as you type. To format text that's already in the message, click and drag across the text you want to change and then click the various formatting buttons. Presto — the old text looks new! To remove some formatting, highlight the text in question and click *off* the format options you don't want.

For some really fun goodies, click the Mail Extras button (along the lower-right side of the New Mail window). This little bonus area offers some great freebies to spice up your e-mail, plus a couple of for-pay services, too. The freebies include a smiley reference guide, simple drawings to drop into messages, a stock of generic e-mail-brightening photos, plus a neat digital stationery maker. The Online Greetings option costs a few bucks, but it's free to explore. Beware, though — once you try them, online greeting cards get *really* addictive!

Linking with Ease

Almost every time I wander America Online or surf the Web for a while, I run across something that's really neat and worth sharing with my friends. In the past, I laboriously copied the Internet address or America Online keyword into a mail message — and sometimes messed it up in the process. Today, though, I never miss an address because I let the America Online software insert the link for me.

Before trying this trick, you have to understand how the Favorite Places area works and what it does for you. If you're not familiar with Favorite Places, flip to Chapter 7 and find out more about it before attempting this link thing.

When you want to include a link to either an America Online keyword or an Internet site in an e-mail message, follow these steps:

1. **Go to the keyword area or Internet site so that it's in a window on your screen.**

   If the keyword area doesn't have a Favorite Places icon in its window, you can't send a link to it. Sorry — it's just how life goes sometimes.

2. **Click the Favorite Places heart in the upper-right corner of the window.**

   A small dialog box appears and wants to know what it should do with your Favorite Places link.

3. **Click the Insert in Mail button.**

   After a few moments of thinking, the America Online software displays a fresh e-mail window with your link ready and waiting in the message body.

4. **Address the message, type a subject and body and then send the message just as you normally would.**

   The America Online software makes this mail-the-link thing easy, doesn't it?

Incoming Missive, Sir!

Sending mail is only half the fun. After you send something, you get a reply! If you think that a mailbox full of junk mail is a lift, just wait until you sign on to America Online and find a message or two in your e-mail box. Someone out there cares!

To check your online mailbox, click the Read button on the Toolbar or the You Have Mail button in the Welcome window. Either way, America Online whisks you away to the New Mail window.

To read a message, either double-click the message in the New Mail window or click it once and then click Read. Your message hops up into its own window. To reply to only the person who sent the message, click Reply. To share your comments with the sender *and* everyone else who received the message, click Reply to All. To send a copy of the message to someone else (even out to the Internet, but not to a fax or postal mail address), click Forward. After you're done with the message, close the window by double-clicking in its upper-left corner.

- ✔ To keep a message in your inbox after you read it, click the message in the New Mail window once and then click Keep As New. Unread messages live in your America Online inbox for 30 days after arriving. After that, they turn into very small pumpkins and are shipped to your local grocery store, never to be seen or heard from again.

- ✔ To save an important message, either print it or save it in the Personal Filing Cabinet (the America Online software's built-in storage spot). To print, click the Print button (it looks like a page coming out of a printer) on the Toolbar. To store the message in the Personal Filing Cabinet, open the e-mail message (as if you're reading it), and then choose My Files➪Save to Personal Filing Cabinet. The America Online software copies the message into your handy filing cabinet. For more about the Personal Filing Cabinet, see the next section in this chapter, "Organizing Your E-Mail Mess(ages)."

✔ After reading a message, it hangs out in the Old Mail area for anywhere from a few days to a couple of weeks after you first look at it. (In the Mail Preferences setting, you can tell the America Online computers to store incoming e-mail for at least seven days — see Chapter 4 for more about that). To reread an old message, choose Mail➪Check Mail You've Read. Doing so brings up the Old Mail dialog box. Double-click the message you want to read.

✔ In these days of rampant unsolicited e-mail (commonly known by its greasy nickname *spam*), the Delete key often gets quite a workout as you browse through your incoming mail. Sometimes the key gets a little carried away, and you accidentally delete a piece of mail that you actually wanted to read. America Online, hearing the plaintive howls of its membership, finally developed a solution: the Recently Deleted Mail area. To read (and even retrieve) a message you accidentally deleted, choose Mail Center➪Recently Deleted Mail from the Toolbar menu. This action brings up a dialog box containing mail that you deleted within the last 24 hours. Double-click a message to read it, click the Keep As New button to put the message back into your mailbox or click the Permanently Delete button to *truly* consign the little sucker to oblivion.

Organizing Your E-Mail Mess (ages)

I absolutely *live* on e-mail. Maybe it's my job or the peculiar people I work with (or perhaps it's my nerdy side showing again — I hate it when that happens), but I spend a great deal of time each day fielding incoming messages and unleashing my own outbound correspondence flood. Thankfully, my faithful digital assistant, the Personal Filing Cabinet, keeps all my e-stuff organized.

The Personal Filing Cabinet tracks incoming and outgoing e-mail, discussion board postings, and e-mail and newsgroup messages retrieved with Automatic AOL sessions. It even covers file downloads. Best of all, it's built right into the America Online software, so you have nothing to download and nothing to buy.

To open the Personal Filing Cabinet, choose File➪Personal Filing Cabinet. The window hops on the screen, looking much like Figure 8-2. The file folders along the left side of the window represent different storage areas. The buttons along the bottom control the Personal Filing Cabinet.

Figure 8-2:
The
Personal
Filing
Cabinet
stores your
digital infor-
mation in
electronic
manila
folders.

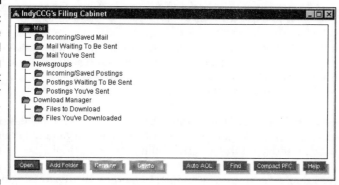

You have much to work with here, and this area is easiest to understand when you play with it. Before turning you loose, here are some basic ideas about how the Personal Filing Cabinet works:

✔ To open a folder, double-click it. To close it, double-click it again. When you open a folder, the software displays all the items the folder contains (which can be a lengthy list). Don't be surprised if you have to scroll up and down to see everything in a folder.

✔ To view a piece of e-mail, a newsgroup posting, or something else inside a folder, double-click the item. Double-clicking an entry in the Download Manager area displays the description for that file, but only if you're signed on to the system.

✔ To create a new folder, click the top folder of the area (like Mail, for example) and then click Add Folder. Type a name for the new folder and then click OK. The new folder appears underneath the top folder. Isn't automated organization amazing?

✔ Folders can be inside other folders, just like in the real world.

✔ Moving things from one folder to another is easy. Just move your cursor over the item you want to move, click and hold down the mouse button, and drag the item to its new home. When the mouse arrow is pointing to the item's destination, release the mouse button. The Personal Filing Cabinet gently puts the item in place.

✔ If you misplace an e-mail message, click Search to have the Personal Filing Cabinet ferret it out. You can search for the item's title or the full text of messages. Spiffy, eh?

✔ In the Mail section of the Preferences option (choose My AOL➪Preferences and then click the Mail button), you can tell America Online to automati-cally store copies of all your mail (both sent and received) in the Mail folder of the Personal Filing Cabinet. The idea is cool, but it eats disk space up pretty quickly. Try turning this feature on and see whether you like it (but regularly delete the old messages that you really don't need to keep).

Catching People with Your Address Book

You start meeting people right away in America Online. Join a discussion, drop in for a chat, or attend a live presentation, and suddenly you have online friends. You also have a problem: How do you keep track of the members of your newfound social club?

It's time to invoke the familiar refrain, "Luckily, the America Online programmers thought of that." Yup, those clever folks from Virginia did it again. Step right this way, and meet the America Online Address Book.

As address books go, this one's simple. It handles entries for single screen names or big, honking mailing lists (assuming that you're into large, noisy name collections).

- For an individual, the address book holds the person's real name, screen name or Internet e-mail address, and notes describing the entry. It also has space for a picture, just in case your friend sends a digital likeness of himself.

- For a mailing group, the entry consists of a descriptive title and a list of the assembled crowd's e-mail addresses.

The address book lists both individual entries and groups in one master alphabetized list. Yes, you read it right — *alphabetized!* After years of waiting, address book entries are finally alphabetized! Hooray!! (I probably shouldn't be this excited about the address book, but it's the nerd side of me showing through — down, nerd, down!)

Adding address book entries

Before you can use the address book to send messages, you have to put some addresses in it. With that marginally deep thought in mind, here's how to add new items to your address book:

1. **Open the address book by choosing Mail Center⇨Address Book or clicking the Address Book button in a new mail message.**

   The Address Book window pops up, all bright and cheery.

2. **To add an entry for a person, click New Person. To build a group entry, click New Group.**

   A blank New Person or New Group dialog box appears.

3. **Fill in the appropriate spaces in the dialog box and then check your work carefully, especially the e-mail address entry (or addresses, as the case may be).**

When you're making a group entry, type the America Online screen names and Internet e-mail addresses one after another, with commas separating them, as shown in Figure 8-3.

Although capitalization doesn't count here, spelling definitely does! For example, you can enter my screen name any way you want (JKaufeld, Jkaufeld, jkaufeld, or jKaUfElD all count), and America Online figures out that you mean me. If you put in **jkaufield** (with an *i*), however, the system gets all confused and doesn't send the mail to me.

Figure 8-3:
Mix and
match
America
Online
screen
names and
Internet
e-mail
addresses
in the same
group.

4. **After you finish, click OK.**

The new entry pops into the Address Book window, in (as I already gloated about) alphabetical order.

Repeat the process until your address book overflows with friends, acquaintances, business associates, and other online contacts.

Deleting address book entries

So now you may have an address book full of stuff, and it's getting unwieldy — plus you can't remember who half these people are. No problem — that's what the Delete button is for. Deleting is a quick and painless process. Here's how to do it:

1. **Open the address book (if you haven't already) by choosing Mail Center⇨Address Book.**

Of course, you can also click the Address Book button in the e-mail message window if that's where you happen to be when the inspiration hits.

2. **Scroll through the Address Book list until you find the entry you want to dispose of.**

3. **Click the description once to highlight it and then click Delete.**

4. **When the software wrings its little hands and asks whether you're *serious* about this deletion business, click Yes.**

   If you just want to see what the Delete button does and how the program will react when you use it, click No. Apologize to your software for even *thinking* of tricking it like that. Shame on you.

Changing address book entries

Because things change at a ridiculous pace, particularly in the online world, keeping your address book up-to-date is a never-ending task. That's why your address book has a Modify button.

Here's the scoop on changing an existing Address Book entry:

1. **Open the address book (if it's still closed) by choosing Mail Center⇨Address Book or by clicking the Address Book button in a brand-new mail message.**

2. **Click once on the entry you need to change.**

   This step highlights the entry.

3. **Click Edit.**

   The Address Entry window comes back. It's the same window you used to create the entry originally.

4. **Make your changes as necessary.**

   Everything is open for change, so make whatever modifications you must. If you're working with a list, you can freely add and delete screen names.

   All the standard Windows text-editing tricks work here: highlight, delete, insert, click and drag, and the rest. Edit (and play) as much as you want.

5. **After you're done with the changes and are pleased as punch with them, click OK to save your work.**

   Click Cancel if you want to abandon our carefully wrought editing and keep the record the way it was.

   Whichever button you click, the Address Group dialog box vanishes, and you're back to the Address Book screen.

Emergency! Saving and replacing your address book

The address book makes your e-mail life so much easier that many people rely heavily on it as part of their everyday online existence. After using computers for a while, though, you quickly find out that even the best technology (yes, even the America Online software) occasionally fails. With the address book, the little word *fails* translates to *toasts your painstakingly assembled and utterly irreplaceable list of e-mail addresses*. In other words, in case of failure, kiss the address book good-bye.

Thankfully, the America Online 5.0 software includes a weapon for defending your precious address book: the Save/Replace button. This two-way tool saves your current address book entries *and* restores a previously saved address book into your America Online software — and it does everything with a couple of quick clicks:

1. **With the America Online software running (but not signed on), select the screen name whose address book you want to restore.**

   Because address books are screen name–specific, make sure you pick the right screen name. (Otherwise, you won't save what you really want.)

2. **Select <u>M</u>ail Center⇨<u>A</u>ddress book from the Toolbar.**

   The Address Book window hops onto the screen.

3. **Click the Save/Replace button near the bottom of the window.**

   As hoped, the Save and Replace Your Address Book window appears.

4. **Depending on your goal (save or replace the addresses), follow the instructions below.**

   - **Saving your address book:** Select the Save the Address Book radio button; then click OK. The Save Folder dialog box appears. Pick the directory to store your addresses and type a name for the saved file (I recommend using your screen name as the filename, since Address Books are unique to each screen name). Click Save to finish the process.

   - **Restoring your address book:** Select the Replace the Address Book radio button; then click OK. The Select File to Restore dialog box jumps into action. Select the directory containing the address book you want to restore; then click on the address book's filename. Click Open to restore the address book entries.

     America Online notes that it made a backup copy of that screen name's current address, so if something goes horribly wrong (like if you accidentally picked the wrong screen name back in Step 1), you can get those addresses back.

You can also use the Save/Restore Address Book feature to copy the address book from one copy of the America Online software to another (putting your home address book onto the America Online software that you use at work, for instance). To copy an address book in this way, save the address book as the steps above explain and then either copy the address book file onto a floppy disk or simply attach it to an e-mail and send it to yourself (that's probably the easiest way to go). Nip off to the computer with the other copy of America Online on it (the "work" computer, in this case) and copy the address book file onto the machine or download it from e-mail, if you went the *all electronic, all the time* route. Next follow the instructions for restoring an address book in the steps above. Now both copies of your America Online software have the same address books. What a deal!

Doing E-Mail the Automatic AOL Way

Do you want to save money? Do you want to save time? Well, then, step right up, folks, step right up and see the working man's miracle, a technological time-saver: Automatic AOL. This little beauty lets you type your e-mail offline, that's right, *offline,* folks, not signed on at all — step back, son, you bother me. Save yourself some money right then and there. But it doesn't stop with that, no siree. It doesn't want to save you a *little* money, folks; it wants to save you a *lot.* That's why it au-to-matically gets your new mail when it's sending the old stuff off. Read your messages, write your replies, and then tell the little fellow to go do it all again. Every time you use it, you can't *help* but save money. Like money in the bank, folks, that's Automatic AOL for you.

Okay, so America Online probably didn't use old-time carnival barkers to announce Automatic AOL, but they sure could have. This technology is incredibly useful, and it's built right into your America Online access software. You have nothing else to buy; no salesperson will call. Even if you belong to the all-you-can-use unlimited online time plan, Automatic AOL still simplifies life by managing all your online communications in one easy tool. And if you still pay by the hour, Automatic AOL is your key to low monthly America Online bills!

To work with Automatic AOL, choose Mail Center➪Set Up Automatic AOL. The Automatic AOL dialog box pops up in the middle of your screen. For all its power and usefulness, Automatic AOL is easy to set up and use.

You don't have to be signed on to the system to configure Automatic AOL — in fact, it's probably a good idea if you aren't.

Here's what Automatic AOL does for you (be sure to sit down before reading the list — it's pretty amazing):

✔ Sign on with one, a few, or all your screen names and gather new mail for offline review.

✔ Send outgoing mail that you wrote offline and saved with the Send Later button.

✔ Automatically download files attached to mail messages (or not, depending on your preference).

✔ Retrieve postings from Internet newsgroups you marked for offline reading.

✔ Retrieve items from your favorite America Online discussion boards (the ones listed in the Read My Message Boards window at keyword **My Boards**).

✔ Post your responses to Internet newsgroups and discussion boards.

✔ Bring down files you marked with the Download Later button in either e-mail messages or America Online file libraries.

✔ Perform all these actions at regular intervals (every half-hour, hour, or two hours, for example) or whenever you tell the program to do so.

Automatic AOL is flexible, so you can do whatever you want. For example, your Automatic AOL session can retrieve new mail, leave attached files online, send outgoing mail, and not mess with the Download Manager. And you can change the settings at your whim whenever you want.

You can choose from two ways to set up Automatic AOL: Either click the Walk Me Through button, which asks you questions and does the settings based on your answers, or follow these steps to set up Automatic AOL by yourself (do whichever is more comfortable for you; heck — do them both if you want):

1. **If you haven't already done so, sign off from America Online.**

   Feel free to get a glass of your favorite soft drink and a handful of snackies before continuing. Food makes software configuration less painful.

2. **Choose ᴍail Center⇨Seṭ Up Automatic AOL.**

   The Automatic AOL dialog box appears.

   If this is the first time you've ever used Automatic AOL, the software throws you right into the Automatic AOL Walk-Through dialog box. If you want the America Online software to take you step-by-step through the whole configuration process (which isn't necessarily a bad idea), click Continue. Otherwise, click the Expert Setup button and go on with the next step.

3. **Click the Select Names button.**

   The Select Screen Names dialog box appears.

4. **Select the check box next to each screen name you want to use with Automatic AOL. Enter the password for each screen name you select. Click OK after you're done.**

   Type the passwords carefully. If a password is misspelled, Automatic AOL doesn't work correctly (and you don't want *that* to happen, do you?).

5. **Tell the software which actions Automatic AOL should take.**

   Table 8-1 has a brief breakdown of the settings, what they do, and how I suggest that you set them.

6. **After all your settings are completed, close the window by double-clicking in the upper-left corner.**

   Congratulations — Automatic AOL is ready to go.

Table 8-1	Automatic AOL Activities	
Setting	*Recommendation*	*Description*
Send mail	Turn it on	Sends any mail messages you write offline and save with the Send Later button. Another must-have feature of Automatic AOL. Use it.
Get unread mail	Turn it on	Copies new mail messages from America Online to your computer so that you can read them offline. Definitely use this option — it's a time- and money-saver.
Download files attached to unread mail	Turn it off	Automatically downloads files attached to mail messages, which can be good and bad. If you get a number of files by e-mail, this feature is useful. In that case, go ahead and turn it on.
Send postings	For advanced use	Posts replies to your read-offline list of Internet newsgroups.
Get unread postings	For advanced use	Retrieves new messages from your read-offline list of Internet news-groups and America Online message boards.
Download files marked for later	Turn it on	Invokes the Download Manager and gets any files you have marked. If you download lots of shareware, this fea-ture shines.

You may have noticed that I ignore the Schedule Automatic AOL button. Although I think that this feature is interesting, I don't want my computer deciding on its own that it's time to call America Online and check for mail. If automating the process sounds like a hot fudge sundae to you (it sounded like cold asparagus soup to me), look on the America Online access software Help menu for help in setting the scheduling options.

I leave out two other settings, namely the ones relating to Internet newsgroups. Using Automatic AOL with newsgroups is a slightly complex process (much like assembling a child's tricycle on Christmas Eve — if you're a parent, I know that you can relate). If you *really* want to do newsgroups with Automatic AOL, sign on to the system, go to keyword **Newsgroups,** and get the details by clicking Read Offline and then clicking the Help button (it has a question mark on it) for help.

Using Automatic AOL is even easier than setting it up (be thankful for small favors, eh?). To start Automatic AOL, choose Mail Center⇨Run Automatic AOL from the toolbar. The Run Automatic AOL Now dialog box appears. If you're happy with the settings you made earlier, click Begin. If you want to briefly review things, click Set Session instead. An information window pops up to give you the blow-by-blow commentary on the Automatic AOL session in progress. After the session is done, close the Automatic AOL Status dialog box.

To read incoming mail, select the appropriate screen name from the main America Online window and then choose Mail Center⇨Read Offline Mail⇨Incoming/Saved Mail from the toolbar. You can read, reply, and do whatever else you want with the messages. After all your replies are done, set off another Automatic AOL session to send them on their way.

If your teenagers have their own screen names, they probably *won't* want to be part of your time- and money-saving Automatic AOL. Why? Well, it's a privacy thing — and you remember how important privacy was when you were young. Because you don't need to type a password to read mail that came in through an Automatic AOL session, anyone in the family could read the teenmail by selecting the screen name and choosing the Mail Center option.

Chapter 9

Chatting the Day (And Night) Away

. . . .

In This Chapter

▶ Connecting with people from all over

▶ Showing off with Member Profiles

▶ Chatting the night away

▶ Keeping your password private

▶ Making a private room

▶ Attending the theater

. . . .

*I*nteracting with your fellow members is at the very heart of America Online. I never saw an online service that's as *into* the idea of community as America Online — and darn it, people in a community should talk to each other. The People Connection exists so that you can chat informally with others, make friends from all over the world, and redeem yourself in the eyes of your mother, who still thinks that you shouldn't spend so much time alone with your computer.

This chapter introduces the People Connection chat rooms and goes into detail about how the whole chat thing works. It also explains the AOL Live theaters, home to some of the finest online presentations ever shown, um, online. Turn off the TV, let the newspapers stack up by the door, and get ready to boldly go where a whole lot of people eagerly await your arrival.

Ambling into a Chat Room

Getting into a People Connection chat room is easy. In fact, you've probably fallen into one more than once by just wandering around the system and clicking a few random links.

To formally set sail for the Wonderful World of Chatting, use keyword **People Connection** or click the People button on the toolbar and then choose Chat Now from the drop-down menu. After a moment of intense thought, the

America Online software launches you into a randomly selected chat room. After you saunter in, look around, and generally get comfy, your screen should resemble Figure 9-1.

Because the People Connection rooms are, after all, for chatting, the *chat text area* fills most of the window. Opposite the chat text is the *people list,* a roster of the members sharing the chat room with you. Along the bottom of the window is the *message box,* where you compose your witty comments before pressing Enter (Return) or clicking Send to share them with the room.

Underneath the people list are the *control buttons,* which work like a transporter beam to various chats:

- ✔ **Find a Chat:** Lists both regular and member-created public chat rooms.

- ✔ **Private Chat:** Leads you to the quiet world of invitation-only chat rooms.

- ✔ **Member Directory:** Sends you straight to the Member Directory window, just like choosing People⇨Search AOL Member Directory from the main menu.

- ✔ **AOL Live:** Whisks you away to the massive America Online online auditorium area, aptly named AOL Live. (For more about AOL Live, flip ahead a bit in this chapter.)

- ✔ **Notify AOL:** Opens the Community Action Team window (for those times when *you're* the only mature person in the chat room).

- ✔ **Chat Preferences:** Opens a dialog box containing the various chat settings (just like clicking My AOL⇨Preferences⇨Chat from the toolbar).

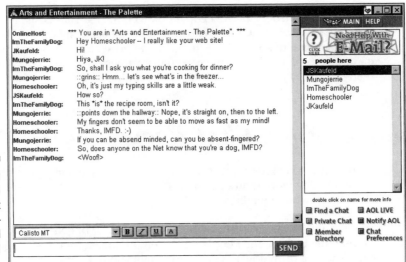

Figure 9-1:
Welcome to
the chat
room —
dive in and
enjoy!

Why you simply must fill out your profile

Before getting too far into the fun and frolic of the People Connection, you need to know about member profiles. Your member profile is a little online dossier you write. It contains whatever you want other America Online subscribers to know about you, such as your real name, your birthday, and the computer you use. You don't have to fill out every line — leaving some parts blank is perfectly okay.

Why fill out your profile? Well, if someone meets you in a chat room or reads a message you

posted and wants to find out more about you, she checks your member profile. People often search the member profiles looking for other America Online members with the same interests. My wife scored an interview in a national magazine because the writer read her profile and liked what she found there.

Making a profile isn't hard. Flip to Chapter 6 for all the details. To make a truly amazing profile, check out Chapter 22 for tricks of the profile masters.

A standard chat room holds 23 people at a time. If you try to get into a room that's full, America Online either offers to send you to another chat room (particularly if you're heading for a Lobby, New Member Lounge, or other popular public chat area) or digitally shrugs you off, saying that the room is full (which it usually does if you try to enter an overflowing member-created chat room). If America Online shrugs, all you can do is wait a few moments and try again.

Even though America Online randomly stuffs you into the first available chat room when you first enter the People Connection, wandering off to some other destination is easy. Just click List Chats and then double-click one of the hundreds (or on some nights, thousands) of chat rooms.

If your kids use America Online, you definitely need to know about the Parental Controls for chat rooms. Check out Chapter 6 for the details.

Finding Conversations among the Keystrokes

It's only fair, both to you and to noncomputer portions of your life, to say this right up front: Chatting in the People Connection is almost too much fun for words. If you like people, thrive on conversation, and enjoy typing, you may as well put a pillow and blanket next to the computer because you've found a new home.

Stop chat room junk mail in its tracks

Although chatting makes the online world come alive with friends (both old and new), it also makes your mailbox strain at the sides with junk mail. Unfortunately, junk e-mailers scan the screen name lists in chat rooms and send out hundreds, if not thousands, of useless, and often downright lurid advertising messages. Left undefended, your mailbox may get 30 to 100 junk e-mails or more during a single chatting session!

So what can a dedicated chatter do to stem the tide? Create a dedicated chatting screen name, that's what! It's your simplest, yet most powerful weapon against junk e-mail.

The idea is simple — and, thanks to the fact that all America Online accounts get up to seven screen names — easy to use. Create a new screen name for your chatting experience and then use the Mail Controls (keyword **Mail Controls**) to block all e-mail to the account. In the member profile for your chatting name, include a note directing people to your e-mailable screen name. That way, the chat room bulk e-mailers won't bother you, but your friends can still drop you a line.

For more about screen names and member profiles, see Chapter 6. To find out more about junk e-mail (and how to fight it), flip back to Chapter 5.

The People Connection chat rooms are the America Online answer to clubhouses, meeting halls, corner pubs, and your living room (except that chat rooms are a little tidier under the chairs). Put simply, chat rooms are digital gathering spots where you and 22 other folks type about life, the universe, and what's for dinner.

When you first arrive in a room, the chat text area is blank except for a brief note from a computer named OnlineHost announcing which room you're in. After a few moments, the chat text area comes alive with messages. (Don't try to talk with the OnlineHost — it never listens.)

The key to a successful chat room conversation is knowing how to read your screen. Flip back to Figure 9-1. The chat text area is a mess, isn't it? That's because whenever anyone types a message in a chat room, everyone can read it. It's like a conference call where everyone talks at the same time *all* the time.

To follow the flow of a chat room, you have to skip around. The chat text in Figure 9-1 shows at least three different conversations. Here's a breakdown of the action.

At the top of the window, Im The Family Dog compliments another room member, Homeschooler, on his Web site. Homeschooler is deep in conversation with someone else at the moment, but he replies to Im The Family Dog near the bottom of the window. Meanwhile, I wandered into the room and Mungojerrie welcomed me. Near the middle of the window, Im The Family Dog and Mungojerrie carry on a little conversation about food.

Around the same spot, Homeschooler and JSKaufeld chat about typing. At the bottom of the window, Mungojerrie tosses out a half-hearted joke (at least it came out that way) based on Homeschooler's last comment.

Tossing your own thoughts into the chat room maelstrom is easy. Basically, start typing. Whatever you type appears in that long, thin box along the bottom of the chat room window. After you're done typing, press Enter (or Return) or click Send. In a moment or two, your words of wisdom appear in the chat text area for all to see. A single chat room comment holds only 92 characters, so choose your letters, numbers, and punctuation marks carefully (or split your thought into two lines — that works, too).

If you type a comment but your text *doesn't* appear in the box at the bottom of the chat room window, click the mouse anywhere in the box. When you see the blinking toothpick cursor way over on the left side of the box, go ahead and start typing again.

There's much to tell about chat rooms, but little of it follows any kind of organization. With that bit of rationalizing out of the way, here are some randomly assembled thoughts and tips about the wild world of chatting:

✔ To get someone's attention in a chat room, start your comment with his screen name. If the person doesn't respond in a minute or two, try it again. If all else fails, send the person an instant message asking whether he saw what you typed.

✔ To quickly read a fellow chatter's member profile or send the person an instant message, scroll through the People Here list until you find the person's screen name and double-click it. A little dialog box pops up. At the bottom of the box are two buttons destined to make your life easier: The Message button sends an instant message to the selected person and the Get Info button displays her member profile. To get back to the chat room, close the little dialog box. Before making another comment in the chat room, click the mouse anywhere in the long box at the bottom of the window and then start typing (otherwise, what you type doesn't appear on-screen).

✔ If a person is getting out of hand or you just don't like listening to him, find the person's screen name in the People in Room list, double-click it, and click Ignore. From then on, nothing he types appears on your screen. (Isn't technology wonderful?)

✔ If you wander into a game chat, someone may ask you to "roll dice" in the room. For wonderful yet mysterious reasons, all America Online chat rooms understand the special command //roll. This command tells the America Online computer to pretend to roll some dice and print the results in the chat room. By default, it "rolls" two six-sided dice (just like you do in Monopoly and other board games). You can also specify the number of sides and number of rolls by typing //roll-dice *xx*-sides *yy* (replace *xx* with the number of dice and *yy* with the number of sides on each die). So, to roll four eight-sided dice, type //roll-dice 4-sides 8.

> ✔ If you see people writing comments like afk, bak, LOL, and ROFL!, don't
> worry — they're not making fun of you. That's standard chat room short-
> hand for things like "away from the keyboard," "laughing out loud," and
> other ever-necessary comments. For a quick primer in chat room-ese,
> use keyword **Shorthand** or check out Chapter 28.

Beware the Password Scammers

I wish that I didn't have to include this section, but I must. Password scam-
ming is alive and well on America Online. The good news is that America
Online actively fights the jerks who do it; the bad news is that more jerks are
always available to replace the ones who get caught.

Don't *ever* give your password to anyone — *anyone* — who asks for it,
whether it happens online or some other way.

Nobody from America Online will ever ask for your password. Period. Never.
It won't happen. No matter what the person says, who the person claims to
be, or what she threatens to do, ignore and report anyone who asks for your
password.

Figure 9-2 shows actual samples of password scammers I bumped into on
America Online. I want to emphasize that: *I did not make these figures up —
they are real.*

If you get an instant message that looks like the ones in these figures, don't
bother to reply or say anything catty (leave that to people like me); just get
ready to ruin the scammer's day. Here's how to report a password scammer
to America Online:

1. **If you're in a chat room when a password-scamming message
   appears, type a note in the room which says that someone is fishing
   for passwords.**

   Be sure to give the screen name of the person who sent you the instant
   message. It never hurts to remind everyone to *never* give out their passwords — think of it as your good deed for the day.

2. **Click the Notify AOL button in the Instant Message window to bring
   up the Report a Violation Here window.**

   Thanks to the wonders of modern software, the system automatically
   prepares a report for the Community Action Team (the America Online
   version of community police), including the screen name of the person
   who sent you the message, the message text, and several other items.

3. **If you want to add any comments with your report, type them in the
   text area at the bottom of the Notify AOL dialog box.**

Figure 9-2:
They
promise
anything to
get your
password.

You don't need to include any extra comments, but this dialog box offers the opportunity anyway. If you do type some notes, they're automatically appended to the report.

4. **After everything is filled out to your satisfaction, click Send Report.**

5. **Close the scammer's Instant Message window and proceed with your regularly scheduled evening.**

If you gave out your password before realizing that the person requesting it was a scammer, all is not lost. *Immediately* (and I mean *right now*) go to keyword **Password** and change your account password. After that, go through the preceding steps and report the scammer.

Enjoying a Little Private (Room) Time

Whether you're talking business or catching up with a friend, the People Connection's private room feature gives you all the benefits of a chat room without the inconvenience of filling it with strange people. Private rooms are great for reunions, parties, brainstorming sessions, and regional meetings.

Private rooms are just that — private. Nobody can get in without knowing the name of the room (a name *you* make up, by the way). America Online doesn't keep a master list of active private rooms. People outside the room can't monitor the discussion in a private room.

Private chat rooms still have *some* limitations, though. For example, a private room holds only 23 people (so you can't have a really *whopping* party). And you get unexpected guests every now and then. Someone thinks up the same name *you* used and {poof!} that person appears in your private room. Don't worry, though — that doesn't happen very often. Also, private chat rooms, unlike their public counterparts, don't include a Notify AOL button in the chat window. To report a problem, use keyword **Notify AOL.**

To create or join the discussion in a private chat room, follow these steps:

1. **Choose <u>P</u>eople⇨<u>S</u>tart Your Own Chat from the toolbar.**

   The Start Your Own Chat dialog box appears.

2. **Click the Private Chat button.**

   The Enter a Private Chat dialog box hops nimbly to the screen.

3. **Carefully type the name of the private room you want to either join or create and click Go Chat.**

   The chat room window reappears, with the name of the private room emblazoned across the top.

If you're creating a new private chat room, just make up any name for it you want. If you're joining someone else's room, type the name exactly as she gave it to you (assuming that she sent you the room name when she invited you in).

If you were heading into a private chat with some friends but find yourself alone in an empty private room instead, make sure that you typed the name right (capitalization doesn't count, but spelling does). If you unexpectedly waltz into someone else's private room, blush profusely, type a brief apology, close the window, and start over at Step 1.

If you spend a great deal of time chatting with folks on your Buddy List, the new Buddy Chat feature promises to make your life a little easier. Flip to Chapter 10 for the details.

Attending Lectures (And Enjoying Them)

Chat rooms cater to small, informal groups of people. For something a little larger (such as, oh, about 500 people), America Online offers AOL Live, where you can interact with popular media figures, captains of industry, authors (yes, even me), and lots of other fascinating folks. AOL Live is a more controlled environment than the chat rooms, but it's still loads of fun.

To get into AOL Live, use keyword **Live**. The AOL Live window appears, looking much like Figure 9-3. All the AOL Live theaters look alike and work in basically the same way.

Figure 9-3:
Appearing
now in
AOL Live!

When you enter one of the AOL Live theaters, you're randomly assigned to a row in the virtual auditorium with as many as seven other people (just like sitting in a theater). To find out who else is in your row, click the People button. A dialog box that lists your row-mates appears. To say something in your row, type your thoughts in the text box along the bottom of the window and click Send (just as in the regular chat rooms). What you type appears in the chat text area, with your row number in parentheses before the comment. In-row comments are visible only to people in the row with you, so you can say just about anything you want.

To ask a question of the person onstage, click the Interact button, type your question in the dialog box, and then click Ask a Question. If the presenter answers your question and asks for more details from you, click the Interact button, type your comments, and click Send a Comment.

Sometimes the audience votes or bids on things. (No, I don't know exactly *what* you vote or bid on, but I have it from the best authorities that the process is very important.) To take part in it, click the Interact button, type your vote or bid (whatever it is), and click either Vote or Bid.

As with chat rooms, you need to know many other things about theaters to make your enjoyment complete:

✔ Take your newly developed chatting skills for a test drive at my *America Online For Dummies* monthly chat. Currently, it's the third Monday of each month at 9pm Eastern in AOL Live (keyword **AOL Live**). For 45 minutes, I answer questions and keep everyone filled in on the latest America Online and Internet game news. It's a hoot (if I do say so myself).

✔ Did you miss a theater presentation you wanted to attend? No problem — just look for a transcript. Use keyword **AOL Live** and click Event Transcripts. Because all transcripts are plain-text files, you can read them with any word processor.

✔ To change rows (if you're allergic to someone you're sitting with), click the Chat Rows button in the theater window and then double-click the row you want to move to. Remember that each row holds only eight people. If the row you choose is full, AOL Live sends you to a nearby row.

✔ For a list of upcoming AOL Live events, use keyword **Live Guide**. Events in this folder are organized by date. Scroll through the list and double-click whatever event looks interesting to get the details.

Recording Your Conversations

For whatever reason (whether it's simple paranoia or something more complex), you may want a record of what went on during a chat. Perhaps you're attending a forum conference center presentation and need to review the chat for ideas. Or maybe you're just feeling a little cloak-and-dagger today and want to spy on your chat room friends. Whatever the reason, keeping a copy of your chats is easy.

To record the chat room you're in, choose My Files⇨Log Manager from the menu bar. This selection opens the Logging dialog box with the name of your chat room in the Room box. Click the Open button in the Chat Log area (near the top of the screen). In the Open Log dialog box, the chat room name automatically appears as your log name (you can change it if you want, by typing a new name for the file). Either click Save or press Enter to open the Log file. From that point on, any new chat text appears on-screen *and* gets saved on your disk drive. Text that was already on-screen before you started the log isn't in the file.

Chapter 10

Dropping a Quick "Hello" with Instant Messages

*Y*ears ago, when the world was young and we thought brick-size desktop calculators and LED watches were still pretty neat, saying "Hi" to your friends meant either calling them on the phone or sending them a quick note through the (gasp!) postal mail. As time went by, immediate gratification won out over genteel manners; thus phone calls became the norm.

The online world took immediate gratification to a whole new level by delivering messages anywhere in the world within moments. It also introduced new problems because the friends who used to live next door now live in the next time zone (or, worse, the second continent on the left just past that ocean over there). E-mail still flies through the wires with the greatest of speed, but it's not interactive — you can't enjoy the back-and-forth exchange of ideas that a good, old-fashioned phone call provided.

Because programmers abhor missing features, the clever developers at America Online came up with the Instant Message system. *Instant messages* blend the immediacy of e-mail with the interactivity of a phone call by letting you type back and forth with someone else on the system. It all happens right now — or, as the computer people say, in *real time* (as opposed to fake time, I suppose) — like a private, one-on-one chat room.

This chapter explores the Instant Message system and details how to send and receive instant messages (or IMs, for short), plus how to shut the little buggers off when you want to concentrate for a while.

Online Telepathy with Instant Messages

Sometimes, you just want to drop a quick "Hi!" to someone you happen to bump into online. That's what the America Online Instant Message feature is for. It's an easy way to have a quick conversation with someone regardless of whatever else either of you is doing at the time (see Figure 10-1). Instant messages are private, too — only you and your correspondent see what passes between you.

Figure 10-1:
An instant message appears.

The top of the Instant Message box tells you the screen name of the person who just "dinged" you. Just below that is the message area itself, where your online conversation takes place. The bottom half of the window is your writing desk, where you compose witty thoughts (and decorate them with the formatting buttons).

Along the bottom of the Instant Message window sits a row of action buttons:

- **Send** ships your message away to the recipient.
- **Cancel** makes the message go away, never to be seen nor heard from again.
- **Get Profile** lists the America Online member profile of the person sending you the message (the same as choosing People⇨Get AOL Member Profile or pressing Ctrl+G on the keyboard).
- **Notify AOL** reports password scammers (more about that later in the chapter), abusive messages, or anything that makes you feel uncomfortable.

Using these little text bombs is easy — here's how they work:

1. **To see whether someone is online, either check your Buddy List or use the Locate command (Ctrl+L).**

   The Buddy List system is a great tool for tracking your friends online. To find out more about it, see Chapter 12.

You can send instant messages only to someone who's signed on *and* has the Instant Messaging option turned on in the America Online Parental Controls area (keyword **Parental Controls**).

2. **If you found your target with the Locate command, click the Send IM button in the Locate dialog box. If you used the Buddy List, click the person's name and then click IM.**

   Either way, the Send Instant Message dialog box pops up.

3. **If it's not there already, type the person's screen name in the To box and press Tab to move the blinking cursor into the text area. Then Type your message.**

   Keep instant messages short — 10 to 12 words is great. If you have something long to say, use e-mail.

4. **After you finish typing the message, click Send.**

   If the message's recipient is signed on and accepting instant messages, the Instant Message window briefly disappears from your screen and then reappears in the upper-left corner.

   If something goes wrong along the way (like the person isn't online right now or has blocked instant messages), the America Online software displays an error message to keep you informed.

When your friend gets the message, she can reply by clicking the Reply button. Her message then appears on your screen, and you can start a running dialogue. (That's assuming, of course, that your buddy *wants* to talk to you today.)

Turning Off Instant Messages Because Sometimes You Just Want to Be Alone

Life on America Online sometimes resembles a huge commune. The moment you sign on, one (or sometimes several) of your friends immediately sends you an instant message and wants to chat. For hours.

If you want to check your e-mail in peace and quiet or perhaps do a little online research, you can easily hang out the Do Not Disturb sign by turning off incoming instant messages. The setting is temporary, so the next time you sign on to the system, instant messages are automatically turned *on* again.

To temporarily turn off the Instant Messaging feature, follow these steps:

1. **After signing on to America Online, press Ctrl+I to open a new Instant Message window.**

   A blank Instant Message window hops onto the screen.

2. **Carefully type the peculiar command $im_off in the To field, type something short (like "go") in the body of the blank instant message and click Send.**

   If everything works right, America Online replies that you're now ignoring instant messages. If you get an error that says something about the user not being signed on, double-check your spelling and try again.

To turn the Instant Messaging feature back on without signing off from the system, just repeat this process and use the command **$im_on** instead.

Catching Password Scammers

Whenever you collect 18 million people in one place (even if it's a virtual place), somewhere in the mix you're bound to find a few undesirable characters. At home, it's the telemarketers. At work, it's the slightly unhinged coworker who lines his cubicle with aluminum foil to block CIA thought-control transmissions. In the online world, it's the password scammers.

These bottom-feeders want only one thing: your account password. Nobody — and I mean *nobody* — from America Online or any other company will *ever* ask for your password. It won't happen! No matter *what* the person says in his message, no matter who he claims to be, he is *lying*. Pay no attention to his drivel. Instead, get ready to report him to America Online.

If someone sends you an Instant Message or an e-mail asking for your password, credit card number, or anything else like that, report the person *immediately* with the Notify AOL button at the bottom of the Instant Message window. Whether the person claims to be from the America Online billing department, a credit card company, or Mars (which is where she *should* be), it's all a lie. You can find out more about this subject in Chapter 5, including a couple of sample scams, plus detailed instructions for nailing — er, reporting — these lowlifes.

Chapter 11

Cogitating, Consternating, and Conflagrating on the Message Boards

In This Chapter

▶ Frolicking in the folders

▶ Peeking at the messages (and adding some of your own)

*Y*ou can't turn around on America Online without running into a discussion. Whether you want to talk about music, mayhem, or something in between (like Branson, Missouri), America Online has a place for you somewhere.

After finding your online home, it's time to join the fray by diving into an online discussion. Of course, you need to know a few things to make sense of the whole thing. This chapter looks at these parts of the discussion world, guiding you through the sometimes obscure path toward joining a discussion group and posting your opinions in the message boards for all to see.

Winding Your Way through the Message Folders

Before joining a discussion, you have to find one. To do that, cruise around in your favorite online areas and look for an item labeled something like *Chat and Messages, Message Boards, Discussion Boards,* or perhaps just *Boards.* Either of those is a strong clue that you found a discussion area with message boards awaiting your thoughts.

TIP

Because details always make more sense if you know the terminology involved, here's a quick romp through the top message-board terms. Ready? Here goes:

- Message boards contain a bunch of individual *topics,* each of which is like a miniature bulletin board.

- *Topics,* in turn, list the member-created discussion *subjects.*

- *Subjects* contain one or more member-written *postings.*

- *Postings* hold your thoughts, carefully arranged and presented for maximum effect among your fellow discuss-ees.

With all that firmly in mind, press onward for a more detailed explanation of the whole menagerie.

After finding a likely-looking message board, you encounter a window like the one shown in Figure 11-1. This window gives you an overview of every *topic* and *folder* in a particular discussion area. The board shown in Figure 11-1 lists a bunch of topics — individual minibulletin boards focused on different discussions. Other message boards may include folders in this window's list. A single folder can hold a number of topics and may even contain other folders. Because the online staffers in charge of each discussion area organize the boards however they see fit, the organizational details of each area vary wildly among online forums.

Figure 11-1: This message board contains several topics and one folder (which leads to more topics).

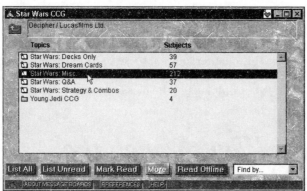

Below the topic descriptions sit the *feature buttons.* You usually see six buttons there. Table 11-1 lists the buttons, along with brief descriptions of what each one does. These buttons are your tools for filtering the postings on a particular message board. Use them well (particularly the Find Since button) to make short work of keeping up with your favorite boards.

Table 11-1	Pressing the Message Board Buttons
Button Title	*Action*
List All	Opens the highlighted bulletin board topic and lists all the messages in it, whether you previously read them or not.
List Unread	Opens the current topic and displays *only* the messages you haven't read.
Mark Read	Marks all the messages in the current topic as though you had read them.
More	Lists the rest of the topics on the bulletin in the window (available only if a particular message board has *numerous* topics on it).
Read Offline	Adds the selected topic to the list of message boards you can *read offline* through Automatic AOL sessions. The list is kept at keyword My Boards.
Find By	Helps you search the message board for specific words or phrases, message posting dates, member screen names, and such. Click the down-arrow to choose the search you want, then follow the on-screen instructions.

Here are a couple of tips and tricks to keep in mind with the message boards:

- ✔ Don't fret if you double-click a message item and America Online replies with a terse message saying `This message is no longer available`. It just means that the message was posted so long ago that it was erased to make room for new ones. ***Remember:*** Old messages never die — they just scroll off the system.

- ✔ Use the Signature option in the Message Board Preferences window to automatically add a few words about yourself to the bottom of each posting. Remember that it's automatic — don't accidentally embarrass yourself.

- ✔ After your first visit to a topic area, save time by using the Find New and Find Since buttons to filter out old messages. That way, you don't have to wade through everything you've already read while the online clock is ticking.

Reading, Replying To, and Generally Browsing the Messages

When you find an interesting topic, double-click its entry to display a window like the one shown in Figure 11-2. These topics are discussion subjects themselves — the real meat of a message board.

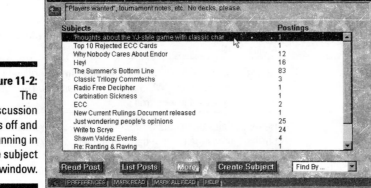

In the middle of the screen is the Subjects list, displaying the first 40 or so subjects that are open for debate. The Subjects list shows the title of the subjects and the current number of responses. To see a message within the subject, double-click the subject entry in this list or click it once and then click Read Post.

The feature buttons along the bottom of the window let you do all sorts of fascinating things:

- ✔ Read Post does the same thing as double-clicking the subject name: It puts you in the discussion message window and displays the first posting for the selected subject.

  When you double-click a subject (or highlight one and click the Read Post button), the message appears in a window like the one shown in Figure 11-3. After all that effort, this window is surprisingly easy to use.

- ✔ List Posts generates a list of all posts within a particular topic, including who wrote the posting, how long it is, and the date and time it was written.

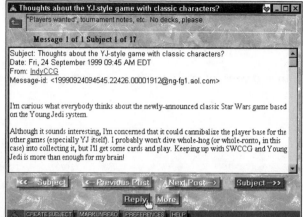

Figure 11-3:
Finally — a
message.

✔ The More button, like its counterpart in the topics window, comes into play only when you have so many messages that America Online can't display them all on the first try. In that case, click More to tell the system that you want to see more messages.

✔ Find Since works just like it does in the topics window — it displays matching messages for each subject within the current topic.

✔ Create Subject is your ticket to making a new discussion subject dedicated to whatever you jolly well want (is that ultimate power or what?).

✔ Cowering along the bottom of the window is the Preferences button (containing your bulletin board signature settings plus other preferences regarding which posts are displayed, how they're displayed, and how many are downloaded).

✔ Mark Read and Mark All Read are down there as well to let you ignore whatever messages you want.

The message text dominates the windows (as it should — after all, that's why you came). Every America Online message begins with a brief header giving the message's vital statistics: subject, posting date, author, and a grim-looking message ID that makes you wonder whether it's harboring some secret code. The message follows.

Along the bottom are a whole raft of feature buttons that do just about anything your heart desires:

- ✓ The forward arrow and backward arrow Subjects buttons move you to the next subject for this discussion.

- ✓ The Previous Post and Next Post display other thoughts on the current subject.

- ✓ Use Reply to add your thoughts to this group (or *thread*) of messages within the subject.

Chapter 12

Where's Your Buddy?
Where's Your Pal?

▶ Creating, deleting, and changing Buddy Lists

▶ Maintaining your privacy

▶ Making your preferences clear

*G*athering your buddies for a chatMeeting is always fun. After all — what would your life have been like these past few years without your best friend (or your cadre of best friends)? When you meet a new friend on America Online, you can keep track of her screen name with the AOL Buddy List feature and avoid the frustrating experience of meeting a new best friend one day and losing her forever the next — all because you forgot her name!

This chapter explores the world of digital friend tracking, including creating, adding to, and deleting from your America Online Buddy Lists. In case you find yourself in a talkative mood, you also find out how to send instant messages to your buddies and gather them for a cozy private chat.

Who's Your Buddy?

At a glance, the Buddy List tells you which of your friends is online. It even organizes your buddies into groups, making the task of discerning the office crowd from the gang at last week's online Jell-O diving competition an easy one. (After all, the difference may be important, even if a few names overlap between the two.)

By default, every time you sign on to America Online, your Buddy List jumps into action, hanging out in the upper-right corner of the screen. (If you don't want the list to always come up, you can adjust the Buddy List's behavior with the Buddy List preferences, covered later in this chapter.) As your buddies sign on and off the system, the list updates itself automatically.

The following sections cover all the important stuff you need to know about building, using, and changing Buddy Lists on America Online. For information about privacy preferences and Buddy List preferences, see the sections "Privacy Preferences: Please, I Vahnt to Be Alone" and "Setting Your Buddy List Preferences," later in this chapter.

What if some of your friends don't use America Online? Are they lost forever? Goodness no! Tell your other Internet-based friends about the cool AOL Instant Messenger program (better known as *AIM*), which lets them send and receive instant messages, create a Buddy List, and do many other nifty tricks. Find out all of the details at keyword **AIM** or www.aol.com/aim (for your *Net.friends*).

Adding someone to a Buddy List

Including people on the Buddy List is a snap. Here's how to do it:

1. In the Buddy List window, click the Setup button.

The Buddy List control window appears, just like the one shown in Figure 12-1.

Figure 12-1: Tweak your Buddy List groups from this window.

If your Buddy List window isn't already on-screen, choose People➪View Buddy List from the toolbar and then click Setup in the Buddy List dialog box. You can also use keyword **Buddy** to dive directly into the Buddy List control window, assuming that you're a big keyword fan.

2. Double-click the name of the Buddy List you want to bulk up with new members.

Depending on your wishes, the Edit Buddies List window hops on the screen, looking as bright and chipper as ever. To create a new list, see the following section, "Creating a new Buddy List group."

3. In the Enter a Screen Name box, type the screen name of your buddy and then press Enter.

Your buddy's screen name takes its place in the Buddies in Group area.

4. **Repeat Step 3 until all your buddies are in there. After you're done with the list, click Save.**

   To prove that it was listening this whole time, America Online replies that your list is updated. The Buddy Lists dialog box then returns in triumph, proudly displaying a new number of entries beside your list.

Creating a new Buddy List group

You've met a whole slew of new people in a particular chat room, on a message board, or through an e-mail mailing list. Keep track of them by creating a unique Buddy List just for them:

1. **In the Buddy List window, click the Setup button.**

   The Buddy List control window appears, eagerly awaiting your new creation.

2. **Click the Create button to make a new Buddy List and add people to it.**

   The Create a Buddy List Group window hops onto the screen, ready to display the result of your creative efforts.

3. **In the Buddy List Group Name box, type a short name (16 letters or fewer) for the new list and then press Tab.**

   The blinking toothpick cursor jumps down to the Enter a Screen Name area, ready to do its thing.

4. **In the Enter a Screen Name box, type your friend's screen name and press Enter.**

   Your buddy's screen name takes its place in the Buddies in Group area.

5. **Repeat Step 4 until all your buddies are in there. After you're done with the list, click Save.**

   America Online replies with a dialog box that says that your list has been created. When you click OK to make the dialog box disappear, the Buddy Lists dialog box returns, proudly displaying an entry for your new list (see Figure 12-2).

Figure 12-2:
The Quilters proudly join my list of friends.

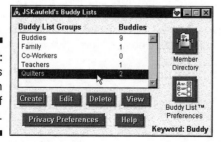

Deleting someone from a Buddy List group

Sad to say, sometimes buddies become ex-buddies. Your interests change, their interests change, and suddenly you no longer correspond. Or maybe your friend simply changed screen names, which means that you need to add his new screen name and delete the old one. Whether deleting a buddy from a Buddy List group is traumatic or transitional, AOL has provided a way to get the job done:

1. **In the Buddy List window, click the Setup button. The Buddy List control window appears.**

   If your Buddy List window isn't on-screen, keyword **Buddy** brings the Buddy List control window to attention, too.

2. **Highlight the Buddy List group that contains the passé screen name or absent friend and click Edit.**

   The Edit List window opens, with the name of your selected Buddy List group emblazoned across the window's title bar.

3. **Highlight your buddy's screen name in the Buddies in Group list and click Remove Buddy.**

   The buddy's screen name jumps to the Enter a Screen Name field. If it was all a hasty mistake, click Add Buddy to reinstate your friend in the Buddy List group.

4. **To remove the screen name from this particular group, click Save.**

   A small dialog box appears that tells you that your Buddy Lists have been updated.

5. **Click OK to make the dialog box go away.**

   The Buddy List control window shows its face again. This time, you see one fewer buddy in the Buddy List group you just edited.

Deleting a whole Buddy List

Once a year or so, you get the urge to clean house. Take a look at your Buddy List groups and see whether the adage also applies there. If you've been hanging on to Buddy List groups that contain no members, groups that track outdated interests, or lists of e-mail business addresses for the job you left 18 months ago, a little window cleaning may be in order:

1. **Click the Setup button on your Buddy List window to open the Buddy List control window.**

If your Buddy List window isn't handily on-screen, use keyword **Buddy** to bring the Buddy List control window to life or choose People➪View Buddy List from the toolbar. Either way, click Setup when the Buddy List window appears.

2. **Highlight the Buddy List group you want to leave forever and click the Delete button.**

   A small dialog box worriedly rushes to your screen, asking whether you truly want to delete the entire Buddy List.

3. **After you click Delete, the Buddy List control window adjusts to the change, displaying one fewer Buddy List group in its collection.**

Be very sure that you want to delete a Buddy List group before you click OK to delete the list. If you mistakenly delete the wrong list, you have to re-create that Buddy List group from scratch. This has already happened to you? See the section "Creating a new Buddy List group," earlier in this chapter.

Renaming a Buddy List group

You woke up this morning and realized that you'd found the perfect name for one of your existing Buddy List groups. Never fear — changing that Buddy List name is a snap:

1. **Click the Setup button in the Buddy List window to bring up the Buddy List control window.**

   If your Buddy List window is hiding from you, keyword **Buddy** calls the Buddy List control window to your screen.

2. **Highlight the Buddy List group you want to rename and click the Edit button.**

   The Edit List window jumps to attention.

3. **Click in the Change Buddy List Group Name To box and type the new name for your Buddy List group.**

   Choose a name that's representative of the whole group or one that helps you remember why you've placed these screen names together.

4. **Click Save to make your changes a reality. A small dialog box appears, notifying you that your Buddy Lists have been updated. Click OK.**

   After the dialog box disappears, you see an updated Buddy List control window that proudly displays your new Buddy List group name.

Watch carefully — it even does tricks!

Now that you have these cool new Buddy List groups, what do you do with them? Well, plenty!

Want to know where your friend is hanging out online? Find her fast by highlighting her screen name and clicking the Locate button.

Quickly send your friend an instant message by highlighting her screen name and clicking the IM button. An Instant Message window opens on-screen with your friend's screen name already filled in.

If you had a more face-to-face discussion in mind, use the Buddy Chat feature to invite your buddy to a private chat room with the two of you (and whomever else you want to invite). See the "Buddy Chat" section, later in this chapter, for all the details.

Privacy Preferences: Please, I Vahnt to Be Alone

You don't have to be a movie star to want a little privacy every now and then. Sometimes, you just want to get away from it all and enjoy a little peace and quiet. That's why the Buddy List system includes a whole collection of privacy preferences.

If you don't want people to track your screen name with a Buddy List, that's easy to set up. Here's what to do:

1. **In the Buddy List window, click Setup.**

   If your Buddy List window isn't visible, choose People⇨View Buddy List from the toolbar to make it magically appear. Then click the Setup button.

   The Buddy List control window appears on-screen.

2. **Click the Privacy Preferences button in the Buddy List control window.**

   You see the Privacy Preferences window jump to the screen, very similar to the one shown in Figure 12-3.

   Although it looks rather daunting, this window is easy to configure. The left side of the window shows two sections — Choose Your Privacy Preferences and Apply Preferences to the Following Features. Each section contains two or more radio buttons; clicking one to select it deactivates all the others.

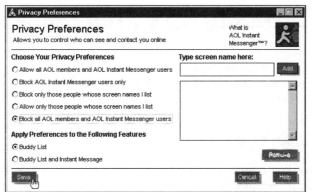

3. **Select the radio button to activate whichever privacy level you prefer.**

   - **To completely block yourself from Buddy Lists all over America Online (including AOL Instant Messenger users on the Internet):** Select the Block All AOL Members and AOL Instant Messenger Users radio button.

   - **To either allow or prevent a few members from tracking you on their Buddy Lists:** Select either the Allow Only Those People Whose Screen Names I List or the Block Only Those People Whose Screen Names I List radio button. Then put the specific screen name you want to block or allow in the Type Screen Name Here box and click Add. Add as many screen names as you want to block (or allow).

   - **To block all AOL Instant Messenger users from trying to communicate with you from the Internet:** Select the Block AOL Instant Messenger Users Only radio button.

4. **Decide whether to apply these preferences for Buddy Lists only or for both Buddy Lists and Instant Messages.**

   I recommend using the Buddy List setting rather than the Buddy Lists and Instant Messages option. The latter option is best if you want to strictly limit who can see you with a Buddy List or send you instant messages.

5. **After you finish setting your privacy preferences, click Save.**

   AOL sends you a dialog box that tells you that you've updated your preferences.

6. **Click OK to make the dialog box disappear.**

   Your Buddy List privacy preferences are now active.

7. **Click the upper-left corner of the Buddy List control window to close it.**

   Continue with your regularly scheduled online experience, free from unwanted interruptions.

Setting Your Buddy List Preferences

Some days, you want sound in your world; other days, the mere thought of extra noise makes your head pound. Set your general Buddy List preferences to match your mood. Opt for or against sounds when your buddies come and go, and tell the system whether you want to see your Buddy List every time you sign on.

To set your Buddy List preferences:

1. **Click the Setup button in the Buddy List window to bring the Buddy List control window to attention.**

   If your Buddy List window is nowhere to be seen, keyword **Buddy** wakes the Buddy List control window, and it jumps smartly to attention.

2. **Click the Buddy List Preferences button to open the Buddy List Preferences dialog box.**

   Look for this button along the right side of the Buddy List control window — it's different from the Privacy Preferences button. You aren't deciding on privacy issues here, but rather how and when your Buddy List appears and sounds.

3. **To see your Buddy List every time you sign on, select the check box that says** Show Me My Buddy List(s) Immediately after I Sign On to AOL.

   The default setting is to display your Buddy List when you sign on. If waiting that few extra seconds for the Buddy List window to load every time you sign on really annoys you, deselect it and use keyword **Buddy View** to see your Buddy List whenever you want to.

4. **Make sound decisions (sorry — I couldn't resist).**

   The two remaining options deal with sound. To hear a sound when your buddies arrive, select the Play Sound When Buddies Sign On check box. To hear sound when your friends leave, select the Play Sound When Buddies Sign Off check box.

   Click only one if you want to be notified by sound only when friends sign on or sign off; click both to hear when they come and go. If your Buddy List groups are large and their members active, the constant noises may grate your nerves after a while. If that happens, use the Buddy List Preferences dialog box to deselect the sound options.

   To hear Buddy List sounds, you need to download the Buddy Sound Installer file. The default sound for Buddy Lists is an opening and closing door; if you select the sound options and don't hear the door when the next buddy comes or goes, click the Go to Sound Library button in the Buddy List Preferences window to open the Buddy List

Sounds information. Then click the Download Buddy Sound Installer Door Theme button to open the download window for the sound installer. Click Download Now to begin the download.

If you want to see other available Buddy List sounds, click the Buddy List Sound Library button in the Buddy List Sounds window. Download any of the sounds in the list that tweak your fancy.

5. **After you finish setting your Buddy List preferences, click Save. America Online produces a helpful Preferences Updated dialog box; click OK to make it go away.**

   You now find yourself back at the friendly Buddy List control window.

6. **If you're happy with the Buddy List preferences and don't want to change anything else, click the upper-left corner of the Buddy List control window.**

   It merrily retires to windowland to await your next summons.

Building an Online Treehouse with Buddy Chat

Instant message conversations have their place, but for extended chatter, using the AOL chat rooms is better. Chat rooms offer a larger text area for scrolling messages and the ability to talk to more than one person at a time. With the America Online Buddy Chat feature, the system quickly creates a private chat room and invites the screen names you specify.

Here's how you create a Buddy Chat of your own:

1. **Select the name of a buddy you want to chat with and then click the Buddy Chat button in the Buddy List window.**

   The Buddy Chat window appears.

   To invite a whole bunch of buddies, click a Buddy group entry (like Family or Friends, for example) rather than clicking a single buddy's screen name.

   AOL fills in the screen names of your selected buddy or buddies, as the case may be. Their names appear in the Screen Names to Invite box.

2. **Alter the buddies in your list as you like by erasing names and filling in others.**

   Invite as few as one person or as many as you can reasonably fit into a chat room (23 people total, including you) and still have a good time.

3. **In the Message to Send box, type a reason for getting together.**

AOL helpfully starts your message with `You are invited to`; either complete it or replace it with a phrase of your own.

Some invitations, like "You are invited to a public beheading," tend to turn people off. Spend a couple of seconds and make it sound inviting if you want your friends to attend your chat.

4. **Normally, Private Chat Room is checked in the Location part of the window. Leave it, as it is to organize a Buddy Chat.**

If you click Keyword/Favorite, you need to enter a keyword in the Location text box. Friends who accept your invitation see one of your favorite places open on their screens.

Opting to invite friends to a keyword is useful if you want to attend the same scheduled chat in an area online or if you want to show them one of your favorite haunts. After everyone has assembled, you can use instant messages to discuss the area and what you enjoy about it the most.

5. **Change any (or all) of the chat room names to make them more friendly.**

The Location text box suggests rather arcane chat room names; usually your screen name and then `Chat` with a few numbers tacked on the end of it. For a good start to your chatting experience, change the name to something a little more noteworthy and interesting.

AOL chooses these chat room names to minimize the chance of having someone you don't know drop in to your private chat room. If you change the chat room name to something more generic, such as `I love dogs` or `Jane`, you may receive a surprise visitor every now and then as someone else thinks up your chat room name. If this happens, simply tell them that you're sorry, but their chat room name is already taken. Most of the time, they leave as quickly as they came.

6. **After you add, alter, and amend your invitation to your heart's content, click Send.**

Your Buddy Chat invitation wings its way to your friends.

To ensure that you're not forgotten, an invitation appears on your screen, too. Figure 12-4 shows you a sample.

The invitation also features an IM button. You may receive an instant message from a buddy in a teasing mood or from someone who had a momentary brain lapse on your screen name's identity.

7. **Click Go to enter the chat room.**

You arrive in the chat room you created and await your buddies. After you're in the room, you find that it works just like a normal private chat — mostly because it *is* a private chat room. (For a quick refresher on private chat rooms, flip back to Chapter 9.)

8. **Greet your buddies as they drop in to the room and have a great conversation!**

Figure 12-4:
Anyone for
a private
Buddy Chat?

Part III
Diving into the Fun Stuff

The 5th Wave   By Rich Tennant

"HONEY! OUR WEB BROWSER GOT OUT LAST NIGHT AND DUMPED THE TRASH ALL OVER MR. BELCHER'S HOME PAGE!"

In this part . . .

Okay, so you're not easily impressed — e-mail doesn't do much for you, discussion boards warm your fires only a little, and chats leave you utterly cold. You tend to repeat the question time and time again: "So what can you really *do* with AOL?" Yet you know that the online world truly is the Next Big Thing and you want to join in the fun.

Welcome to Part III — your field book for the Digital Age, offering tips for finding the who, what, and where of digital life; techniques for researching the topics that tweak your curiosity; and suggestions for picking out the *perfect* game to play while frittering away the hours. To make this part complete, I also include an Internet chapter, with the low-down on everything from gophers to the Web.

Chapter 13

Finding People, Places, Things, and Information

*I*f I could have a nickel for every time someone asks me how to find things in the online world, I'd ask for a dollar instead. (A nickel doesn't buy *anything* these days.) Whatever the payment, I would be up to my eyeballs in money. That's because tracking stuff down on America Online and the Internet is (ahem) challenging — or at least it *was* challenging before those clever programmer types invented the supercool *search systems*.

Whether you want something specific or feel like browsing aimlessly for a while, start your hunt here, with the various search systems available through America Online. This chapter reveals the search oracle's mystic secrets, starting with the Search button and continuing with a romp through all your search-related tools. Whether you seek an online area, Web page, favorite quotation, obscure fact, e-mail address, or business phone number, the America Online search tools make quick work of the job.

Finding People: Sniffing Out Friends, Acquaintances, and Other Novel Folks

Even though the world of America Online is packed with information covering every topic under the sun, it's the people that make life fun — people who populate the chat rooms, fill the message boards, and pack the audiences at online events. No matter what brought you to America Online, the community is what keeps you there.

Find it all with AOL Search

It's time for a quick experiment.

With no special equipment and nothing up my sleeve (at least nothing that household remedies can't treat), I shall now attempt to link two ideas within the recesses of your mind. Ready to begin? First, think of the word *look*. Got it? Good. Now, use keyword Search to open the very slick AOL Search window. Softly repeat the word *look* as you gaze at the AOL Search window. Whenever you want to *look* for something but you don't know where to start, think of AOLSearch, the single best America Online starting point for the whole search experience.

From this one window, reaching all the system's search services is a snap. Whether you seek people to meet, places to visit, or things to do, AOL Search has the tools you need.

The tools in this section help you find people, wherever they may be. Each tool takes a slightly different spin on the problem, from locating friends signed on to the system to discovering friends-to-be among the millions of other America Online members.

Locating folks to see who's around

The America Online Locate command gives you a quick way of finding your friends. If you know your pal's screen name, the Locate command tells you whether your compatriot is signed on at the moment and also reports whether she is in a chat room. If your friend is chatting the light fantastic in a public chat room, auditorium, or conference room, the Locate system automatically offers to take you right to that chat. (Ahh . . . this is definitely one of those "Isn't technology wonderful?" moments.)

Speaking of technology, America Online *also* includes a way for you to prevent people from finding you with the Locate command (and through Buddy Lists). To find out more about the built-in privacy options, stealthily slink on to Chapter 10.

To quickly find someone online with Locate, follow these steps:

1. **Either press Ctrl+L or choose People⇨Locate AOL Member Online.**

   The Locate Member Online dialog box appears on-screen, ready and willing to do its thing.

2. **Type the screen name in the dialog box and either press Enter or click OK.**

   The system searches hither, thither, and even Yonkers to see whether the person you seek is signed on to America Online or the European AOL services.

   If the person is signed on right now (and if he didn't block you through the Buddy List system's privacy preferences), America Online displays the Locate dialog box, as shown in Figure 13-1. The system giddily announces that it found him and tells you whether he is in a public chat room or private chat room or just skulking around the system waiting for you. If your pal is in a public chat room, the dialog box also gives you the room name and offers a Go button so that you can join him there. The dialog box also offers a button to send the person an Instant Message.

   If the person you seek is not online at the moment, a vaguely sad dialog box tells you. In that case, be sure to check your spelling because America Online doesn't say "Whoops, you misspelled the screen name" — instead, it looks for a person with the screen name you typed, whether or not it's a valid America Online screen name.

Figure 13-1: Hey — I'm signed on!

Searching the member directory

It doesn't matter whether you like to fly kites during rainstorms while dressed as Ben Franklin or meditate in front of the TV considering Zen and its effects on game show hosts. With more than 18 million members of America Online, you're *very* likely to find people just like (or significantly similar to) you somewhere on the system. The trick is finding them — and being found yourself.

To ensure that you are found, fill out your online profile. If you haven't done your profile yet, there's no time like the present. Sign on to America Online, choose My AOL⇨My Member Profile from the toolbar and mark your place in this book and fill out the profile dialog box. After you finish, click Update to save your profile information and then come back to the book (yes, I'll wait for you). Now that your profile is done, you're part of the member directory. Congratulations.

If you want an incredibly fancy profile that's sure to make people stop and say "Hey, that's an incredibly fancy profile," flip to Chapter 22.

Now that your information is in the system, try searching the member directory for friends-to-be. To do that, follow these steps:

1. **Choose People⊅Search AOL Member Directory or use keyword** Members **to bring up the Member Directory dialog box.**

   The Member Directory Search dialog box appears.

2. **Type something that describes the people you want to find: a hobby you enjoy, the city you're from, your occupation, or whatever else you can think of.**

   Short descriptions work best. Check your spelling — you don't want a typo standing between you and your friends-to-be!

3. **Click Search to see whom you can see.**

   If America Online reports that it can't find anyone, check your spelling again (it never hurts) or search for some other unique characteristic. If everything works, the dialog box overflows with possible new friends. (Okay — it doesn't _really_ overflow, but that's poetic license for "there are so many entries that a scroll bar appears next to the list.")

4. **Double-click anyone who looks interesting. Jot down the screen name (or add it to your address book), write a "Hi, how ya doing?" e-mail message, and see where it goes from there.**

When you reach this last step, remember that you get only one chance to make a good first impression. Make your introductory e-mail message witty, genteel, interesting, and, most of all, polite. If the person in question never writes back to you, don't take it personally — just search the member directory again and look for someone else to correspond with instead.

Finding friends with the AOL White Pages

Even though America Online has more than 18 million members, that number pales against the countless millions who inhabit the Internet worldwide. Even though nothing exactly like the America Online member directory exists for the Internet, the America Online white pages system makes a good start.

The AOL white pages is just what it sounds like — a white-pages-style listing of names, addresses, phone numbers, and e-mail addresses for United States residents. Because the information in the online white pages is drawn from publicly available sources (such as the paper-based white pages), the odds are good that both you and your friends are already listed. Even though you're in the system, there's no guarantee that the information about you is accurate. (Ah, the joys of information in the electronic age, eh?)

In addition to address and e-mail information for individuals, the system also includes a whole section devoted to business information. The business search system works in much the same way as the version for individuals, so just pay attention to the prompts as you work through the dialog boxes, and your business searches should go as successfully as your other explorations.

Searching the Switchboard system takes only a few steps. Here's what to do:

1. **Either use keyword** White Pages **or choose People⇨Internet White Pages from the toolbar to open the AOL white pages system.**

   The Web browser pops up, filled to the brim with the White Pages Web site.

   If you want to look for an individual's e-mail address or for business information, scroll around the AOL White Pages window until you find a link to the Web Yellow Pages. Click here to start your business search.

2. **Fill in whatever information you have about the person (such as the name, city, and state), and then click Search.**

   The White Pages system chews on your information for a while and then displays its search results.

3. **If the system found your person (or a group of people, if you did a more general search), it lists the name and address it came up with from the white pages database.**

   If you see more than one name, scroll through the list until you find the specific person you want.

   On the other hand, if the system doesn't find your person, try leaving off the first name or shorten the name to just the first few letters. Searching for Dave, for example, won't find your person if he's listed as David. Try using Dav for the search because that matches both variations.

Finding Places: Tracking Interests and Meeting Informational Needs

Do you ever sit in front of your computer, staring at the America Online screen, knowing that what you want to know just *has* to be in there somewhere? If only you knew where to look . . . (insert wistful sigh here).

The next time that feeling strikes, fire up one of the America Online topical search systems. These routines search not only the content areas within America Online but also the wealth of stuff on the World Wide Web to match you with precisely the place you want.

When you're looking for a particular topic, start with AOL Search (keyword **Search**) first, and then use NetFind (or one of the other Web search engines discussed in the "NetFind" section, later in this chapter) as a backup. To zero in on specific information (like tips and reviews), use the Search & Explore options within each channel. Remember that areas inside America Online usually offer both informational and community links (like discussion boards and chat areas), although most Web sites are information-only connections.

Find It on AOL

To track down an online community for your favorite topic, try the handy AOL Search system. AOL Search takes any word you type (like *homework, finances,* or *photography*) and looks for that subject among the America Online forums and services, as well as a voluminous database of interesting Internet sites. The system lists everything it finds relating to your subject.

To start searching , sign on to America Online and follow these steps:

1. **In the big white box near the top of the America Online screen, type the word you're looking for and then click Search.**

   After a moment, the Web browser pops up, displaying the results of your search, just like in Figure 13-2. The system splits your results into sections: Recommended Sites (features Web sites and America Online areas), Matching Categories (lists of related sites), and Matching Sites (other individual Web sites and America Online areas that match your search term).

   If the system displays a window apologizing that it couldn't find any matches for the topic you entered, don't worry — you didn't do anything wrong. Instead, close the gee-I'm-sorry-I-failed-you window and search with a different word. If you run out of terms, take your search out to the World Wide Web through NetFind, discussed later in this chapter.

2. **Browse through the search results to see what America Online found for you. To view something on the list, click its entry. To see more matching sites, click one of the Next links.**

   When you click an item in the results list, the information hops into view, either in the Web browser window (where the search information was just a moment ago) or in an entirely new window (if the area lives inside America Online itself). Pretty cool, eh?

3. **After you're done with that particular area, go back to the Search Results window to look for other items of interest.**

   If the stuff you looked at replaced the search results window, use the Back button on the navigation bar to flip back to the search information. (Or, if all else fails, just start your search over again.)

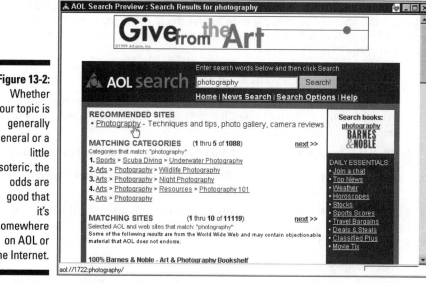

4. **To start another search, close the various windows and start over at Step 1.**

   If you don't feel like looking for anything else right now, feel free to close all the search-related windows. (There's no penalty for tidiness.)

Surfing — er, Searching — the Channels

When the folks at America Online redesigned the channel lineup, they moved things around, pushed the content areas into different cubbyholes, and generally gave the whole place a clean, freshly painted look. They also added a cool tool to your arsenal of goodies: a vastly improved channel search system.

Although every channel needs a search option, not every channel has one. As I write this, the Teens channel doesn't offer a search option (but I guess that makes sense — would teens listen to the computer either?). And the Health channel includes search systems focused on finding particular health problems, but nothing that scours the whole Health channel.

The search system includes cool features, like content limits that control where you want to find information and a filter to adjust how narrowly or broadly you want to search. All in all, the channel search system is a big improvement over the old way of searching the channels. You do, however need to invest a few minutes in figuring out how to make the channel search system work.

To simplify that task, I present you with the following steps. They guide you through the channel search process in an utterly painless way. (If your personal pain quotient is low today, feel free to slam your head into the wall between steps.) Here's what to do:

1. **Go to a channel you want to search.**

   Click Channels on the toolbar and then select the appropriate channel from the drop-down list. The Channels window appears, displaying the selected content channel.

2. **Click the Search item or the Search & Explore item for that channel.**

   After a moment of deep thought, the channel's Search and Explore window pops up.

   The Search window occasionally hides in the channel windows (it's a little shy — you know how software sometimes gets), but if you look carefully, you can find it.

3. **Browse through the list of available topics on the item list.**

   When you find a description that looks interesting, click its *hyperlink* (the colorful underlined text) to visit the area.

4. **If you don't see anything you like, click the Search button at the bottom of the window.**

   A little search window appears, complete with cool-looking text boxes, time settings, and goodness only knows what else.

5. **Carefully enter the term (or terms) you want to find into the Enter Search Word(s) box.**

   Gud speeling iz a must-hav sorta item here, sew pulhezzee be kareful.

6. **Click the down arrow next to the danglingly named** `Find Articles Within the Last` **and select a time frame for the search system to explore.**

   For most searches, leave this item set to *All Articles*.

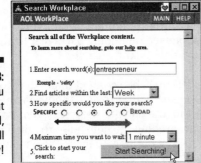

Figure 13-3:
What you
type is what
you find,
so spell
carefully!

7. **Choose how specific you want the search to be by clicking the appropriate radio button.**

   By default, the system uses a simple *AND* approach, so if you search for *John Adams,* the search engine returns any document with the words *John* and *Adams.* To search for the exact phrase you type, click the radio button next to the word `Specific`. To loosen the search and turn it into a fuzzy, I-want-this-and-things-like-it search, click the button next to the word `Broad`.

   To figure out all the nuances of manually adjusting your search, click the Help link at the top of the search window.

8. **If you feel impatient today, adjust the Maximum Time You Want to Wait setting and impose a deadline on the search system.**

   The search system usually works so fast that it never even gets close to the wait time. (This setting reminds me of the "Close Door" button in elevators — it lets you do something with your frustration, but doesn't accomplish anything else).

9. **Click the Start Searching button to do the dirty deed.**

   After the search chugs away for a few moments, the Search Results window appears.

10. **Scroll through the search results list and click whatever looks interesting to see it.**

    To start another search, click the link at the bottom of the Results window.

Digging a little deeper

The Search system has more than one button and a cool window. In fact, lots of searching resources are all over America Online. The trick, as usual, is knowing where to look. (Yes, it's frustrating when you can't find the sites to help you look for things, but at least *now* you know where they are!)

The following bullets point out the other search-thingies lurking on the America Online toolbar menus and skulking around the system:

- **Channel Guide (keyword Channel Guide):** Get a quick overview of the 19 channel areas within America Online, plus links that take you directly to the various areas within each channel.

- **Search Featured Chats (keyword Chat Search):** Scour the service's content areas for interesting scheduled chats. Just type your topic of interest and click the Search button to see where it's the Subject of the Day!

- **Find Public and Member Chats (choose People➪Find a Chat from the toolbar):** Go to the Search Featured Chats window, where you can browse through the featured chat or member chat room lists or search through the chats by room name to find *precisely* the one you want.

✔ **General America Online Help (keyword Help):** Cruise through the Member Services area for tips and information about life in the online world.

NetFind

It seems like almost everybody (including the local plumber) offers information through the World Wide Web these days. That diversity makes the Web an incredible repository of information — like a library filled with the collected knowledge, opinions, and ramblings of a measurable percentage of the world's populace. Sounds almost too good to be true, doesn't it?

Well, you're right — there is a catch. Although the Web world is filled to the brim with cool stuff, organizationally speaking it's a mess. Imagine a library organized by a tornado, with assistance provided by every kindergartner in your hometown. Not a pretty picture, is it?

Shortly after the Web came to be, many clever people built indexes and search systems to tame this wild digital frontier. Some of these tools catalog sites and then help you search the list by a keyword you entered. Others take a slightly different approach by building a topic index you browse by clicking on-screen menus. Both systems have their advantages, depending on what you want to find and how you feel like looking for it.

The America Online foray into the world of Web searching is NetFind. NetFind gives you the best of both worlds, by offering both a searchable database *and* a browsable subject index — although the list of subjects is somewhat limited right now:

✔ **Go topic hopping through NetFind:** Just click one of the links in the Time Savers or Web Centers areas in the bottom part of the window. Each of these leads to more-detailed lists. Just keep clicking until you dig your way down to a particular site that meets your needs. If you click your way to the bottom of the barrel without finding a good match, try a keyword search instead.

✔ **Use NetFind's fill-in-the-blank search option:** Type in the box at the top of the NetFind window a word or two describing your topic and then click the ever exuberant Search! button. After chewing on your request for a few moments, NetFind returns with a list of matching sites. To view any of the matches, just click the site's entry. Sometimes, NetFind uncovers so many possible matches that they don't fit on one screen. In that case, NetFind presents a Next button at the bottom of the window. Click that button to view the next page of matching entries.

If NetFind can't come up with anything that matches your topic, it quietly tells you of its failure and often implies that the problem is somehow your fault. Don't believe it — it lies. If this happens during your search, take your topic to another of the Web's search engines, listed in Table 13-1. Some engines, notably Yahoo!, provide automatic links to other popular search systems when they display your search results (just in case you want to try your luck elsewhere).

Table 13-1	Search Engines for Scouring the World Wide Web
Search Engine	*Web Address*
AltaVista	www.altavista.com
Deja News	www.dejanews.com
Excite	www.excite.com
Infoseek	www.infoseek.com
Lycos	www.lycos.com
Yahoo!	www.yahoo.com

Browsing through some great resources

Sometimes nailing down precisely what you want to find isn't easy. Instead of being a simple, cut-and-dried topic, your goal is more vague — sort of an I'll-know-it-when-I-see-it feeling. Even so, you still need some places to start looking. The general areas listed in the preceding section may meet your needs, but sometimes a more narrowly focused source sparks your imagination in a way that a more general one can't.

The following list identifies a selection of searchable resources from all corners of America Online. Some areas offer news, and others come bearing general introductory notes. All these resources are free, which makes them my friends by default:

- ✔ The king of all general references has to be the Research & Learn channel's More References window (keyword **More References**). Just look at the list in that window — topics ranging from etiquette to personal finance, plus even more that scrolled off the screen! No matter what kind of information you seek, the More References list makes a great starting point.

- ✔ Every schoolchild in the United States knows that it's hard to stump the encyclopedias (keyword **Encyclopedias**). Putting these general reference guides online makes browsing and searching their content even easier.

✔ In addition to the encyclopedias, America Online offers many other classic references, such as a dictionary (keyword **Dictionary**) and a thesaurus (keyword **Thesaurus**). AOL goes a step further by offering specialized word references, too, like Word Histories (keyword **Word Histories**), Other Dictionaries (keyword **Dictionaries**), and the beginning connoisseur's friend, the Wine Dictionary (keyword **Dictionaries**, and then double-click Wine Dictionary on the list).

✔ Writers require strong research areas to find facts for their stories, but sometimes they also need information that's a little off the beaten path. For days when you either want a good laugh or feel like adding to your storehouse of the odd and mystifying, check out Straight Dope (one of my favorite areas, at `www.straightdope.com`), Mad World (keyword **Madworld**), and the ever popular Urban Legends forum (keyword **Urban Legends**).

✔ What report, theme, or presentation couldn't use a good quote to spice it up? Choose the best sound bites from several volumes of quotations behind the Research and Learn channel's Quotations folder (keyword **More References,** and then double-click Quotations on the list).

✔ When your research sends you looking for ethnic information, try areas like Ethnicity (keyword **Ethnicity**), Black History Reference (keyword **BH Reference**), Jewish Community (keyword **Jewish Community**), NetNoir (keyword **NetNoir**), or Hispanic Online (keyword **Hispanic Online**). Each one includes resources, discussions, and chats that may lead you to still other resources in the Great Out There.

✔ Digging into the world of business? Check out Business Research (keyword **Business Research**) for general corporate information and a searchable library of press releases; Company Research (keyword **Company Research)** for financial reports; and the news by company ticker system (keyword **Company News**) for the latest news wire tidbits about your favorite firms.

✔ Looking for some culture in your life? Search a list of more than 250,000 theatre, dance, and other arts events all over the United States and Canada in CultureFinder (keyword **CultureFinder**). When you find an event that makes your heart sing, buy tickets right there. Culture doesn't get any easier than this!

✔ It's a frightening thought, but the federal government is the single largest publisher in the United States. It also generates more statistics than should be allowed by law. To dip into the wellspring of numbers bought with your tax dollars, check out the Federal Statistics Web site, at `www.fedstats.gov`.

If you need to collect information about a topic on an ongoing basis, check out the News Profiles system, at keyword **News Profiles.** You define what kind of stories you want to see, and the News Profiles system scours the news wires, automatically forwarding any matching stories directly to your mailbox. Setting up a profile takes only a moment, but it keeps going and going, just like an electronic news version of that annoying pink bunny.

Finding Cool Programs and Nifty Files

After working through the initial euphoria (and the first credit card bill) of owning your computer, the next thought that usually goes through your mind is something like "I wish that the computer could do X," where X is some incredibly important task that none of your current software and hardware setup comes even *close* to performing. Worse, if you're like most people (myself included), X is quickly followed by Y, Z, and a whole horde of functions starting with peculiar math symbols you barely remember from school.

It sounds like you need software — and lots of it at that! Purchasing commercial programs to accomplish everything is a great idea, but your credit card is still on life support from getting the computer. Copying your buddy's program is out of the question (the software makers frown on that in a big, ugly, nasty way). What's a computer owner to do? Search the file libraries of America Online, that's what!

The hundreds of file libraries on America Online contain programs that process words, mangle (sorry, *manage*) data, implode unfriendly aliens — the list goes on. And these programs keep your budget happy because they're either *freeware* (free programs donated to the world by proud developers) or *shareware* (try-before-you-buy programs that require only a small payment to the author). You may even find demonstration versions of commercial applications.

To help you find the software needle in the online haystack, America Online created the Software Search system. This system quickly puts the software you need right into your hands — or, more precisely, right on your hard drive, which is an infinitely better place for a program (software stains wickedly if you get it on your clothes).

Get into the File Search system by using keyword **Software Search.** A little dialog box happily pops up, asking whether you want to search for brand name (also known as *expensive*) programs or if you prefer to cruise through the shareware file libraries. Unless your credit card is well on its way to a full recovery, click the button for downloading shareware. When the Software Search window appears, type a description of what you need, and then click Search to see what's out there. For a thorough, step-by-step walk through finding files and downloading them, flip to Chapter 15.

By default, the Windows search system appears, but Macintosh software isn't far away. To switch to the Mac search system, click the Mac Search button at the bottom of the Software Search window.

In the unlikely event that you can't find what you want in the voluminous America Online digital catacombs, point your Web browser to either Download.com (www.download.com) or Shareware.com (www.shareware.com). These two sites (both part of the huge CNET Web presence) carry software for almost any use and occasion, including business applications, utilities, games, and more. There's no cost to use the areas (and no salesman will call).

America Online For Dummies Channels Directory

The 5th Wave

By Rich Tennant

"From now on, let's confine our exploration of ancient Egypt to a site on AOL."

In this directory . . .

Cable TV is a fixture of modern life. These days, people expect to sink into their favorite couch, chair, or yoga position (ouch!) and flip aimlessly among 763 different channels of equally mindless programming. Thank goodness society sets its sights so high.

These 19 channels are America Online's version of cable TV (and a mighty nice substitute it is, too). The channels sit at the heart of America Online, creating a structure for all of the other information areas on the system.

In keeping with their central position, this directory devotes page after page to the channels, describing what the channel offers, covering the primary information areas inside each channel, and listing keywords for quick access to everything. It's truly the informational surfing experience. (Now if I could just find my remote control. . . .)

America Online For Dummies Channels Directory

Some days, nothing feels as good as camping in your favorite chair, sucking down a cold soda pop, and channel-surfing the moments away. After all, with the hundreds of channels available on TV, you're bound to find something that tickles your fancy (even if it's just the relaxing sight of the different channels flipping by).

Even though the channels themselves provide some small amount of entertainment value, their main purpose in life is to organize the TV programs so that consistently finding reruns of *The Man from U.N.C.L.E.* doesn't completely whack our brains. Combined with a good printed reference, the various TV channels make viewing less of a chore and more of a time-consuming obsession.

The 19 channels on America Online do the same thing — organize information, that is, not turn our online time into an obsession. (If you're like me, you're quite capable of doing the online obsession thing on your own, thank you very much.) The channels give you a ready-to-use, subject-oriented guide to all the content on America Online. Just pick the channel that sounds like it matches your interests, and start browsing. You never know what you may find!

If you want a truly wild trip through the America Online content areas, try keyword **Random**. It sends you to a randomly selected online area somewhere in the wilds of the system. You never know quite where you'll end up, but that's what makes it fun!

Welcome Channel

The AOL Welcome channel (keyword **Welcome**) ranks right up there as one of the world's best inventions since the concept of evenly apportioned bakery goods (sorry — make that *sliced bread*). The Welcome Channel rolls a little bit of everything into one place, presenting it all to you on a quick-to-peruse digital platter.

In addition to the ever-changing Today on AOL area in the middle of the channel window, the Welcome Channel offers links to America Online's most popular areas.

AOL Help

Keyword **Help**

Despite what the computer company ads say, your computer doesn't *always* do things right the first time — sometimes it fails on the second, third, seventeenth, and eighty-sixth times, too. When you feel overwhelmed, frustrated, or want to drop-kick your modem over the balcony, check the America Online Help area for tips and tidbits to make your online life better.

Chat

Keyword **People Connection**

Want to pass the time with some new (or old) online friends? Click the People Connection button and join the fun. This button takes you directly to the main People Connection window, where a world of people talk in a universe of chat rooms.

My Places

Keyword **My Places**

Sure, it's already full of great online places to visit, but the Welcome Channel still needs a personal touch before it's truly your digital home away from home. My Places, a new arrival with the America Online 5.0 software, lets you add five links of your choice to the Welcome Channel

window. Unfortunately, you can't include *anything* you want because My Places makes you choose the links from a preset list created by Those That Make Lists at America Online. Even with its lack of flexibility, My Places still makes your life easier. (For more about the *truly* customizable areas of the America Online software, flip back to Chapter 23.

My Weather

Keyword **Weather**

Although looking out the window gives you a snapshot view of the day, sometimes your plans require a bigger weather vision. For moments like that, click My Weather. If you know the zip code, then the Weather area knows the forecast.

Online Calendar

Keyword **Calendar**

Thanks to the My Calendar button, your schedule is never far away. Best of all, you can't accidentally leave it behind in a restaurant, taxi cab, or luxury ocean liner.

Online Mailbox

Keyword **Mailbox**

Click here to dive deep into your online mailbox. If the mailbox's flag is up and letters peek out, then new message await your attention.

Parental Controls

Keyword **Parental Controls**

Even though America Online gives a neighborhood feeling to the online world, the kids still shouldn't wander around unsupervised. Focus your child's online time (and keep their fingers out of the digital cookie jar) by setting the Parental Controls for their screen names. Chapter 6 explains the controls in detail, so head there for more information.

Search

Keyword **Search**

America Online and the Internet both offer amazing amounts of cool information. The Search system makes finding the good stuff quicker and easier than ever. Find both Web sites and America Online content areas with one-stop searching.

Top News

Keyword **News**

All day, every day, news pours in from around the world. The Top News area displays the current top headline, and links you straight to the News Channel (covered later in this section) for everything from the news of the world to the tidbits of your neighborhood.

You've Got Pictures

Keyword **YGP**

Turn your film photos into beautiful digital images (suitable for e-mail or a Web site) with You've Got Pictures. Like the mailbox icon, the little roll of film on the Welcome Channel window changes to show that your pictures are ready.

Computing Channel

When computers made their first appearance in the 1940s, they were an incomprehensible morass of wires, tubes, huge boxes, and cooling fans. Thanks to the wonders of modern technology, the computer of the 1990s bears little resemblance to its long-antiquated counterpart. Computers are now an incomprehensible morass of boards, chips, little boxes, and cooling fans. Fills you with hope for the future, doesn't it?

Whether or not you comprehend the morass, you still need a place to go with your questions, concerns, and general complaints. On America Online, look no further than the Computing channel (keyword **Computing**). It covers all your computer woes from hardware to software, from laptops to palmtops. Gather all those computer questions you have lying around, wade into the Computing channel, and demand answers.

The channel window has two main sections. The middle of the window sports the features and departments area. The buttons here lead to the true informational depth of the Computing channel. Next to that, on the right side of the window, are the Spotlight areas. Sometimes fun, sometimes educational, but *always* useful, these buttons change frequently, highlighting all kinds of timely content on the Computing channel.

Build Your Web Page

Keyword **Build Your Web**

The Build Your Web Page department shows you how to create your AOL Web presence. Whether you need the let's-start-at-the-beginning basics or you want a piece of clip art to jazz up your Web site, Build Your Web Page contains stuff you can use to take advantage of the Web space that comes with your America Online account. The Build Your Web Page area even offers daily help sessions and weekly classes to assist you in creating your own Web page.

Chat and Messages

Keyword **Computing Communities**

If your life is (horrors!) devoid of computer people or if you just want to swap computer tips with whoever wanders by, check out the various chat and discussion areas in the Chat & Messages department. They are great places to find solid technical help because you never know *whom* you may run into there. One night, I bumped into a couple of consultants having a deep discussion about Windows NT as a network server (don't laugh — it *was* interesting!) and soaked up all kinds of cool things about networking in the process.

Computing Superstore

Keyword **Computing Superstore**

Keeping your computer happy takes time, effort, and software. Whether you long for the latest in spreadsheets or the time has come to retire Old Faithful, look to the Computing Superstore for one-stop shopping online. The Superstore carries cameras, modems, monitors, and memory. Research a computer, grab a gift for your favorite geek, or search for a specific computing product all from the Computing Superstore window.

CNet Consumer's Guide and Product Search

Keyword **CNet Buying Guide**

Owning a computer means many things, among them the freedom to spend every loose piece of money you have on new stuff to keep your machine happy (because, goodness knows, you don't want to upset the computer). Use the hardware and software reviews to help you find the best digital goodies at the most wallet-friendly price.

On the other hand, stay far away from the **Search for a Specific Product** option. This poor tool can't find its way out of the vegetarian section of a rib joint's menu. For a much easier (and infinitely more useful) solution, visit the CNet Web site directly at **www.cnet.com**; then click either the Product Help link (near the top of the main CNet window) or the larger Software link (near the bottom). Browse through the listings directly — it only takes a moment.

Daily Download

Keyword **Daily Download**

You never know what's coming next at the Daily Download, but it's always interesting.

Pick up screen savers, music programs, games, graphics, and more in this never-ending parade of unique and useful software.

Download Center

Keyword **Download Software**

When you want new software for your Windows, DOS, or Macintosh computer, start the search in the Computing channel's Download Software department. This area offers freeware, shareware, demonstration software, sound files, and graphics files in popular Windows and Macintosh formats; hundreds and hundreds of TrueType fonts; and ready-to-use template files for popular commercial programs, like Microsoft Publisher, Aldus PageMaker, PrintShop (Sierra Online), and many others. And, of course, you can plop down your credit card for some online software purchasing, too.

Get Help Now

Keywords **Help Desk**

Did your computer ever go *ping, beep,* or (my personal favorite) *bzzzrp-sproing-wugga-wugga-wugga?* During the work day, those peculiar sounds usually mean a quick call to your friendly computer support technician (followed by a bit of a wait while the support folks draw straws over who answers your question). At home (and in many small businesses) those same sounds usually precede weeping, wailing, and gnashing of teeth as you try to figure out what on earth just happened to your faithful machine.

Rather than cry yourself a river (or at least a small in-office pond), sign on to America Online (assuming that part of the computer still works) and check out the Get Help Now area. It's chock-full of hardware and software assistance, plus nightly *ask the expert* chat sessions.

Online Classrooms

Keyword **Online Classrooms**

Find out all about computer hardware, object-oriented programming, World Wide Web page design, and more at this Mecca of online education, the Online Classroom department. Regular classes cover the basics of computer hardware, software, programming, graphics, and almost anything else you can imagine. Most classes are free, although some require a small fee.

Search and Explore

Keyword **Computing Search**

Keeping up on the latest information in the fast-moving world of computing is a never-ending (and nearly impossible) job. Things change so quickly that the information you got yesterday may change by tomorrow (heck — by then, it may have changed *twice!*). To keep as close to current as possible without pulling out all your hair in the process, use the Computing Channel's Search & Explore tool. It scours areas throughout the Computing channel for news, tips, and just about anything else relating to your topic of interest.

Entertainment Channel

If you take America's top entertainment capitals (New York City, Hollywood, and, of course, Branson, Missouri) and digitally roll them into one place, toss in a computer game or two, season the concoction with a touch of Las Vegas in the summer, and then hang Christmas tree lights on it, you come *close* to the flavor of the America Online Entertainment channel (keyword **Entertainment**). Close, mind you, but still not *quite* there.

This channel simply *is* entertainment. No matter what you're into, you can find it all on this channel (within the bounds of good taste, of course — no accordion players need apply). Movies, theatre, music, sports, trivia, entertainment news, online games, and even places to mix and mingle with new people — the Entertainment channel is all that and more.

The window layout puts you on the front row of an informational extravaganza. Sitting in center of the window like a bunch of studio executives are the channel's main areas. Each area focuses on a different facet of the entertainment industry, from movies (my favorite) to books (my other favorite) and Fun and Games (my other-*other* favorite). Arrayed along the right of the window are the featured areas, the online version of this week's hot entertainment properties. Like the real-life version (stars of the moment, as it were), the featured areas change regularly. Finally, a group of four buttons at the bottom of the window whisk you away to America Online's main entertainment information areas — places like People Magazine, Entertainment Asylum, E! Online, and Entertainment Weekly.

Books

Keyword **Books**

I have to be honest: I love books. Sure, I write them (although I don't play an author on television), but *reading* is truly one of my joys. If you love books as much as I do, there may be help for us yet. Turn to the Books department to indulge yourself in the latest tidbits about the newest titles and the hottest authors.

Celebrities

Keyword **Celebrities**

Get the goods and the gossip on the celebrities that you love (or just love to hate). From news to no-no's, the Celebrities area dishes up a little bit of everything on Hollywood's hottest.

Entertainment Search

Keyword ESearch

Thank goodness for the Search & Explore option! (Okay, so it's very late and my naturally nerdy side *is* showing a little — but can't a guy get excited about something that takes your request, digs through a ton of material, and then delivers your answer in record time, all without asking anything in return?) The Entertainment channel's Search & Explore area uses the Web-based search system like its fellow channels, so you have a set of tweakable tools at your service, plus the ever-popular A–Z Channel Guide. Whenever you simply can't find what you need (at least in entertainment information), turn to this area for help.

Fun and Games

Keyword Fun & Games

Hollywood wants very little from us — just most of our money and all our attention (plus some well-timed applause). In exchange, the entertainment industry offers, well, entertainment. It's not a bad exchange, when you get right down to it. In keeping with the whole Good Times concept, the Entertainment channel presents the Fun & Games department. Enjoy all kinds of free fun, from trivia contests to little arcade games, and all with an entertainment industry twist. It's fun (and free)!

Home Video

Keyword Home Video

Remember when "watch a movie" involved leaving your living room? Thanks to videocassettes, laser discs, and DVD, your couch is the front row of the Bijou whenever you feel like watching a flick. If home is your video castle, pop over to the Home Video department. Pick up new release information, reports on the most popular videos, general stories about the home video market, and links to online video and DVD stores (to indulge in a little *personal* market research, of course).

In the News

Keyword Entertainment News

It's like simple math: Stars garner attention; attention draws reporters; reporters write stories; stories become news. Thus, thanks to obscure and unmemorable theories learned to escape eighth grade math class, you end up with the statement *stars equal news*. (Mark this page — you never know when some online math teacher may throw a pop quiz at you about this stuff.) Given the stars and news equation, it's no wonder that the Entertainment channel includes a direct link to all the entertainment industry news you could possibly want. This area includes entertainment headlines, a couple of top stories, and links to still more entertainment news sites and wire services.

Movies

Keyword Movies

When I think of entertainment, the silver screen immediately pops into mind. Movies *define* Hollywood, and they dominate a big part of the entertainment industry. If you're a movie fan, the Movies department is waiting to thrill you. Turn to this area for the latest news, reviews, and inside scoop on who's doing what and when the results will show up at a theatre near you.

Music

Keyword Music

Before reading this section, you simply *must* put your favorite CD, tape, or even one of those big vinyl things on your stereo and crank up the volume. With tunes filling the air, you're ready to find out more about the Music department, the America Online haven for music makers, listeners, and lovers. The areas in this department cover all kinds of music, plus the artists, labels, and technologies behind the beat. You can even find online music and culture areas, like *Rolling Stone*, MTV, and SonicNet.

In addition to general features, the department organizes itself into basic areas by musical genre, giving each one its own button in the main Music department window. Each of the genre areas includes its own discussion boards and chat areas, plus tons of links to other online fan areas and Web pages. Keep your eyes peeled for special items in each area, too.

Speak Out

Keyword **ECommunity**

Do you have a favorite movie star, follow a particular television series, enjoy a good book, or love great music? (Hey — how's *that* for an inclusive question?) Swap thoughts and tidbits about your preferred media darlings in the entertainment message boards and chat rooms. The boards cover all facets of the frenetic entertainment industry. The chats include everything from spur-of-the-moment ranting opportunities to every-week scheduled fun.

Television

Keyword **TV**

I've heard it said that television is a vast wasteland, but I'm reasonably sure that the quote wasn't uttered by any current media executive. After all, with direct broadcast satellites, megachannel cable TV systems, and at least four different editions of HBO, there has to be *something* worth watching out there.

To cut through the tripe and find the shows with the most promise, turn to the TV Today department. Its witty repartee and insightful analysis (tempered with more than a little old-fashioned public relations hubris, I might add) promise to fill all your tube-related desires.

Families Channel

The kids are in bed (or safely away at college), the house is neat, and you're too tired to go anywhere. Maybe you spent all day matching wits with a 4-year-old (and losing more than you care to admit), or you need some advice on living day by day with a teenager. Rather than spend the last daylight hours sitting numbly in front of the tube, hop on to America Online and nimbly check out the Families channel (keyword **Families**).

America Online combined all the home and parenting areas in one handy channel. From the Families Channel window, you can read up on your child's current phase, research group entertainment options, or discover new project ideas your family can complete together.

Unlike many of the channel windows, the Family channel window contains just a few items (after all, your familial world is complex enough as it is). The window's right side displays the current *featured areas,* which change frequently during the week (the digital equivalent of the seasonal-products aisle at your local department store). The left and center sections offer the *department buttons* — your links to all the good stuff on the channel.

Babies

Keyword **Parenting Babies**

Baby powder, nursery furniture, and teeny-tiny diapers evoke feelings of "Ah, isn't she cute?" in almost everyone. Join the baby party in the Babies department. Whether your bundle-turned-baby is gnawing on your furniture as you read this book, or you simply want to remember the baby days-gone-by, this department supplies some excellent information, message boards, and chat opportunities.

Family Activities

Keyword **Family Activities**

Everybody loves a good time — particularly when it involves everybody in the family! For tons of great activity ideas, take a trip to the Family Activities area. Whether you need a seasonal suggestion, insight into some cool games and toys, or ideas for a family trip, the Family Activities area delivers the goods.

Family Entertainment

Keyword **Family Entertainment**

Entertainment options abound in our high-tech world. Unfortunately, a lot of them definitely *aren't* for the family. Dig into the entertainment realm from a family perspective in the Family Entertainment section. It includes TV and movie reviews, plus perspectives on books and music. Proving its deep appreciation for serious entertainment, the Family Entertainment area even covers theatre, dance, and other performance art.

Family Life and Genealogy

Keyword **Family Living**

Each family, although unique in its own right, shares delightful traits with other families. Explore the ties that hold families together as well as those that link various families one to another — commiserate with other parents, share your newfound adoption joys (or the pain of your search), and find out how to keep track of online friends through the areas and forums available through Family Ties.

Grade Schoolers

Keyword **Grade Schoolers**

From puppy love to the first report cards, the Grade Schoolers area eases the transition from *he's just a baby* to *look what we did today*. Whether the kids attend a public or private school, or if you choose to teach them at home, the grade school years bring their own unique brand of fun

and challenge. Use this area to uncover tips about how your child learns, how to focus their blooming energies, and when to give them space.

High Schoolers

Keyword **High Schoolers**

It's the last great stop before heading into the Real World. High schoolers need specialized love and support (and so do their parents). With adulthood calling your kids while empty nest syndrome threatens your solitude, visit the High Schoolers area to share your thoughts and concerns. The section includes college preparation and selection help, tips for talking to teens, and a link to America Online's new Teens channel (where the kids share and explore the world from their perspective).

Middle Schoolers

Keyword **Middle Schoolers**

The kids made it through the elementary grades. They carry on conversations (frequently in a language you and I don't quite comprehend), and they show amazing interest in projects, friends, and the world around them. The Middle Schoolers area helps you and your kids through the newly-teenage years, when life's changes often don't make sense to anyone (particularly those involved).

Newsstand Department

Keyword **Families Newsstand**

Sometimes you want to curl up with a cup of hot cocoa and a good magazine. When those moods strike, turn to the Families Newsstand department. The department contains links to several family-oriented magazines that maintain an area on America Online. From *Consumer Reports* to *Country Living*, and from *Teen People* to *Seventeen Online*, you can find articles from the magazine's current issue, some "Best of the Best" from past issues, and even some online content you won't find anywhere else.

Hot Tip: If you completely fall in love with a few of these magazines by reading their online versions, most of the forums contain subscription information so that you can receive the magazine via postal mail. Often you can subscribe to the print version of the magazine while you're online. If you don't find exactly what you're looking for on the item list, try the Magazine Outlet button (keyword **Magazine Outlet**) for subscription information on hundreds of magazines.

Pregnancy

Keyword **Parenting Pregnancy**

Expecting a new bundle at your house? Spend some time preparing for junior-to-be by visiting the Parenting Babies area. Research baby names, calculate the costs of your new little guy, or find a perfect name for your baby-in-waiting. If it's your first, spend extra time in the Being Pregnant area for answers to the myriad questions rolling through your mind (and body).

Preschoolers

Keyword **Parenting Preschoolers**

As school time nears, so do another huge round of changes in your child's world (and in your world, too). The Parenting Preschoolers section picks up with pre-kindergarten and developmental topics like make-believe play, vaccinations, food allergies, and the myriad things which make the preschool years so memorable (in a happy way, I mean).

Search and Explore

Keyword **Families Search**

Sometimes things aren't where you think they should be. In the same way that I leave coffee cups all over the house and then go on roundup missions before the next dishwasher load, America Online periodically drops forums into channels where you wouldn't think of looking for them. If you think that you may be missing something on the Families channel or you simply want to see what's out there, use the Search and Explore department to view the breadth of Families.

Toddlers

Keyword **Parenting Toddlers**

Last year, she was cuddly and cute. This year, she's on the warpath. It sounds like you need a visit to the Parenting Toddlers area. Post your questions to the discussion boards, map your child's development, or pick up cool online activities for you and your little one (or ones). The area also features health notes, wellness tips, and development information to demystify the changes taking place in your child (and protect your sanity at the same time).

Games Channel

Whatever your pleasure, the Games channel (keyword **Games**) covers it. Drop in for a dogfight between classic World War II fighters, match wits and drinks with a few dozen ogres in the local inn, race to remember the name of Dudley Do-Right's horse in a national trivia challenge, engage a new friend in a friendly game of chance, and then download the a bunch of new maps for Quake II. Hmm — not bad for your first 15 minutes!

The Games Channel window is split into three distinct areas. Starting on the left are the games themselves, including the Game Parlor (keyword **Game Parlor**), Game Shows (keyword **Game Shows**), and Xtreme Games (keyword **Xtreme Games**).

Along the bottom of the window lurk the Games channel departments. That's where the fun really starts, as you link up with other gamers, swap tips, download programs, and generally wreak havoc with your computer. Taking up the right half of the window are the current featured areas.

These areas are usually devoted to various premium games, although the game shows and general information areas pop up from time to time.

Remember: All the games in the Game Parlor and Xtreme Games belong in the *premium* category, although I'm happy to report that the price to play dropped recently from *waay too high* to *reasonable value for the $$*. Each games tells you the cost to play. By default, only the original master screen name (the first one you made when you signed up for America Online) can play the premium games. To allow your other screen names into the area, go to keyword **Parental Controls** and change the Premium Services setting.

If online games make your heart flutter like nothing else in the world, pick up a copy of *Games Online For Dummies* (written by yours truly and published by IDG Books Worldwide, Inc.) to find out more about the incredible world of multiplayer, online gaming.

Games Insider

Keyword **Games Insider**

When you want gaming information of almost any kind, go straight to Games Insider, the America Online one-stop gaming warehouse. Games Insider links you to sites all over America Online, including gathering places like Gamers Forum (keyword **Gamers**); news and help areas like Games Help (keyword **Games Help**); and discussion areas for swapping tales of success and prowess (keyword **Games Chatbox**). The department even includes a feedback link for sending your thoughts and suggestions to AOL Games Central.

The Game Parlor

Keyword **Game Parlor**

Even though the rough-and-tumble super-3-D action games garner most of the headlines, the truth is that *more* people play

online card games than those explosion-laden digital destruction fests. On America Online, that means visiting the Game Parlor, the home of card, board, and other games of quiet persuasions. Your playing options in the parlor include classic card games, like gin, hearts, spades, and poker, plus arcade-style multiplayer games such as Jack Nicklaus Golf, Splatterball, and Virtual Pool.

Game Shows Online

Keyword **Game Shows**

Few things in life beat the fun and value of the Game Shows Online department, including the America Online Games channel. What's so great about online game shows? They're challenging and engaging, of course, and (hang on to your hat) they're *free!* That's right — free. What a deal! Enjoy the multiplayer challenges of games like Strike-A-Match (keyword **Strike A Match**), Slingo (keyword **Slingo**), and Take 5 (keyword **Take 5**), or settle down in front of the computer for a quiet round of crosswords (keyword **NYT Crossword**). All that and more awaits you in Game Shows Online.

Games Store Department

Keyword **Games Store**

What good is reading about the hot new games if you can't go buy a few to add to your collection? With that marketing-driven thought in mind, check out the Games Store, the America Online answer to catalog shopping for the hard-core computer gamer. The store carries games in just about every genre, including action, strategy, sports, and role playing. It even includes a special section for joysticks and game classifieds, just to make sure that nobody walks away empty-handed.

PC Games News

Keyword **PC Games**

Why buy a computer these days? I can think of only one reason (other than to use America Online) — so that you can play games! Indulge your love of things that go bang, crash, and r-o-o-o-o-oar in the night by visiting the Games channel's PC Games department. Whether you want to download a demo of the new game you just read about, join a lively discussion about weapon selection in Quake III, or try your hand at an online game of skill against a few hundred of your fellow gamers, everything you want is in PC Games.

Search & Explore Department

Keyword **Games Search**

Gamers don't have much time on their hands (if they did, they could play more games). To make the most of your online (non-game-playing) time, use the Games channel's Search & Explore system to help you find information right now. This channel uses the new and improved search system, including the flexible I'm-thinking-of-a-word search window, the A–Z Games Channel Guide, the Best of AOL Games area, and the channel's slide show, dedicated to how wonderful life is on the Games channel.

Video Games News

Keyword **Video Games**

If your favorite games live on a Nintendo 64, Sega Dreamcast, or Sony Playstation, the Video Game News area has your name written all over it (and the maintenance crew wants to discuss that with you, by the way). Console games rule the day in this area, with areas devoted to news, gossip, tips, and chat about your favorites.

Hot Tip: If you love classic arcade games (like Asteroids, Centipede, and Tempest) or home video-game systems (such as the Atari 2600 and the original Nintendo system), relive your glory days with a visit to Dave's Video Game Classics (**www.davesvgc.com**). This site offers *emulators* (programs to make your computer behave like the brains behind the video games of days gone by) and the actual programs for your favorite arcade and video game classics. It's all free (well, some of the emulators are shareware, so

you should pay for one if you fall in love with it), so give it a try!

Xtreme Games

Keyword **Xtreme Games**

If a game explodes, roars, flies, stomps, shoots, or otherwise involves mayhem and digital carnage, it probably hangs its gunbelt in Xtreme Games, the America Online gateway to the best in action games. Whether your interests lean toward fantasy role-playing or high-tech vehicular battles, Xtreme Games includes something to make you smile. In addition to the games listed in this area, try keyword **Gamestorm** for still more multiplayer action titles. Like Xtreme Games, the goodies in Gamestorm carry a per-hour fee, so choose wisely what you shall enjoy.

Health Channel

Everyone wants to be healthy. Millions of Americans lower their fat intake, partially eliminate meat from their diets, and begin an exercise program in an effort to maintain or regain health. The America Online Health channel (keyword **Health**) helps you along the way, with departments devoted to illnesses, living healthfully, support groups, and the various stages of life.

The channel window features a health topic search system, ready and waiting to deliver the information you need. Below that sit several health focus areas, containing links for current health articles, health-related areas, plus the ever-present message boards and chats. The right side of the window displays the featured areas, special spots within the Health channel that are worth an extra look.

Hot Tip: The featured areas change frequently, so if something really appeals to you, save it in your Favorite Places (see Chapter 7 for more about that).

Alternative Medicine

Keyword **Alternative Medicine**

As the health industry grew, so did health customer concerns over expensive chemical therapies, lengthy treatments, and complex drug regimens. As health technology advanced, many doctors rediscovered herbs and other natural remedies. Soon, alternative medicine itself grew into a full-fledged health industry. Learn about alternative treatments, herbal remedies, and much more in the Alternative Medicine area.

Children

Keyword **Children's Health**

Nothing is quite as joyful as a healthy child. Healthy children run, leap, jump, and ask millions of questions. Use the Children's Health department for information to enhance the health of the children in your life. Look in this area for information about topics that range from the snuffly-nosed cold and otitis media (ear infection) all the way to extremely serious illnesses, such as leukemia. You also find info about school-related health issues, such as attention deficit disorder and other learning disorders. Pick a folder and dive in.

Conditions and Treatments

Keyword **Conditions**

When you or a loved one suffer from an illness of some kind, you long to find more about it, discover ways to cope, and meet other people who can relate. In the Conditions & Treatments department, you can meet all three goals at one time. The department contains folders on many different illnesses and health issues, from allergies and cancer all the way down to skin illnesses. Select one of the areas and find out about it. In most cases, the specific illness window contains information about online support groups, where you can connect with members who understand.

Dieting and Nutrition

Keyword **Dieting**

Need to shed a few pounds before terming yourself completely healthy? (Goodness knows I do — writing isn't exactly an aerobic activity.) Seek help and guidance in the Dieting and Nutrition area. Starting with the basics of good nutrition and losing weight, the area covers a lot of ground on the way to a newer, smaller you. The Success Stories section earns a particular mention, because some days you just need a little boost to keep you going.

Doctors, Insurance, HMOs, & More

Keyword **Doctors**

As the population counts echoed from the baby boom, the health care industry exploded in both size and complexity. When you felt ill, you used to simply pick a doctor and schedule a visit. Today, thanks to insurance restrictions, HMOs, and the ever-rising cost of medical care, it's a bit more complicated than that. If the whole health-and-money thing confuses and confounds you, visit the Doctors, Insurance, HMOs, and More area. It demystifies the often-frustrating world of health care with information about treatments, insurance, and more. Take a stand for your health — dive into this section to find out how!

Fitness and Sports Medicine

Keyword **Fitness**

There's more to fitness than push-ups and jumping jacks. Perhaps you prefer burning calories with mountain biking, weight lifting, tennis, running, or walking. Whatever your activity, the Fitness and Sports Medicine area delivers the information you need. Swap ideas with fellow aficionados, explore a ton of fitness tips, and garner some insight on how your body works (and why it hurts when you put your arm *waaaaay* over your head, like this. Ow!).

Health and Beauty

Keyword **Health and Beauty**

Beauty means more than picking the right cosmetics and making sure that your clothing colors match. The Health and Beauty section guides you through the world of beauty from a healthy perspective. Covering everything from balding and body image to skin care and sun protection, this area provides the health information you need.

Men

Keyword **Men's Health**

Men have special health needs, too. That's why the Health channel created the Men department — to discuss men's health issues apart from the general illness or healthy living departments. Look in this area for information specific to men and the bodies they inhabit: male baldness and hair loss, cancers that affect only the male body, and other illnesses and problems men may incur.

Message Boards, Chats & Experts

Keyword **Health Talk**

You (or someone you love) struggles with a health problem, and you want to talk about it? Turn to the Message Boards, Chats & Experts department for support and help. Select the support group that interests you, and open its folder to find out more. Some support groups meet in scheduled chats several times a week to discuss various topics; others meet only once a week. Browse through the entries for your topic of choice for the details.

Online Pharmacy

Keyword **Pharmacy**

Ah, how times change. Neighborhood pharmacies gave way to larger chains, which now battle with groceries and discount department stores for your prescription dollars. As if those choices weren't enough, now the online world boasts its own digital pharmacies. The Online Pharmacy area links you to several online health and wellness vendors, all of whom offer special discounts for America Online members. Give one a try!

Seniors

Keyword **Senior's Health**

Just as children sometimes suffer with specific age-related illnesses, the senior set faces its own unique challenges at the other end of the age spectrum. Look in the Seniors department for information about arthritis, glaucoma, osteoporosis, and a range of other concerns. You can also find a folder named Parenting & Caregiving, which contains links to support groups and Web sites designed to help the elder caregiver.

Tests, Calculators, and Tools

Keyword **Test Yourself**

For a little healthy fun in your day, visit the Test Yourself area. This area offers all kinds of healthy tests and quizzes (no surprise there), plus a variety of other interactive informational sources, like the calorie calculator, nutrition database, and recipe finder. Munch through the chocolate quiz, take an IQ test, measure your risk for Diabetes, check your nutritional knowledge, and much more.

Women

Keyword **Women's Health**

Women's health demands specific information. Find what you need to know in the Women department. From information about cancers that affect only women to eating disorders and pregnancy, Women successfully delivers information unique to the female body's health.

Interests Channel

Several years ago, a research study stated that people who regularly engage in hobbies or follow special interests outside of work concerns live longer, happier lives. The adage is one my family follows religiously; my photos and computer games proudly take their places beside my wife's textile studio and the kids' Lego blocks and chess sets.

Once in awhile, though, lacemaking loses its charm and you want to research a new hobby or meet a fellow hobbyist. On those days, visit the Interests channel (keyword **Interests**), where interests and hobbies await you. Select from the channel's eight departments to explore your favorite interest.

Auto Center

Keyword **Autocenter**

Whether you're thinking about a new car purchase this season or you find all cars fascinating, you can find a wealth of information in the AutoCenter department. Read about new cars, browse classified ads for used vehicles, and share your love of automobiles (or motorcycles) in *Car and Driver* or *Wheels*. The area even includes a new-car showroom, for your online browsing pleasure.

Food

Keyword **Food**

Humans don't survive long without food, but some of us have taken culinary interest to an art in itself. Make the Food area your destination when you don't know what to fix from the leftovers in the fridge, or when you have friends coming for dinner tomorrow night and you're at a complete loss for ideas. The Food area provides recipes, informational articles, and tips on a whole host of food-related topics. My personal pick is the Recipe Finder, a really cool search system featured front-and-center on the Food area window.

Hobbies

Keyword **Hobbies**

Read reviews of new books on the market, find out who located that antique whatzit you've been looking for everywhere, meet fellow star gazers in Astronomy, or swap roots with researchers in Genealogy. No matter whether you enjoy creating items from scratch, rebuilding cars for fun, or collecting yesterday's toys, the Hobbies area leads to pastimes online. Check out this department to brush up on an old hobby, maintain your skill level in an interest you enjoy, or research a new hobby or two for the winter.

Home & Garden

Keyword **Home**

More than its life as a structure, *home* evokes feelings of warmth, security, and brightness. The Home and Garden section gives you the tools you need to create your own haven. Transform your house for each season and enhance your home's coziness with decorating tips, home improvement instructions, and craft and gardening projects. Be sure to check the Home & Garden Index button for tons of great destinations.

Interests Newsstand

Keyword **Interests Newsstand**

Does your favorite hobby or interest magazine have an area on America Online? Use the Newsstand department to find out. Newsstand links you to the forums maintained by publications like *Boating Online, Car and Driver, Cycle World, Video Magazine,* and *Wine Spectator*.

Pets

Keyword **Pets**

Sharing your home with a furry roommate brings its own set of challenges and joys. Whether your friend is a dog, cat, gerbil, mongoose, or tarantula, concerns abound. Is your pet getting the right food? What signs of sickness do you look for? How do you redirect those less-than-desirable behaviors? Find answers to these questions and more in the Pets department. You may even meet and fall in love with a whole new section of the animal kingdom. Use the links in the main Pets window to read the latest Pet Connection article, browse the Pet Web Site of the Week, or locate useful supplies or that perfect gift for Fido.

Pictures

Keyword **Pictures**

Explore traditional photography, digital photos, and video in the Pictures department. Pictures contains information for beginners as well as serious amateurs. If you're just beginning your photographic journey, start with *Popular Photography* or the Photography Forum. The Pictures department features a lot of information about digital photography, in case your new digital camera and your computer long to know each other a little better. Dive into scanners, image editing (there's more than one way to get the family dog out of the picture), graphic file formats, and more. It's all there, just waiting for you!

Search & Explore

Keyword **Interests Search**

Use the Search & Explore department to locate some of the best portions of the Interests channel. Search for specific articles online that pertain to your interest, or look at the channel's contents in alphabetical order. The Best of AOL Interests button gives you a list of some of the Interests channel's favorite spots — to find your own favorites, however, you may want to cruise through the other departments and see what you find. For more information about using the Search & Explore department, refer to Chapter 7.

International Channel

Despite what I learned during my southern Indiana childhood, the world is made up of more than the United States (I guess that's why they call it *the world* instead of just *the U.S.*). Africa, Asia, Australia, Europe, North America, and South America all await you in the Great Out There. Of course, all that travel takes either big bucks or lots of frequent-flier miles, so if you're a little low on both but still want to find out how the rest of the world lives, the International channel (keyword **International**) is for you.

Prominently displayed on the right side of the window is the *HotMap,* a highly technical and cool-sounding term that I made up just now. The HotMap's seven pulsating buttons (one for each continent on the map) are your main links into the International area. They lead to windows filled with Web links, discussion boards, chat areas, and other information about the continent you clicked. Both to the left and beneath the HotMap are featured areas of the International channel.

In the bottom left of the window sit the most distinctive offerings on the entire channel: links to the International America Online versions for Canada, France, Australia, and the United Kingdom. For a taste of other international AOL's, click a continent on the ol' International channel HotMap, and then click the service you want to see. (If the continent window only shows an *AOL Access Numbers* button, then there's no local version of America Online in that part of the world.)

Business

Keyword Intl Business

Before you pack your bags for an international business trip, take a peek at the International channel's Business department. Find essential business etiquette for your destination country and check the current currency exchange rate — taking the time to know what's proper (and how much it costs) may save your business transaction. If you invest internationally, dig into economic numbers for your favorite locations here as well.

Classifieds

Keyword Classifieds

Looking for an international bed and breakfast, an opportunity to study abroad, or a job somewhere outside the United States? Does your company need workers from outside the United States or Canada? You may find what you're looking for in the Classifieds department. AOL members post ads for business, travel, study, employment, real estate, and collectibles. Oh — you also may find some international personal ads in this area.

Country Information

Click the Country Information button (no keyword)

Research countries of the world continent-by-continent through this dialog box. The Country Information window provides the same information as the International channel's HotMap, but does it by opening folders rather than clicking dots. Select any continent from the item list. The only exception is Antarctica (perhaps because you find few people, many penguins, and little culture down there).

Cultures

Keyword Intl Cultures

Foods and traditions beloved in one country are often taboo in another. Pastimes and sports that delight one nation bore or astonish another. Differences such as these carve a country's niche in the world and help to develop each country's uniqueness — that special something we call *culture*. America Online devotes an entire department to cultures around the world. For an interesting genealogical twist, research your family's cultural heritage for a better picture of where you fit in the world.

Fun & Games

Keyword Intl Fun

Quick! Think of your favorite online games. Name That Flag? Foreign Language Trivia? No? How about international trivia games, like Trivia Info in French or Tiger Trivia in German? If none of these comes to mind, you're missing some of the most unusual games on America Online. In these games, along with the other sections in the Fun & Games department, you find out about leisure-time events such as films and music and meet international friends-to-be, all while practicing a foreign language. Not exactly your middle-school foreign language course, is it?

Global Meeting Place

Keyword Global Meeting Place

Where do you go online for a rousing international chat session? How do you locate an international pen pal? If you're studying a particular culture but live far away, how do you meet people from those countries? America Online answers those problems with the Global Meeting Place. This area links you to chats in languages other than English, members' family immigration stories, and international lifestyle and people areas. Don't be shy — drop in to an international chat and say hello (or "Bonjour", "Guten Tag", or whatever appropriate greeting you come up with).

News

Keyword **Intl News**

Nothing keeps you up-to-date on another country like reading its news. A country's culture, concerns, biases, and beauty all emerge from the pages of its news articles. Whether you want to improve your knowledge of a specific country, maintain your knowledge of a nation you miss desperately, or find out about the world in general, the International channel's News department provides the means. Use the sections listed in this area for business travel, international newspapers (many in languages other than English), and weather around the world. Discuss late-breaking stories from distant shores in the International News chat room (click the Chat button). For a more deliberate conversation, post your views on the International News message boards, located behind the Message Boards button.

Search & Explore

Keyword **Intl Explore**

Find out what gems await you on the International channel by taking a trip to the Search and Explore department. Use the A–Z International Channel Guide for an alphabetical overview of the channel's contents; although the guide looks exhaustive when you scroll through it, it doesn't contain each country by name or individual small areas under the larger keywords. You may be better off, on the International channel, to use the extensive departments list rather than the A–Z directory.

Travel

Keyword **Intl Travel**

Ready to grab your passport and board the plane for exciting destinations? Before packing your laptop — maybe even before booking your flight — sign on to America Online. Check out the International channel's Travel department for information about possible travel destinations, tips to help you plan (and pack) wisely, and ideas for what to see while you're there. If your budget dictates vicarious travel, look in Tales from Road Warriors for some interesting travel stories. In addition, Your Travel Memories holds downloadable travel photos of exotic places.

Kids Only Channel

"When I was a kid. . . ." Do any words put as much fear and trepidation into a child as the threat of yet another parental tale of the good ol' days? (How about "We're disconnecting cable TV"? That may come close.) Kids, here's something for you to lob back when Mom and Dad get into reminiscence mode: "Yeah, but you didn't have your own online hangout. We're talkin' *digital treehouse* here."

America Online set aside a channel just for kids and marked it plainly, too. Kids Only (keyword **Kids Only**) offers activities, forums, discussion areas, research sources, and interactive hangouts specially designed for kids ages 5 to 14. Heck, it even includes homework help (where was this channel when I was a kid?).

Warning! Most of the people who hang out in Kids Only are there to have a good time and learn stuff. Unfortunately, it seems like a few bad apples always try to spoil things for the rest of us. If you run into a person in a chat room who's being obnoxious, if someone sends you an instant message that makes you feel weird, or if *anyone* asks for your password, get help from a Kids Only guide. To do that, either click the Kids' Help button near the bottom of the Kids Only Channel window or click in the address box on the navigation bar (the big white space just under the toolbar at the top of your screen), type keyword **KO Help**, and press Enter. Follow the instructions on-screen, and help will arrive shortly!

Art Studio

Keyword **KO Art**

Expand your creativity in the Art Studio, the Kids Only channel's answer to arts, crafts, theatre, and writing all rolled into one. Try your hand at drawing, show off your wordsmithing talents, and create some neat crafts. Wherever you go, the best and brightest minds in all of Kids Only are waiting to meet you.

Hot Tip: For a truly artsy time, take a side-trip to Blackberry Creek (keyword **Blackberry Creek**). It's a wild club for young writers, artists, and storytellers. Take a moment to check it out!

Chat

Keyword **KO Chat**

Kids, like adults, *do* love to talk, discuss, and chat. Even though the topics may focus on some slightly different subjects from other online areas, the Kids Only chat rooms make great places to meet and be met by other online kids. The Chat department houses the channel's special chat and discussion rooms, plus a broad variety of kid-centric discussion boards.

The Kids Only channel sponsors six regular chat rooms, organized by topic. During the school year, these special chat rooms open up after school hours and close in the evening (so if you're home sick from school, no chatting for you — but you should be in bed anyway!). During the summertime, the rooms run most of the day, so when it rains, you may want to drop in for some online talking time. Specially trained Kids Only staff members hang out in the rooms to keep the chats moving and on-topic.

Hot Tip: It's easy to pick out Kids Only staff members because their screen names always begin with KO, for Kids Only. If you have a question or problem, always feel free to ask a Kids Only staffer — they want to hear from you!

Clubs

Keyword **KO Clubs**

Come one, come all! Join a club and have a ball! (Sorry, no more poetry. I promise.) Taking its place as one of the best places to have fun and meet new people on the whole Kids Only channel, the Clubs department gives you a place to follow your interests and find cool friends in the process. Just pick your favorite hobbies (or a hobby you've always wanted to try), find the club that matches them, and join the fun!

Games

Keyword **KO Games**

Games, I firmly believe, are the only reason computers exist. Well, games and America Online access — but that's strictly it. Everything else is just icing on the digital cake. The Kids Only Games department takes this idea and runs with it, proving beyond any doubt that the best things in life explode, fly, drive fast, or make peculiar *boinging* sounds. The Games area offers so many diversions that I may find it hard to stay focused long enough to write this paragraph. (Whoops, sorry — it's now tomorrow. I got sidetracked, but I promise to finish this section without getting lost again. Really.) Take your brain for an entertaining and even *educational* (remind Mom and Dad about that one frequently) spin through some of the most entertaining games, puzzles, and contests anywhere in the online world.

Homework Help

Keyword **KO HH**

Stuck on that geometry assignment? Need a little push to get through an English paper? When homework closes in around you, leaving you more than a bit frustrated and forlorn, turn to the Kids Only Homework Help department. You can find the energy and tips that help you over the hump (and, more important, open up time to spend in the Chat and Clubs departments with your friends).

Remember: The folks you find waiting in Ask a Teacher *don't* do your assignments for you, no matter how much you beg and whine. They *do* offer all the help they can and go to great lengths to make sure that you find the resources you need. Putting the pieces together, though, is still your job.

Kids Only Help

Keyword **KO Help**

When things aren't working quite right or something a little unexpected happens, it's time to get help. That's why the Kids Only Help department exists — to answer questions, help you through the technically tricky stuff, and generally make you feel comfortable in the big online world. Kids Only Help covers everything from basic online life to the perils of the Web. If you have a question, dive right in and find the answer. That's why Kids Only Help is there!

Kids Only NetFind

Keyword **KO Web**

The Web (even apart from its fairly eerie name) sometimes sends stout adults into fright-filled spasms. Because kids aren't the least bit fazed, of course, by little things like new technology, the Kids Only Web department focuses on getting around the Web and finding new places to visit instead of spending a bunch of time explaining how the whole thing works.

Hot Tip: If, despite being a member of the technoliterate younger set, you need some information about how the Web actually works, don't worry — I won't tell a soul. Find out everything you need to know about the Web in Chapter 17.

News and Sports

Keyword **KO News & Sports**

Catch up on the news from a kid's point of view or play ball — or whatever other sport activity you enjoy — in the Kids Only channel's nod to the action-packed world

of information: Kids Only News and Sports. In addition to all its regular sports coverage, the News and Sports department profiles well-known athletes and newsmakers, giving you some insight into what they like, how they started out, and what they do to stay on top of in their area sport. Uncover new tidbits about your favorite sports stars and swap notes about the sports you love on the News and Sports discussion boards (in the More News and Sports window) right here, in the Sports department.

TV Movies & Music

Keyword **KO TV**

Whether you love cartoons, comics, or celebrities, the TV, Movies, and Music department brings everything you want to know about your favorite shows and starts right to your computer screen. You never know exactly what (or who) you may find, so visit often. (After all, if you aren't *watching* television, you may as well *read* about it.)

Lifestyles Channel

How do you show the world who you really are? What parts come together to make you unique? Your beliefs, ethnic background, and stage of life all play a part. Celebrate your uniqueness on the Lifestyles channel (keyword **Lifestyles**), and find other members who believe, live, and dream in much the same way as you.

Divided into 11 departments (including the mandatory Search & Explore entry), Lifestyles helps you connect with people who share your background, your dreams, and your views of the world. If you've found something about yourself you want to change, the channel also includes a Self Improvement department to support you along the way. Don't be shy — select an interesting-looking department, hop right in, and explore a facet of Lifestyles.

Ages & Stages

Keyword **Ages & Stages**

Drop in to Ages & Stages for age-appropriate fun, whether you're 23, 43, or 63 or beyond. Select a forum and find people like you, no matter which stage you occupy. Ages & Stages includes focus areas for retirees, baby boomers, Generation Xers, and more. In the More Ages & Stages area, take a look at The Knot for wedding advice, Third Age for the over-40 crowd, Military City Online for veterans.

Ethnicity Department

Keyword **Ethnicity**

Where does your family originate? Did they journey across the seas to come to North America at some point, or did they begin already planted here? Which country's traditions did you adopt, either through your family or through society in general? Connect with others who share your traditions and your background when you visit the Ethnicity department.

Hot Tip: The department lists ethnic groups from practically all over the world, with the possible exception of Antarctica. Despite all its good intentions, however, America Online missed including at least one important international ethnic community in the listing: the Irish. Use keyword **Irish Heritage** to dig up information about the Irish in America and the country of Ireland (and be sure to point out the inequities of being forgotten by the Ethnicity department).

Gay & Lesbian

Keyword **Gay;** Keyword **Lesbian**

Find lots of information and many kindred spirits in the Gay & Lesbian department. Visit all kinds of online services, including a great resource directory, or check out the cities most open to gay travelers. OnQ and PlanetOut in particular offer some well-developed online communities, plus solid information and discussion areas.

Check out the PlanetOut News (keyword **PNO News**) for a well-focused look at important headlines from the gay, lesbian, and transgendered viewpoint.

Newsstand

Keyword **Lifestyles Newsstand**

Life and the myriad facets it involves makes a great writing topic. There's so much to say, so much to remodel, so much to plant — the possibilities (and subscriptions) are endless. That could be the reason the Lifestyles Newsstand department boasts so many titles for your online reading enjoyment. Whether you want something homey (like *House Beautiful*), something Earthy (like *Country Living Gardener*), something with wedding bells (*Town & Country Weddings* comes to mind) or something with classic lines and topics (like *Victoria*), the Lifestyles Newsstand is the place to go.

Romance Department

Keyword **Romance**

A little wine, a gourmet meal for two, and a glowing fire in the fireplace — with soft music wafting through the air. Who wouldn't be in heaven? Indulge your romantic fantasies (and maybe find someone to share them with) in the Romance department. Before jumping in with both feet in a search for Mr. or Ms. Wonderful, be sure to read the Do's and Don'ts Online article (scroll down a bit in the Romance window list box to find it), along with the Safety Tips. Both are designed to keep you and your friends safe while online.

Search & Explore

Keyword **Lifestyles Search**

Looking for something in Lifestyles and can't quite put your finger on it? Search & Explore helps you find what you need. Either search by topic for articles anywhere in Lifestyles or check the A–Z

Channel Guide to be sure that you haven't missed anything. To see an overview of the Lifestyles channel, try the Lifestyles slide show.

Self Improvement

Keyword **Self Improvement**

An important anniversary rolls around, you pass one of life's milestones, and you wake up one morning deciding that you, or something about you, could be better. The Self Improvement department understands, and helps you in your quest for change, whether you want to drop a few pounds, tone your voluntary muscle groups, or connect with somebody who understands. If you need a support group or support information, look in areas like iVillage. For the physical side of life, browse Shape Up America. For a group experience, join one of the Self Improvement communities.

Spirituality

Keyword **Spirituality**

Your belief system dictates your lifestyle. Dip into the Spirituality area when you can use a little encouragement or you want to know more about others' belief systems. This area lists all the major world religions, plus new religious movements and links to general spirituality-oriented topics. To access the main belief areas quickly, including some topical Web sites, click the buttons along the left side of the window. The Christianity, Judaism, Islam, Hinduism, and other buttons take you to their featured areas in a flash. If you don't see your particular belief brand listed, try the More Spirituality Resources link, near the bottom of the page.

Teens

Keyword **Teens**

Nobody understands life as a teenager — except, perhaps, another teenager. That's why, in the name of preserving (or perhaps promoting) teenage sanity, America Online created the Teens channel. With hot colors, cool topics, and the kind of new-topics-every-second focus that the teen attention span demands, the Teens channel fills the bill. Flip ahead in the directory for lots more about *the* place for online teens — America Online's Teens channel!

Weddings

Keyword **Weddings**

Planning a wedding? Sure, you need flowers, invitations, dresses, and a great band for the reception, but the *first* thing you need is the Weddings area. Thumb through tons of announcements, picture yourself in any of several thousand wedding gowns, set up a wedding (and beyond) budget, and research cool locations for the ultimate honeymoon. The Weddings area brings it all together for you — except the "find the mate" part, that is. (That's still up to you.)

Women Department

Keyword **Women**

Discuss women's issues and loves in AOL Women. You can relax, drop in to the Women Talk chat rooms, and meet other women who think like you do. Or explore how women feel about relationships and family in two of the department's sections. Whichever section you decide to explore first, you can find plenty to engage your mind and emotions in the Women department.

Local Channel

According to the wise old sage (who probably moonlights at the automobile club), "Getting there is half the fun." Thanks to the cool stuff on the America Online Local channel (keyword **Digital City**), you may think that *not* getting there is almost *all* the fun (virtually speaking, of course).

The Local channel is America Online's Digital City area in disguise. Digital City chaperones you through a slew of cities all over the United States. Big cities, small towns, and quaint burgs await your virtual visit. Each Digital City entry offers the best in tourist information, city maps, travel tips, and hot sightseeing spots, all available without leaving the comfort of your home. Who could want more?

Occupying most of the channel window is the *HotMap,* my own highly technical term for the clickable U.S. map image. To the left of it are the Digital City departments, with their links to local news, movies, the search area, and more.

To visit one of the cities on the HotMap, click its red button. A window opens, inviting you to explore that city's news, entertainment, people, sports, travel, and communities. Read current news articles, find out which movies fill your city's screens, read personal ads, or dive into a city's chat room by clicking any of the items the city window's department list.

Autos Department

Keyword **Local Autos**

If you live near one of the Digital City's areas and you're in the market for a new car, the Digital City AutoGuide could save you some work. Access car dealerships' Web sites, read about new cars from manufacturers' Web sites, and get a quote from Auto-by-Tel, all in one place. Digital City's AutoGuide makes that new car purchase (horrors!) an almost pleasant experience.

City Index

Click the City Index link (no keyword)

If poking an online map with your mouse pointer doesn't sound like much fun, use the City Index option to find the Digital City you desire. This link brings up a dialog box listing all of the cities covered by the whole Digital City area. Scroll through

the list, find the city you want, and double-click its entry to see everything there is to see.

Classifieds Department

Keyword **Local Classified**

Trying to find a pedal car from the '50s, a job halfway across the country, or an apartment to rent? You may just find what you want in the Classifieds department. Select a city and see what its classifieds contain. Some of the cities offer general classifieds entries, and others give information under headings like Suburban Shopping.

Directory Department

Keyword **Local Directory**

Looking for someone or some business? Save some time and frustration by looking through the Digital City Directory. Click the city where your friend lives or the business resides, and then, after the Digital City Directory window appears, follow the on-screen steps to find the object of your quest (if it's a business). To find a person, do the same thing, but click the White Pages link (look in the lower-left side of the Departments area). After the White Pages window appears, follow the on-screen steps.

Employment Department

Keyword **Local Employment**

Looking for a job in your current area, or perhaps thinking about following through on the cross-country change of scenery? Whatever your situation, the Digital City Employment department may contain the answer. Choose your city from the list and then browse through the myriad employment listings. It could be the start of that dream career!

Hot Tip: After looking through this area, check the Classifieds department (keyword **Local Classifieds**). The Classifieds often contain employment listings (and even if they don't, you can always browse through the fun stuff, like used floor lamps, garage sales, and office furniture).

Local News

Keyword **Local News**

The Local News window offers your choice of the top local stories from any city on the whole Digital Cities channel. Scroll through the list until you find the right city (or at least one that's close to you) and then double-click the city entry for your fill of important headlines.

Movie

Keyword **Local Movies**

Thinking about heading out to a movie tonight? After checking the reviews in the Entertainment channel's Movies area (keyword **Movies**), head over to the local Movie area to find out where your chosen title is playing, um, locally. Scroll through the city list until you find the local metropolitan area, and then find your movie in the local listing. Is this easy or what?

Personals Department

Keyword **Local Personals**

Looking for a friend? Seeking a companion? Trying just to find someone to do things with? Don't give up until you check the Personals department. Like the other local departments, Personals lists all the available cities. To find your future honey, double-click your city (or the city you *think* may house the human of your dreams) and start looking. Good luck!

Real Estate Department

Keyword **Local Real Estate**

Before you pull up stakes and travel halfway across the country for a new job, use the Digital City Real Estate department to help you locate that perfect house or rental. The Real Estate department contains listings for many cities; choose your destination and then search the database to find a home listing, look up possible rentals, or determine your purchasing power.

Search & Explore

Keyword **Digital City Search**

Seeking a topic that just doesn't fit under one of the regular Digital City departments? (I know the feeling — it seems like *all* the things I look for online are just a little different from what's out there.) The only thing left is a romp through the Digital City Search department. Just type your topic, set your date range, fiddle with the other options, and then whack the Start Searching button. In no time at all, the system (hopefully!) finds what you need.

News Channel

Keeping up with the news gets harder all the time — so much to think about, so many things vying for your attention, and so little time to pursue mundane trivialities like staying informed. What's a hoping-to-be-informed person of the new millennium to do? Check out the America Online News channel (keyword **News**) — that's what.

The News channel promises quick and timely stories, delivered right to your screen. This area covers the world — headlines from the Middle East to late-breaking cricket scores in Great Britain to soccer in Brazil (and there's plenty of United States news, too). You can even use a search function to pick and choose from the news of the day and keep up on the stories important to you.

For its size, the News channel window packs quite an informational wallop. Scrolling through the upper-left side of the window are the hour's News Headlines. Click a particular headline or anywhere in the Headline area for a window with capsule versions of the moment's top stories. On the window's left side sit the current CBS News slide show story and a link to Opinion area (also known as The Land Where Arguments Happen). Further down are the department buttons, leading to the various news detail areas. For more about each department, flip through the listings below it. Rounding out the window are the Features (along the bottom) and the top stories (along the right side). To dive in to any of them, click the little button next to the story that interests you.

Business News

Keyword **Business News**

If holding a thumb to the pulse of business sounds like your kind of fun, the Business department is definitely the place for you. (Of course, you *may* need to get out a little more, but that's something to think about later.) The Business department tackles business from all angles, offering a high-level summary of current goings-on, plus detailed stories covering the economy, technology, international business, the financial markets, industry notes, and consumer briefs. To truly inundate you with information, try the business newsstand option, which unleashes the online versions of your favorite business magazines (like *Brill's Content, Business Week,* and *Financial Times*).

Entertainment News

Keyword **Entertainment News**

Stroll down the red carpet into the heart of Tinseltown with a stop in the Entertainment News area. One click and you're knee-deep in the top movie, music, and theatre stories, many straight from the industry's primary source of truth and public relations, *Variety.* You also receive a selection of the best people-oriented tales rolling through the news wire. Topics in this area include the entertainment industry, online world, art, culture, film, theatre, music, television — the list goes on and

on, as you can tell. Whenever you need to take a break from the stressful stories pouncing on you elsewhere on the News channel, chill out in this area. It really helps — I promise.

Family News

Keyword **Family News**

News never stops, but there's a lot more to the latest happenings than simple facts and figures. How does the news impact your kids? How do parents explain a world of violence, destruction, and poverty to innocent eyes? The America Online Family News area helps answer hard questions like that, while delivering a whole range of family-centric news and information at the same time. This area is a *must visit* site for parents and grandparents alike.

Health News

Keyword **Health News**

The health industry booms with money, political power, and social interest. A swirling mass of activity like that ensures a constant flow of news-worthy tidbits, which the Health News area collects for your benefit. Read the top health stories from the newswires; then go in depth about new drug approvals, innovative health treatments, and the perils (and profits) of Big Health.

Life

Keyword **Life News**

Need a left turn into the oddness of life? Feel like taking a walk on the lighter side of the news? For a relaxing topper to your news-gathering time, visit the Life News area. The Mad World area (keyword **MadWorld**) makes the whole trip worthwhile, with its mix of odd and peculiar news items from around the world. The area's chats, message boards, and trivia games deserve an honorable mention, because they're a scream. Visit here when you have some time to kick back and enjoy the fun — it's a spot worth savoring.

Local Department

Keyword **Local News**

On the Internet, finding out what's happening halfway around the world is easy. Unfortunately, it's much tougher to get the latest information from halfway around the block. The Digital City Local News department changes that. Scroll through the city list until you find your local metropolitan zone and then double-click its entry to zip straight to the local news, weather, and sports.

News Search & Explore

Keyword **News Search**

If you're not a browser (and with the volume of stuff in the America Online news area, I can hardly blame you), try the News Search feature. News Search thumbs through stories from the other Today's News sections, helping you to zero in on stories *you* find interesting, not the ones the helpful wire service editors chose for you.

Use either keyword **News Search** or the News channel's Search button to open the News Search dialog box. Type a few words that describe the kind of stories you're looking for and then press Enter or click List Articles to see what's out there. After a few moments, the window fills with story headlines that contain the word or phrase you typed. See Chapter 14 for tips on searching the News channel.

Newsstand

Keyword **Newsstand**

Welcome to the world of magazines with windows rather than covers, with e-mail addresses rather than phone numbers, and with interactive chat areas rather than letters to the editor. This world is the Newsstand department, one of the News channel's most interesting areas.

When I wrote this book, the list of publications in this area seemed, well, short. Because the new channels were just going

into effect, the odds are high that more magazines will populate the digital racks by the time you read this. For now, be sure to check out *Time.com* (keyword **Time**), *George* Online (keyword **George**), and *The Chicago Tribune Online* (keyword **Chicago Tribune**), which aren't anything to shake a mouse at, by the way.

Politics Department

Keyword **Politics**

Nothing makes headlines quite like the political process. Between new legislation, research announcements, and old-fashioned dirty laundry, the political news machine never stops running. Plug into this constant stream of Beltway tidbits with the Politics news area. It includes the latest scoop on the White House, Congress, the judiciary, and almost anyone (and sometimes *anything*) else that draws a government paycheck and lives within a campaign contribution of Washington, D.C.

Sports News Department

Keyword **Sports News**

Is news of the sporting scene important? Take a look at the Sports News department, and then tell me what you think. With a slew of main categories, plus the wonderful More Sports area (in the Explore AOL Sports drop-down menu), you can find more news in this area than any three fanatics could want. All the major sports (professional baseball and basketball, and college basketball and football, for example) have their own categories, although my favorite has to be More Sports. Where else can you follow baton twirling, cricket, inline skating, and paintball from the same news window?

U.S. and World News

Keyword **USworld**

U.S. and world headlines sit atop the news areas list in Today's News. The stories in this area are, for the most part, what's known as *hard news* — violent storms, political maneuverings, international incidents, and the discovery of a thousand tax returns predating the birth of Christ stashed in a van behind some Chicago post office. In short, it's front-page stuff. New stories are added every hour or so, depending on how the news day is going. If you're a serious newshound, checking this area every couple of hours should keep you on top of all major world developments.

Weather Department

Keyword **Weather**

You won't find a better way to track the weather than with the Weather News area. Whether you're trying to figure out what to pack for your trip or wondering whether it will rain on your way to work, Weather News has your info. The department offers a variety of forecasts, reports, and satellite images. Use the U.S. Cities Forecast to make doubly sure that you take the right clothes on your next excursion. For hardcore weather aficionados, visit the Weather Mall (every time I see that entry, all I can think of is *dehydrated boxed rain* and *lightning-in-a-can*) for more weather-related stuff than anyone really needs.

Personal Finance Channel

Money makes the world go around. (I think that some laws of physics are involved, too, but you get the idea.) It also keeps you up at night, makes you work 50 hours a week, and leaves you feeling vaguely defeated after paying the month's bills.

Suppose — just suppose for a moment — that you controlled your money. Pretty neat thought, eh? That's what the Personal Finance channel (keyword **Personal Finance**) is all about. It covers saving,

investing, dealing with credit, owning a home, and lots of other stuff. You can find help for tuning your portfolio and for finding out what exactly a portfolio is and whether you can take it out in the rain.

The channel window is your doorway to the online world of personal finance. The prominently displayed quote box and market indexes welcome you to the channel. In addition to displaying the current value of these popular investment barometers, the index names link directly to the day's performance chart. The area also includes buttons for the popular America Online Quotes and Portfolios systems.

Below the stock area are the department buttons, which lead to the nine Personal Finance focus areas. Right under the departments are buttons for the four financial centers. Look there for online banking, real estate, insurance, and mutual fund information. On the right side of the channel window are today's featured financial areas.

Opinions aren't information

Before wading too deeply into the Personal Finance channel, I want to reinforce something you probably already know: *Opinions are not information, and vice versa*. Although you may not think that this statement is groundbreaking, it's important to keep in mind on the Personal Finance channel.

The forums and services on the Personal Finance channel contain a great deal of cold, hard data: financial calculations, sales reports, stock price fluctuations, and company histories. They also harbor many warm, soft opinions floating around in the discussion areas. To get the most from the Personal Finance areas (and not lose a bunch of money on wacky investments), you have to carefully discern the difference between the two. Suppose that someone posts a message saying, "You're an idiot if you don't buy SciPhone Video and Tanning because it's going through the roof!" That is an *opinion*. If you read a news story that says SciPhone Video and Tanning just won a huge contract to install hundreds of its patented combination satellite TV/video conferencing/pay phone/tanning booths in the Pentagon, that's *information*.

My advice to you is simple: Don't let someone else decide on your investments for you. Everyone has a right to an opinion — just don't blindly adopt someone else's as your own.

Watch for sharks

A long time ago, a wise and learned person taught you an important lesson: Don't believe everything you read. Before you get too carried away on the Personal Finance channel, please write down that lesson in big letters and tape it across the top of your monitor.

Don't get me wrong — Personal Finance contains some wonderful places. Areas such as Vanguard Online (keyword **Vanguard**) and Fidelity Online Investments Center (keyword **Fidelity**) clearly lay out the facts and perils of investing. However, remember that not everything on the Personal Finance channel is like that.

Keep a particularly tight grip on your wallet while perusing the investment discussion boards throughout the Personal Finance channel. Most of the messages are from small investors like yourself — but some sharks lurk in those waters, too. It's your money, so rely on *your* research and intuition.

If you're new to investing, do the smart thing: Remember the disclaimers in the

Personal Finance areas. Nearly all the services have them. They say things like, "Don't take this as professional advice" and "Watch who you give your private information to," and "Please, oh please, oh please, don't send money to anyone without reading the full prospectus."

Hot Tip: If you're really, really new to investing, do your money a favor and buy a copy of *Personal Finance For Dummies, Investing For Dummies,* and *Mutual Funds For Dummies,* all published by IDG Books Worldwide, Inc. The author, Eric Tyson, did such a good job on all three of them that they even made sense to me (and that's saying a lot).

Active Trader
Keyword **Active Trader**

Trading stocks for long-term gain means picking the right stock and then sitting on it over time. For those type-A personalities with money to burn, camping on a stock just doesn't fly. Those folks trade actively, and they need an information source that meets their needs. Enter the Active Trader area, a compendium of financial knowledge for the most active of trading minds. The Active Trader area offers a one-stop landscape of all major market indices, the wonderful Investment Snapshot tool for quickly reviewing all the news about a particular ticker symbol, plus a whole set of departments and special focus articles.

Advice & Planning
Keyword **Advice & Planning**

Every stage in life comes with its own unique physical, emotional, and monetary challenges. Even though you just have to buck up and endure some of them (such as the teenage years), the right planning and advice promise to smooth the way during others. That's why the Advice & Planning department exists — to offer sage advice and an understanding shoulder just when you need it most. Starting with the wooly world of singledom and carrying you on past retirement, the Advice & Planning areas offer sound suggestions for managing your money at every step along life's way. Take a look at the tips for where you are right now, as well as the ones covering where you're headed in the coming years. You won't find a substitute for good planning — and a few ways to catch up if you discover that you started planning too late. Don't let money slip through your fingers!

Banking and Loans

Keyword **Banking**

Banks are part of life, so banking information should be part of your world, too. The Banking and Loans area offers some information about banking in general, plus several links to online banking companies. Personally, I wish the area spent more time on education and less on marketing, but such is life sometimes. The area's most useful feature is the State Banking Centers box near the bottom of the window, which lists banks in your state that comprehend online banking. Perhaps there's one near you!

Business News Department

Keyword **Business News**

Put your finger to the pulse of the world's business headlines with the Personal Finance channel's Business News department. It links you directly to the News channel's Business News area, offering up the latest tidbits in technology, the economy, the markets, and the international scene. To focus on stories from a particular segment of industry, check out the Industry News area. The Newsstand deserves a special mention, thanks to its plentiful links to online versions of everything from *BusinessWeek* to *The Chicago Tribune*.

Insurance

Keyword **Insurance**

Insurance made no sense to me for quite a while. (Granted, I was a kid at the time, but I nourished an inordinate love of business for my age.) After growing into the marginally odd human I am today, insurance makes even less sense. If you feel the same pain and angst when faced with the myriad insurance questions of life, turn to the Insurance area for help. This area explains the most common types of insurance, offers an online quote system, and even includes message boards to discuss your questions.

Investing Basics

Keyword **Investing Basics**

Attention new investors: Your informational ship just came in! For a good introduction to the basics of making money with stocks, bonds, mutual funds, and other investments, carefully work through the eight Becoming an Investor steps in the Investing Basics department. They're free, insightful, and won't try to sell you anything — which is more than you can say for many so-called investment managers out there.

Warning! This bears repeating: Be *very* wary of whom you accept investment advice from, particularly if you find the tips on the message boards or in the broker areas. You worked hard for your investment dollars, so treat them with the care they deserve.

Investing Forums

Keyword **Investing Forums**

Heard a hot tip about your favorite company? Want to argue the merits of one stock over another? Feel like venting about the performance of your mutual fund? For these and other communicative moments, turn to the Investing Forums, the community discussion areas on the Personal Finance channel. The stock discussion boards are organized alphabetically by stock ticker symbol. Just browse through the board list, dive into the right letter, and find the folks talking about your favorite stock. Further down the list from the stock boards are the general investment message boards, plus areas for futures, mutual funds, stock index options, and trading strategies.

Warning! Remember that what you read in these areas are *opinions* that can be posted by *anyone*. Before pinning your life savings to some hot advice you discover in this area, be sure to read the sections "Opinions aren't information" and "Watch for sharks" a few pages back.

Investment Research

Keyword **Company Research**

Many people think that making money with investments is a matter of luck — a case of being in the right place at the right time with the right type of zebra on the right color leash during the right phase of the moon. Even though the Fates play a role in stock market success, the people who consistently win at the money game do it through careful research. The Investment Research department puts a whole library of financial information at your fingertips (or at least at the tip of your mouse pointer). All the important corporate filings and financial statements live in this area, including the always popular 10K and 10Q reports required by the Securities and Exchange Commission, as do historical quotes, company profiles, and detailed stock reports.

The Markets

Keyword **MNC**

Look into the Market News Center when you need current numbers or trend graphs for stocks, bonds, currencies, or futures. Data for the major United States economic indicators, like the Gross Domestic Product (GDP) and the Consumer Price Index (CPI), live in this

department too, along with current information and daily trend lines for international stock indexes, such as the Japanese Nikkei, German DAX, and the British TFSE.

Mutual Funds

Keyword **Mutual Fund Center**

If investing in individual stocks fills you with a bit of dread, don't let that stop you from putting money away for the future. Turn your investing sights on mutual funds, where the "pros" managed the details while you watch your money grow. The Mutual Fund Center offers insight and information about funds from all over, plus a free fund lookup service from the Morningstar folks.

Personal Finance Live

Keyword **PF Live**

Hear top experts in financial matters from all over the country in the privacy of your own computer in the Personal Finance Live department. These presentations bring you the latest tips for saving, investing, retiring, and tax planning. Best of all, AOL doesn't charge you any extra for hearing these titans of the money world — it's a regular part of America Online! Some events, like the Sage and Motley Fool chats, take place on a regular daily or weekly schedule, and others are special this-night-only happenings. Keep an eye on upcoming events by checking the schedules in this area and in your favorite chat areas. If you miss an event, dig around in the Transcripts area to see what transpired without you.

Portfolios

Keyword **Portfolios**

Good investors don't leave all their financial eggs in one basket (even if they do, you can bet that the basket lives in a bombproof refrigerator). Because most investments are a mix of stocks from several different companies, keeping up with your holdings on a symbol-by-symbol basis would take forever. You need a tool that monitors your whole stock portfolio at one time — and, as luck would have it, America Online provides one, in its Portfolios system. This system helps you manage your stocks by grouping them into one or more portfolios and displaying a single window that gives you an at-a-glance summary of how everything is performing. Because you are building the portfolios, everything about them is up to you. Create them according to industry, investment risk, or whatever other way you want.

Quotes

Keyword Quotes

Many years ago, a brass-and-glass ticker-tape machine busily spewing forth a constant stream of letters and numbers in your office was a tangible sign of success. Today, society measures success differently (and it's a darn good thing, too, because those ticker-tape machines were noisy). Late-breaking stock market news isn't the sole domain of the rich and powerful anymore. Instead, this information is freely available to everyone on America Online, through the Quotes system. To check the current price (actually, the *mostly* current price because data in the Quote system is delayed about 20 minutes) of a particular stock, just enter the stock's symbol in the Symbol box and click Get Quote. If you don't know the stock's ticker symbol, click the Symbol Lookup link for help.

Real Estate

Keyword Real Estate

Measured by total dollars spent at one time, the two largest purchases most people make in their lives are their home and their car. (For the nerds of the world, of course, it's usually home and *computer,* but I digress.) Although the multithousand-dollar outlays demand special care and attention, their complexity often leaves us utterly bewildered and at the mercy of a

sharp-tongued sales rep. To overcome the bewilderment and arm yourself for battle with real estate agents, turn to the Real Estate department. Apartments and home-buying both earn spots, as do a variety of other sources for finding, buying, and moving into your new house. Because loans and insurance are usually also must-have items, the department offers links for them, as well.

Taxes

Keyword Tax

Although some people would disagree with me, the word *tax* really contains three letters and not four. But that knowledge doesn't make its monetary bite any less painful. The only remedy for that is the advice awaiting you in the Personal Finance channel's Tax Planning department. Rustle through the areas in the Tax Planning department for the latest tax news, forms, and planning tips, plus the best in tax-focused forums. Tax software is enshrined in its own special section, with support and discussion forums as well as file libraries covering all the major packages.

Search & Explore

Keyword PF Search

The Personal Finance channel has so much stuff that you can't possibly look through all of it by hand. But your computer can make short work of whichever searches you require, thanks to Search & Explore. You can browse through a thorough A-to-Z list of the areas on the Personal Finance channel, along with a Best of Personal Finance area, with selections of the neatest and most useful spots the channel offers. Or use the Search button just below the A-to-Z list for a classic channel search window. Stay away from the AOL Search button on the right side, unless you want to search the whole Web for your topic of interest.

Research & Learn Channel

Here's a wild statistic for you, from one of my favorite authors and information architects, Richard Saul Wurman: A single weekday edition of *The New York Times* contains more information in its pages than the average person in 17th century England was exposed to during his *entire lifetime* — and he didn't even have direct-broadcast TV! Is it any wonder that people sometimes feel overwhelmed when they're trying to look up even the simplest informational ditty?

America Online created the Research & Learn channel (keyword **Research & Learn**) as a tool to rescue you from the anxiety of not knowing where or how to uncover the information you need. Its links include sites inside America Online and treasure troves of goodies on the Web. The channel covers all kinds of subjects, from business to health, and still finds room on its shelves to tackle the day-to-day need for dictionaries, encyclopedias, and other standard reference books.

Looking relaxed and helpful, the Research & Learn channel window offers subject areas and references on the left side of the window. These choices sit atop the main content on the channel: the research areas you long to see. Opposite the window from the subject area buttons are the current featured areas, which change with Swiss watch-like regularity.

Ask a Teacher

Keyword **Ask-a-Teacher**

The America Online homework help areas may be some of the system's best-kept secrets. Regardless of age level, your favorite students (or you, for that matter) can get a gentle push in the right direction toward solving those awful homework problems. The helpers in this area don't just blurt out answers. Instead, they're careful to help students find the answers themselves.

Careers

Keyword **Workplace**

Everybody wants a good job for their child when the time comes, but the best way to get there is by planning now. The Careers link whisks you away to the Workplace channel, home of some great career information. Flip ahead to the Workplace channel section later in this directory for more details.

Courses Online

Keyword **Courses**

Want to expand your knowledge without leaving the house? Thinking about picking up a new skill or adding another college course? If that sounds like you, check out the Courses Online area on the Research & Learn channel. This area links you to several online-based education options, including both enrichment courses and classes for college credit.

Hot Tip: If you want computer classes, check out the Computing channel's Online Classroom department. It offers all kinds of great courses, many of which are *free* — yes, you heard it right — they're free.

Dictionary

Keyword **Collegiate**

The Research and Learn channel also includes a link to the Merriam Webster online dictionary, a handy tool for resolving those online Scrabble squabbles in record time. Don't forget about the online thesaurus at keyword **Thesaurus**, either. I spend more time with that reference than with anything else on my bookshelf.

Education

Keyword **Education**

Preparing for a good education means different things to different people. The Education area, in a burst of public-spiritedness, offers something for everybody. Students learn study skills, parents get some great K-12 resources and college-planning links, and school teachers and home educators earn classroom materials.

Encyclopedia

Keyword **Encyclopedias**

Sometimes you need just the basic facts — and you need them right *now*. If your research question isn't large, or if you're just starting out and need some general information to launch your quest in the right direction, turn to the Research & Learn channel's Encyclopedia area. Between the two online encyclopedias available to you through America Online (plus a slew of specialized ones on the Internet), the odds are good of finding the information you need.

Geography and Maps

Keyword **Geography**

Okay — I'm a sucker for maps. But that's only *one* reason that the Geography and Maps in the Research and Learn channel scores so many points with me. Whether you need a do-it-yourself map with customized driving directions, a generic city map, or a layout of something larger (like a state or country), this area hands it to you for free. For fun, try your hand at the geography quiz and map games, too!

Health

Keyword **RL Health**

There's a lot more to health than knowing where the asprin bottles are. The Health area links you to the main departments of the Health channel, America Online's center for health and wellness information. For the details of what's available, flip back to the Health channel section, earlier in the directory.

History

Keyword **History**

Study and explore the world of the past in the History area. Special focus areas include biographies, folk tales, inventors and inventions, plus the ever-popular quizzes and games section.

More References

Keyword **More References**

As though the rest of this channel weren't enough, the America Online research folks just couldn't resist the temptation to toss in a few more reference resources. They jammed all the stuff they could think of into the More References area and then sat back with pleased grins all around at a job well done. Some of the items in this area, like the dictionary and the encyclopedias, already appear elsewhere on the channel (they're repeated here to make them easier to find — or perhaps because somebody messed up and forgot to take them out). Others, like the online thesaurus (keyword **Thesaurus**), Word Histories (keyword **Word Histories**), and the Web-based Robert's Rules of Order, are only found here, to the Research & Learn channel.

More Subjects

Keyword **More Subjects**

There's a lot to research and learn in the world, and the poor Research and Learn window just wasn't big enough to hold everything. Rather than leave out anything important, the America Online programmers created the More Subjects area, home to all the stuff that wouldn't fit. It includes buttons for the Arts, business and money, government, sports, and more.

Phone & Addresses

Keyword **Phonebook**

Keeping your personal address list and phone book current is a challenge for almost anyone. Unless your circle of friends is particularly limited, the odds are good that, thanks to moves, job changes, and the other vagaries of life, your stock of jotted-down addresses and phone numbers goes stale in short order. (Of course, you often don't find out about the problem until it's absolutely vital for you to find that person, which helpfully throws a little more stress into your world.) Before giving up on the friend thing entirely and committing yourself to a life of solitary noncommunication, seek refuge in the Phone & Addresses section of the Research & Learn channel. This area provides links to online white and yellow pages, search pages that cover e-mail addresses and toll- free phone numbers, plus all kinds of other clever goodies, like area code and zip code lookups.

Reading and Writing

Keyword **Reading**

Nothing brings life to a day (or relaxation to the evening) like time spent with a good book. The Reading and Writing area indulges your literary whims with reading and writing-related links to both America Online areas and goodies out on the Internet. My picks include the Classics Quizzes, Literature and Literary Figures section, and the Quotes area (nothing is quite like a good quote).

Science

Keyword **Science**

For a quick study of all things scientific, visit Research and Learn's Science area. The area's links explore space, chemistry, backyard science, and the latest news from the science community.

Search & Explore

Keyword **RL Search**

The Research & Learn channel sports the system's new supersearch area in its Search & Explore department. In addition to A–Z Channel Guide (which, like several other channel guides, seems a little short compared to the number of items listed in the channel's areas), it also includes the fill-in-the-blank search window (sitting behind the Search button, near the bottom of the window).

Shopping Channel

Shopping is a drag. You leave your comfortable home, brave the wilds of modern transportation, and then walk around some glitzed-up store, following carefully marked paths just the right size for a thin 11-year-old. After bumping into innumerable displays and more than a few other shoppers, you clutch the prizes of your quest and head for the recycled cattle queues — pardon me, checkout lanes. After a certain amount of mooing time, you make your purchase and begin the trek homeward.

Online shopping is *nothing* like that. You don't mess around with crowded stores, pushy clerks, long lines, or wailing children (yours or anyone else's). Your goods arrive at the door of the comfortable home, which you never left. What a deal.

If this kind of stress-free shopping experience sounds interesting to you, the America Online Shopping channel (keyword **Shopping**) is the place to go. This area has a variety of stores for your browsing and purchasing pleasure. Better still, many of the items for sale include online pictures to show you exactly what you're buying. You can even use a special classifieds advertisement section to help you clear out the old stuff and make room for the new. (Can life get better than this?)

Like an unusually good mall, the Shopping channel is laid out in an easy-to-navigate format. The center of the window features the various departments, where everything from apparel to zydeco CDs await you and your credit card. On the opposite side of the window are the Shopping channel's featured items. They change often, much like the seasonal goody aisles at your favorite department store. Almost hiding down at the bottom of the screen are the Customer Service and Gift Reminder buttons, to help you in times of gift-need.

Choose a Department

Keywords **Apparel, Art and Collectibles, Auctions and Outlets, Books and Music, Consumer Electronics, Department Stores, Flowers and Gifts, Food and Wine, Health and Beauty, Home Shop, Home Office and Business, Jewelry, Kids and Babies, Pet Shop, Sports and Outdoors, Travel & Auto;** Computing department uses menu access only

There's nothing like starting big — and, on the Shopping channel, that means hitting the departments. With more than 250 stores spread across 16 departments, you're likely to find just about anything you want or need to purchase right there.

Each department contains a number of stores that either cater to the department's focus area or offer a selection of related products that's part of a bigger mix. Don't be surprised to find some of the larger stores, such as J.C. Penney (keyword **Jcpenney**) or Hammacher Schlemmer (keyword **Hammacher Schlemmer**), listed in several departments. Most of the stores at these keywords are open to everyone, although some, like Netmarket (keyword **Netmarket**), reserve the best deals for paying members.

Customer Service

Keyword **Shopping Services**

Shopping and customer service — you can't have one without the other. (Well, I suppose you *could*, but nobody would shop there.) To make the online shopping experience fun and hassle free, the Shopping channel offers all kinds of help in the Customer Service department. The area provides customer service links for all the Shopping channel vendors, a free channel newsletter, and online merchant ratings (to find out how other customers liked a particular Shopping channel vendor). For some in-person shopping, the Customer Service department links you to a local mall locator system (just type your zip code to find the nearest mall).

Free Gift Reminder

Keyword **Reminder**

Apart from the stores, my favorite item in the shopping channel is the Free Gift Reminder service (keyword **Reminder**), which reminds you of those important dates you simply *can't* forget (but which I work so hard at putting out of my mind).

Quick Gifts

Keyword **Quick Gifts**

The Quick Gifts idea zone comes to the rescue when you overlook the reminder notice sent by the Free Gift Reminder service. It presents you with a great variety of gifts and gift certificates, all of which include 48 hour shipping anywhere in the United States. When you need a gift *now*, turn to the Quick Gifts area for the goods to save your bacon!

Search Department

Keyword **Shopping Search**

Like the other channels, the Shopping Search department boasts the Type Here to Search window, plus the A–Z Store Listing (for quick access to whatever store tweaks your interest). In addition, the window also includes the shopping discussion boards, with help for finding items and advice for picking the best product, plus seasonal topics, like holiday recipes and memories. (If these boards sound pretty cool to you, use keyword **Shopping Boards** to hop straight into them.)

Store Listings

Keyword **Store Listings**

The Shopping channel gets bigger and better every day. Bigger, of course, means more products to see, but it also means more places to look. To quickly find a particular store (or for a leisurely browse through a directory of the whole online mall), try the Store Listings department. Clicking the button in the Shopping channel window gives you an alphabetical list of all stores, plus alphabetical lists of stores in the various categories (Apparel, Books & Music, and Office Products, for example).

Sports Channel

The smell of the engines, the roar of the crowds (or do I have that backward?), that little *schussing* sound the skis make right before the announcer says, "Oh, that had to hurt!" — the world of sports brings to life all kinds of sights, sounds, and fascinating medical opportunities. It also fills the news wires and magazines with scores, stories, gossip, and colorful photographs. In fact, the sports world generates so much information that, out of sheer self-defense, America Online dedicated an entire channel to it: the aptly named Sports channel (keyword **Sports**).

Unlike many of its department-filled brethren, the Sports channel includes only three main areas: Scoreboard, Team Pages, and Talk About It. Each of these departments merits, of course, its own special coverage below it. In addition to the three departments, the main channel window provides quick access to focus areas for football, basketball, baseball, and many other popular sports. Along the right side of the Sports channel window, you see the spotlight areas, highlighting the day's top sports stories.

Choose a Sport section

In the midst of the Sports channel sit a bevy of sports buttons — auto racing, baseball, golf, hockey, and more. Each button leads to immense mountain of news, details, trivia, and such that sends even the most hardened fan into joyous overload. Each sport's window displays top stories for the sport in general, plus provides tabs for more information (things like schedules, organizations, and such as that). Drill down as far as you want, because you can find plenty of depth everywhere you look.

Hot Tip: Click the buttons on the channel window for easy access to the various sports, or use the name of the sport (**Baseball, Basketball, Auto Racing,** and too many others to list) as a keyword to zip straight to the window you want.

Scoreboard

Keyword **Scoreboard**

When you want the scores and nothing but the scores, turn to the Scoreboard area. As its name suggests, this is *the* place for fresh statistics on your favorite NFL, NCAA, NBA, and NHL contests. In addition to quick scores, the Scoreboard department also serves a sampling of the day's best individual performances. As a bonus, the department also includes links to the top sports stories and a couple of often-changing feature areas.

The real gold in the area lives beneath the various league buttons. Each of these buttons leads you to a sports fan's dream scoreboard, filled with statistics for current games, previews of coming games, and enough raw box scores to put your calculator in a coma for weeks. In a neat touch, the football preview and summary windows even provide a weather button so that you can find out what kind of climate your favorite team has to endure in the game.

Talk About it

Keyword **Grandstand**

Sports fans love their teams. They read about the teams, go to games, swap insight, and second-guess plays. Stringing together these disparate pastimes is the undying need to talk endlessly about *their* team. That's where the Grandstand enters the action. Talk about your favorite teams, engage in some fantasy league action, and generally indulge your sports fanaticism with others like you. The Grandstand (through the Talk About It link) makes a great home for online sports fans like you!

Team Pages

Keyword **Team Pages**

Fans unite! If you love the Falcons, the Bucks, the Blackhawks, or some other brand of athletic animal, share your dedication with fellow fans in the Team Pages area. Every team in the NFL, NBA, NHL, MLB, and NCAA (and possibly a few stray college professors who were sucked into the initial-laden maelstrom) gets a whole page of scores, stories, schedules, rosters, and every other piece of information a *true* fan needs. Add to that the message board links to the Grandstand area (the next section in the directory), and you have a fan paradise wrapped up in digital clothes.

Teens Channel

Being a teen can be tough. You're wading through middle school or high school, wrestling with hormonal changes in your body that would qualify a lesser human as

an EPA Toxic Cleanup Site, and no matter how hard they try, your parents just *don't* get it. Sounds like you need a little time with your online friends in America Online's teen hangout extraordinaire, the Teens channel (keyword **Teens**).

Looking hip and informative at the same time, the Teens Channel window puts the online world at your fingertips. The channel's main departments (all six of them) sit on the left side of the window, while the right shows off the featured areas for the day, the week, or the moment.

Friends

Keyword **Teen Friends**

Friends are where the fun is, so check out the Friends department for the latest in high and low-tech fun. Discuss culture and entertainment in the message boards, read about the latest video games, and generally have a cool time with those you know online. Life doesn't get much better, eh?

Fun

Keyword **Teen Fun**

All work and no play gets a lot done, but really leaves you ready for some break time! When you're ready to kick back and unwind, the Teens Channel's Fun department awaits! Talk about movies and music, dig your teeth into an online fan club, pick up some pix of your favorite bands, or indulge your creative side in Teen Writer. It's all here, so give it a try.

Go Chat!

No keyword — button access only

Teens and talk — a match made in online heaven! America Online knows what teens want, so the Go Chat button takes front and center position in the window. It leads you to the teen chat window, home of a slew of teen-focused chat rooms. Get something to drink and perhaps a bowl of snacks, because you're gonna be here for a while.

Go Post!

No keyword — button access only

Don't feel like diving into the fast-paced world of the teen chats? Try swapping opinions in the message boards instead! The boards in the Teen Channel's Go Post area cover everything from movies to music, plus style, books, and video games thrown in at no extra charge. Share your thoughts, reply to others, and make your voice heard!

Life

Keyword **Teen Life**

Weighty issues swirl around today's teens — stuff that mom and dad never dealt with when *they* were in high school (okay, and some stuff that they *did* wrestle with). School violence, increased pressure for great grades, plus the always-on peer pressure from friends and classmates is enough to make even a solid and self-confident teen worry every now and then. When life gets you down, visit the Teen Life area. Check out the news, share your concerns, and generally recharge your mind.

Style

Keyword **Teen Style**

If it's *in,* then it's in Style, the Teen Channel's window on the fast-paced world of teen chic. The area offers links to the hottest style areas on America Online and the Internet, and provides instructions for creating some cool accessory touches from scratch.

Travel Channel

Suppose that you're trying to plan this year's vacation. So, where and when will it be? Perhaps Carnivale on the French Riviera . . . Oktoberfest in Munich . . . or does your budget have something a little closer to home in mind, like the annual Pork Belly Push in beautiful, metropolitan Floyds Knobs?

Whatever your plans (or budgetary constraints), make the most of your vacation with the help and forums available on the America Online Travel channel (keyword **Travel**). All kinds of news and information await you here. The area's hidden gem is the marvelous collection of member-populated discussion boards containing first-hand insights and tips of the travel trade (which help you find those marvelous out-of-the-way restaurants that make trips worth taking). You may even find out a thing or two about your hometown if you're not careful.

Like an old hand at globetrotting the days away, the AOL Travel window uses every bit of space to pack lots of goodies. The departments sit carefully stacked in the center of the Travel window. To their left are the travel resource buttons, your on-screen travel guides and agents. Opposite the working sections of the channel, you find the featured areas. A single click on any of them sends you careening off to an online destination filled with fun, frolic, and whatever else the travel agencies manage to pack into it.

Business Travel

Keyword **Business Travel Center**

"Attention, business travelers: For the latest information on your flight, don't bother picking up the white courtesy telephone. Instead, please report to the Travel channel's Business Travel department. You don't have to wait, and numerous digital agents are there to make the inevitable inconveniences more bearable. Thank you." Even though you won't ever hear that message echoing through the halls of your favorite metropolitan airport, it doesn't change the fact that the Business Travel department is a true miracle for busy corporate fliers. This department is the kind of place travelers love — one-stop shopping for America Online access numbers, airport information, flight details, frequent-flier programs, weather forecasts, and much, much more.

Destination Guides

Keyword **Destinations**

You know that you need to go, but where will you head? Another city, another state, or maybe even another country? Are you a plan-it-yourself person, or do you long for the organized approach of group travel? The Destination Guides button focuses resources for picking the right destination to mollify your wanderlust.

Maps and Directions

Keyword **Maps and Directions**

Sure, we live in a world populated with AAA branches, but not even the automobile club knows where *all* the addresses are (and besides, they don't have all the maps). Thanks to the Maps and Directions area, maps aren't a problem any more. Between the interactive driving directions, the instant maps of any United States address, and the marvelous library of city, state, and regional maps, the Maps and Directions is a cartographer's (or at least a traveler's) dream.

Member Opinions

Keyword **Member Opinions**

Particularly in the world of travel, nothing beats firsthand experience. Sure, the guidebooks paint swell pictures with broad brushstrokes. But that's nothing compared to the photographic detail provided by someone who has walked the streets, eaten in the cafés, and gotten lost in the subway system (and, for the record, I *wasn't* lost — I just took the wrong train from the wrong platform). To help you soak up information from the experience of others, the Travel channel includes the Member Opinions department.

The message boards and chat rooms in this friendly haunt are great for swapping real-world answers to tricky travel questions. No matter what kind of information you need, the advice of a friendly, seasoned traveler is usually mere steps away. This area is also the home of the Travel channel's newsletter, a must-have item for any traveler's kit.

News and Features

Keyword **News and Features**

The News and Features area acts like its own complete news office, offering a combination of features and news, seasoned with the travelogues and destination tips unique to the traveler's needs. Personal favorites here include the occasional article about really odd destinations, plus many money-saving tips and passenger rights information.

Reservations Center

Keyword **Travel Reservations**

With the dust nearly settled, the Reservations Center awaits to take your order and send you on the road. It's all-inclusive, offering airplane, bus, and even train reservations, plus hotels and rental cars. A few clicks, and your trip's myriad details are done.

Resource Center

Keyword **Travel Resource**

Remembering every little detail before a trip requires more than most of us can give. Stop the mail, pack the dog, feed your clothes — oh, did I mention that you *still* need to keep all the other confusing details of life straight at the same time? And I haven't even mentioned figuring out your destination. I'm amazed that anyone travels anymore. The collection of forums and services in the Resource Center department makes the all-important planning stage of your trip a smashing success. Find restaurants, flight information, currency-conversion tips, unusual sights to see, and more. (Okay — who put the dog in my suitcase?) It even includes a minisearch system for quick access to the information you need.

Search and Explore

Keyword **Travel Search**

You can find so much on the Travel channel that you almost need a book to find it all. (Hmm . . . come to think of it, you *do* have a book, but I digress.) To ensure that you find on the Travel channel everything you can possibly want, the programmers assembled the Search and Explore department. The window offers two different approaches to the department's information. On the left is the A–Z Guide to the Travel channel, with its browsable list of travel-related areas. Below that sits the Search button that whisks you away to a classic enter-something-to-look-for system, complete with controls to govern how wide or narrow you want the search to be.

Travel Bargains

Keyword **Travel Bargains**

With your destination firmly in place, it's time to consider your pocketbook. Can you get there within your budget? Sure — if you put the Travel Bargains area to work for you. Dig through the Bargain Box, prowl Dynamite Deals for Families, and discover the intricacies of inexpensive airfares in this penny pincher's nirvana.

Travel Interests

Keyword **Travel Interests**

To some people, *vacation* means piling into the minivan and hitting the road. For others, the word conjures up visions of golf courses stretching to the horizon, endless miles of beach, or playing a rousing game of Dodge the Tree on a mountainside at 70 miles per hour. Whatever your vacation dreams, the Travel Interests department points you in the

right direction. The department organizes travel information, suggestions, message boards, and chats by lifestyle (family travel or romantic getaway, for example) and by type of activity (cruising, golf, skiing, and the like). In addition to the main areas, the window includes a couple of pull-down menus offering even more lifestyle and activities options.

WorkPlace Channel

Work makes the world go round. At least, it makes the economy go round. If you're like most people, you spend most of your waking hours at some sort of job. You wake up, putter off to work, make a difference in the world through what you do, and wander back home to collapse in front of the computer at night. Perhaps you own the business — in that case, you relax only when someone whisks you out of the country for a couple of weeks!

Filled with its ups and downs, its unique hassles, and the camaraderie that comes only from spending long hours together, the workplace takes its place as a fixture in American culture. America Online recognizes this and presents the WorkPlace channel (keyword **Workplace**). WorkPlace gives you business help, career guidance, and job-finding tips. You can network with others in your field, find out about a completely different career before you take the plunge, or discover how viable a home business may be.

Business News

Keyword **Business News**

What happened today in your corner of the world? Keep current on business happenings, company news, the economy and investment markets, and technology through the Business News department.

Rather than wade through the general news window for specific business news, go directly to Business News and read all the news you want to know.

Career Center

Keyword **Career Center**

What do you want to be when you're grown? Although you may have known when you were 12, others (me included) still wonder when they'll grow up and have to make that final decision. No matter where you fit in the flow, the Career Center provides welcome tips and guidance. The Career Center gives you professional forums where you can meet and network with others in your field, tips for advancing your career in the direction you want it to go, and some much-needed help with finding that first job — or changing your career path. Delve in and discover the priceless career assistance that awaits you.

Career Finder

Keyword **Career Finder**

Feeling a little out of place in your current job? Or perhaps your career grew in fits and starts, bringing you to a point where you aren't sure what happens next (and you *really* aren't sure if you even like the options)? Whatever the case, the Career Finder may hold the insight you need. Take a personality test, browse careers suited to your style, and compare them with other job prospects.

Chats & Messages Department

Keyword **Business Talk**

On those days when you feel like connecting with someone, drop into the Chats & Messages department for a rousing chat room conversation or to browse the business message boards. Two weekday standards, Your Business Lunch and Your Business Dinner, invite different special guests each day. Topics range from public relations to starting your home business

and from Internet marketing to effective management.

Click with your Colleagues

Keyword **Professional Forums**

How do you advance in your chosen career? Where do you find information about jobs related to yours? When you're looking for real-life information about a career different from yours, where do you turn? Begin your search in the America Online Professional Forums department — and maybe end it there, too.

Professional Forums provides more than message boards. Look in the forums for scheduled chats that discuss your profession, recent news articles specifically related to what you do, and links to work-specific Web sites. Whether you're working in a particular profession or thinking about taking the plunge, check the Professional Forums department first.

Post a Résumé

Keyword **Post a Resume**

The online revolution touched everything. Engaging in communication, buying goods, selling products, playing games — it's all online now. Since businesses took the online leap, it only makes sense that job hunters should take the plunge, too. The WorkPlace channel puts in the Post a Résumé department all the tools you need to send your résumé into cyberspace. The department leans heavily on the *how-to* side of things with step-by-step instructions for creating and posting your résumé, links to free résumé critiques, a database of hundreds of sample cover letters, and even a Question and Answer discussion board.

Research and Directories

Keyword **Business Research**

A particular company catches your eye. Maybe you want to work for that company.

Or perhaps you want to invest in the product or service it provides. No matter what your reason (even if you need a subject for your latest term paper), the Business Research department offers several different online sources to speed your search. Within the forums listed in Business Research, you can look up abstracts from articles published in major medical journals, search for news related to a specific company, read past business articles written about your subject, or read about trends in home businesses.

Start-Up Businesses

Keyword **StartUp**

When you own your own business, whether it employs only you or a thousand people, you can use all the help you can get. Especially when you're a one-person shop — and you need to fulfill federal requirements, keep up with inventory, take care of your phone and mail needs, and still get something done during the day — you may think that the 24-hour day provides only half the necessary hours for you to get everything done.

Take a deep breath, fix yourself a soda (ice cream or not), and drop in to the Start-Up Businesses department. This featured area provides all kinds of business help. From information about starting your own business to regional government resources you may be able to tap, the Start-Up Businesses department is one-stop shopping for business owners.

Workplace Humor

Keyword **Lighter Side**

No matter how much you love your job (or how much like the rest of the world you are), sometimes you need a smile, a laugh, or some other quick recharge of your spirits. When the burdens of life weigh a little heavily on your shoulders, drop by the Workplace Humor department for a quick lift. With features like the Dilbert Zone (keyword **Dilbert**) and the

member-submitted joke of the day from iVillage (keyword **iVillage**), you won't be morose for long.

Work the Net

Keyword **Business Services**

As a business owner or swamped professional, you don't always have the time to run to the store for office supplies. Sometimes, researching a new purchase costs more in time than the item is worth. If these statements describe you and how you think, you'll love the Business Services department (known here by its lively moniker, Work the Net).

Chapter 14

Tracking News, Weather, Markets, and More

· ·

In This Chapter

▶ Browsing through the news
▶ Collecting stories with a session log
▶ Checking on the weather
▶ Examining the business side of news

· ·

*N*ews plays a big role in our lives. It's our link to the community, the country, and the world. (I can almost hear the national anthem playing!) America Online must think that news is very important because it offers so many kinds of news — headlines, international, business, technology, feature; the list goes on — and costs you nothing extra because it's part of normal America Online service. Is this a deal or what?

Thankfully, America Online gives you lots of tools for dealing with the influx of news, weather, sports scores, and stock prices. This chapter looks at your options for picking up news, ranging from a casual romp through the channel to a detailed analysis of the markets.

Look back at this chapter two or three times over the coming months. Your information needs change over time, and a quick peek here may open up precisely the news source you need.

Getting the News

Most of the online news lives (no surprises here) on the News channel, as shown in Figure 14-1. It displays top headlines from business, politics, entertainment, and the world in general. The News channel also provides links to in-depth coverage in the various news departments. Each department, in turn, narrows the focus, giving you an ever-more-carefully winnowed collection of stories.

Some of the most interesting news areas sit deep inside the News channel. For example, reading a relatively short news wire story about massive changes in how investors view online businesses is one thing, but reviewing an in-depth analysis of those same events in the Economist Intelligence Unit (keyword **EIU**) or the Financial Times (keyword **FT**) is another thing entirely. Other sources, like *Time* (keyword **Time**), CBS News (keyword **CBS News**), *BusinessWeek* (keyword **Business Week**), the Nightly Business Report (keyword **NBR**), and *The New York Observer* (keyword **NY Observer**) provide equally deep and unique perspectives on the news beyond what the wire services have the time and capacity to provide.

Filling your mailbox with news you want

A little-known feature of the America Online news system could save a *bunch* of time if you like to watch for stories about particular topics or companies. Considering all the resources on the News channel, you often don't have time to sift through tons of stories to find that all-important informational nugget. The America Online News Profiles service (keyword News Profiles) solves this problem for you by delivering directly to your mailbox the latest stories about the topics *you* choose.

To build a news profile, go to keyword **News Profiles** and follow the instructions in the How

to Create a Profile section. Start with something simple, like a single topic (mine was *espionage*) or a company name. Let the profile do its thing for a couple of days so that you can judge how many new e-mail messages it adds to your box. Adjust the items in your profile or the story-limit setting to manage the incoming story flow.

This service comes at no extra charge with your America Online account, so it's definitely worth a look. One word of caution: If you track a popular topic (like *Microsoft* or *Clinton lawsuits*), your mailbox fills up in no time!

Click the Search button to search all the news channels for topics that interest you. Here are a few tips for searching the News channel:

- ✔ If the system can't find any stories that match your search, try searching for something more general (*music* rather than *new rock groups,* for example).

- ✔ Likewise, if you're suddenly the proud owner of hundreds of matches, narrow your search terms (*small business* rather than *business*) to cull the reports you really don't want. Also, try limiting your options with the special search commands (see Table 14-1 for more details).

- ✔ To make a more detailed search, try using the tools AND, OR, and NOT. The table shows you how.

Table14-1	Special News Search Commands	
Command	*Example*	*Description*
AND	government *and* waste	Links two words or phrases; finds only articles that contain *both* examples
NOT	software *not* buggy	Finds only articles that contain the first word or phrase and do not contain the second; prevents unwanted matches (and occasionally provides moments of humor)
OR	Windows *or* Macintosh	Finds articles that contain either example *or* both of them

Better still, the News channel periodically brings breaking events directly to you through *AOL Radio,* the America Online audio technology. AOL Radio plays both live and prerecorded audio news directly through your computer's sound card and speaker system. As I write this book, AOL Radio is used only periodically when a breaking story or important news event pops up — it's not a regular feature you can simply hop into at any time. (If that kind of thing tweaks your interest, check out RealPlayer, at the Web site www.real.com. RealPlayer does much the same thing as AOL Radio, but it also includes regular radio stations, news, talk shows, and more.)

Rolling Your Articles into a Log

With so many easily accessible news areas, you can spend all day doing nothing but wandering from place to place, browsing through the stories. Obviously, that can affect your regularly scheduled day. Luckily, a tool built right into your America Online software captures all the stories you see on-screen and packages them into a single file, which you can put on your laptop, print on paper, or even download to your personal digital assistant.

The tool is the *session log* (part of the Log Manager that's built into your software), the America Online answer to a very fast-writing scribe. The session log automatically copies into a plain text file on your computer any articles you display. What's an *article?* It's a news story, picture caption, bulletin board posting, or other text that appears in a window on-screen. Menu items and things like that don't count — it's only paragraphs of text that land in the log files.

Follow these steps to create a session log of your reading activities:

1. **Choose My Files⇨Log Manager.**

   The Log Manager window, small though it is, hops on the screen.

2. **Click the Open Log button in the Session Log portion of the dialog box.**

   The Open Log window, shown in Figure 14-2, appears.

3. **America Online automatically offers to name the file SESSION.LOG, which is fine for most purposes. Click S̲ave.**

   If you want to save the session log files for posterity, you may change the name to today's date instead. If you reuse the same name each day (always naming the file SESSION.LOG, for example) when you click Save, Windows asks whether you want to overwrite the old file with a new one. Click Yes when it asks.

4. **Browse through the news stories just as you always do.**

   From this point on, your session log file is active and working behind the scenes to capture all the stories you display on-screen. Do what you normally do: Find a story that looks interesting and then click it to bring it up in a window. You don't need to actually scroll through the story yourself; just making it appear in the window is good enough for the session log.

5. **After you finish looking through the stories, choose My Files⇨Log Manager to open the Log Manager, and click Close to save the log file.**

   Your file is safely tucked away on your computer. At this point, you can do anything you want with it, including opening it in a word processor, printing it, or copying it to another computer or a personal digital assistant.

If you copy the log file into a personal digital assistant (such as a Palm Pilot or Franklin REX), remember to erase it when you finish indulging your desire for news. Otherwise, the stories take up the very valuable (and limited) memory space in your little device.

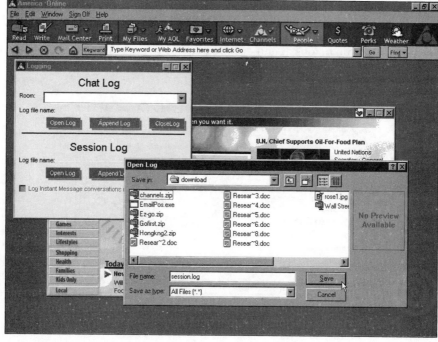

Figure 14-2:
Using the
default
name,
SESSION
LOG, works
well for
most
everyone.

The Weather Outside — Is It Frightful?

How much you care about the weather seems to depend directly on where
you live (I wonder whether anyone in Hawaii, for example, *really* checks the
forecasts, except during storm season) and which generation you belong to.
My parents, for example, were denied weather forecasts as children, so they
watch the cable-TV Weather Channel radar for fun. I, on the other hand, took
off on a trip into Canada without stopping to realize that late-fall-leaning-
toward-winter means a much different thing when you're 700 miles farther
north. (Although my cotton jacket froze solid on that trip, I managed to survive by wrapping my head in socks.)

To avoid problems like this in your life, check out the America Online
Weather area, at keyword **Weather.** It's one-stop shopping for every kind of
weather information imaginable (plus some you just don't *want* to imagine).
There's even a weather store, where, presumably, you can take home your
very own cumulonimbus cloud and whip up a storm in the privacy of your
own home.

Among other things, the Weather area (shown in Figure 14-3) offers a quick forecast for anywhere in the United States, plus detailed forecasts for both the United States and the world. It even includes satellite and radar images for you to look at and download (they're great for school projects or as practice maps for budding meteorologists).

Figure 14-3:
No matter what kind of weather you want, it's available in the Weather window.

Watching the Markets

Considering the amount of work and worry some people put into fretting over their stock market investments, stuffing all your cash into a mattress suddenly looks like a marginally attractive idea. At least you don't spend all your time wondering whether your funds are safe, because what kind of thief is going to walk off with a big . . . um . . . did you happen to see where my bed went? Hmm — perhaps there is something to be said for putting your money in stocks, after all.

If you've parked some money in stock investments, you probably want to see how your investments are performing. America Online offers two unique tools for tracking your stock market money. The first is the Quotes system, which pulls up the almost current (delayed by 20 minutes) price for whatever you want. The other system is Portfolios, which makes short work of watching a whole group of stocks. The following sections look at each of these tools individually.

Quotes (keyword Quotes)

The only way that checking stock prices could be easier than the America Online Quotes system is if the system could read your mind — but if it did that, who knows *what* it would discover? Perhaps the world is a better place if we just keep the Quotes system the way it is and not let computers peer into our thought processes.

Getting a stock quote takes only a moment. Here's what to do:

1. **Open the Quotes window by using keyword** Quotes **or clicking the Quotes button on the toolbar.**

   Whichever way you choose, the Quotes window hops into action.

2. **Type the company's stock ticker symbol in the Symbol box and click Get Quote.**

   After a moment or two, the stock's information appears in the lower section of the Quotes window (see Figure 14-4).

   If the window mechanically mutters `no quote information available`, double-check the spelling of the ticker symbol you entered. If worse comes to worst, click the Lookup button to find the symbol you need.

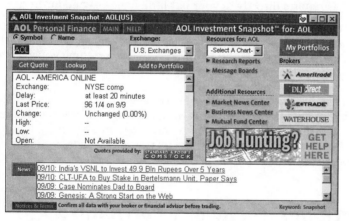

Figure 14-4: Things are looking good for the stock of the day!

Repeat the process for however many stocks you want to see. To track a number of stocks, it's easier to use the Portfolios system, as discussed in the next section. That system gives you some extra perks, by offering more information about your particular investments.

In addition to the stock price search system, the Quotes window offers a host of newsy goodies of interest to both serious investors and part-time plunkers. Here's a quick rundown of what's waiting there:

✔ The Market News Center (keyword **MNC**) offers quick graphs for everything from the Dow Jones Industrials to the Japanese Nikkei 225, plus selected news headlines.

✔ News by Ticker (keyword **Company News**) delivers recent articles from Reuters, the Associated Press, the PR Newswire, and the Business Wire for any company you choose. Just enter the company's stock ticker symbol, click Search, and enjoy your collection of news.

✔ AOL MarketDay (keyword **MarketDay**) wraps the day's financial news in one easy-to-use window. It includes a blow-by-blow description of the day's stock price moves, live market commentary, and links to several other AOL-based financial information areas.

✔ AOL Business News (keyword **Business News**) takes you to the Business window of the News channel, for the latest in wire stories of business deals and the companies that make them.

✔ Historical Quotes (keyword **Historical Quotes**) thumbs through previous years of pricing to clearly show how a stock has performed in the past. (Remember, as the gurus say, previous performance is no guarantee that we won't all lose our socks on this sucker the next time around.)

✔ Investment Research (keyword **Investment Research**) delivers stock reports, financial statements, earnings reports, and the EDGAR 10K and 10Q reports directly to your hot little hands — and for free.

✔ For moments when you want another opinion or want to buy something *now,* the Brokerage Center (keyword **Broker**) and the Mutual Fund Center (keyword **Mutual Funds**) supply everything you need, from final analysis information to links to online brokers.

Invest carefully, and don't believe everything you hear on the Personal Finance discussion boards. To repeat this warning, and to hear several others like it, flip to *America Online For Dummies Channels Directory,* the minibook in this book (you can tell that you're there by the yellow pages), and check out the Personal Finance channel.

Portfolios (keyword Portfolios)

The other side of the America Online built-in stock-tracking tools is the Portfolios system, at keyword **Portfolios.** Unlike its little brother the Quotes window, Portfolios easily handles a whole, well, portfolio of stock investments. Your portfolio shows, at a glance, your positions for all stocks, including the number of shares, the stock's current price, the price you paid for it, and your total gain (or, horrors, loss).

All the tools you need for creating and managing a portfolio live in the Portfolios window. Your first portfolio, cleverly named Portfolio #1, is automatically created when you tell America Online that you want to add a stock to your portfolio. Open your portfolio by either double-clicking it or clicking once to highlight it and then clicking Display.

With your portfolio open on-screen, you can do any of the following:

- ✔ **Add another stock to the portfolio:** Use the Add Item button. You need to know the stock ticker symbol, number of shares, and the price you paid for the stock.

- ✔ **Remove a stock:** Click the stock you want to get rid of and then click Remove. When America Online asks whether you're sure, click OK.

- ✔ **Transfer a stock to a different portfolio:** Click the stock and then click Transfer. America Online displays a nice dialog box asking to which portfolio you want to move the stock. (Of course, you need at least two portfolios before trying this little trick. For more about making a new portfolio, see the text after this list.)

- ✔ **Edit an entry:** Click the entry you want to change and then click Edit. You can adjust the number of shares and the purchase price, but you can't change the ticker symbol. To do that, you need to delete the entry entirely and then create a new one.

- ✔ **Check the details:** Click the stock entry you want detailed information about and then click Details. After a moment or two of serious consideration, the system displays a window filled to the brim with expanded price information, links to recent news stories, and buttons to create historical charts.

- ✔ **Refresh the display:** Click Refresh to get the latest prices for all stocks in your portfolio.

You can create and manage multiple portfolios through the system as well. To do that, go to the main Portfolios window at keyword **Portfolios**, and then pick your task from these items:

- ✔ **Create a new portfolio:** Click Create Portfolio. When asked, type a name for the portfolio, and click OK. The new portfolio appears in the Portfolios window.

- ✔ **Delete a portfolio:** Click the portfolio you don't want anymore and then wave solemnly at it while clicking Delete Portfolio. When the system asks whether you really, *really* want to delete the portfolio, click OK.

- ✔ **Rename a portfolio:** Click the portfolio with the weird name and then click Rename. When America Online asks you for a new name, type it, and click OK.

Be careful when you're deleting a portfolio. Make doubly sure that you clicked the correct portfolio because after you click that fateful OK button, that portfolio is gone forever. There's no Oops key, so don't let mistakes happen to you.

Chapter 15

Frolicking in the Games

- -

In This Chapter

▶ Sorting out the free games from the premium ones

▶ Playing the coolest games on the system

- -

Games, games, games — they're a great pastime, a relaxing way to spend an evening, and a challenging contest aimed at sharpening your mental blades. They're also one of the top reasons people buy a computer in the first place (whether they admit it or not).

Being part of the America Online community brings a whole new dimension to games. Rather than play a game *against* the computer, how about playing the game *through* the computer with a live opponent hundreds of miles away? Whether you want to challenge others or swap tales of gaming in the good old days, the games and game forums on America Online are definitely the place to do it.

This chapter looks at the free and premium (as in *not free*) games available through America Online and offers some tips about online games to try and love.

If There's No Free Lunch, Are There at Least Free Games?

Yes, Virginia, free games *are* on America Online. And the system also has pay-per-play games that charge an hourly fee. No, the fee doesn't apply to all games on the system. Yes, it does cover some. Yes, you get plenty of warning before entering a pay-by-the-minute gaming area, so you can't accidentally wander into one. That would be like "accidentally" driving your car through a shopping mall and then claiming that the pedestrians didn't get out of the way fast enough.

Most of the for-pay (or *premium*) games live in two areas of the Games channel: the Game Parlor (keyword **Game Parlor**) and Xtreme Games (keyword **Xtreme Games**). The individual games are provided and supported by two big-league online game companies — GameStorm (keyword **GameStorm**) and WorldPlay (keyword **WorldPlay**).

As their names imply, each game area focuses on different kinds of games. The Game Parlor contains classic parlor games, like backgammon, chess, cribbage, hearts, and spades. Just to keep things interesting (and, I think, because they couldn't figure out where else to put them), it also includes some nonparlor games, like Jack Nicklaus Online Golf Tour (keyword **Jack Nicklaus**), Splatterball (keyword **Splatterball**) and Tetris: Head-2-Head (keyword **Tetris**).

The Xtreme Gaming side of the world offers action-oriented titles, like Air Warrior III, Cosrin, Dragon's Gate, Harpoon Online, Legends of Kesmai, Magestorm, Multiplayer Battletech, and Warcraft II. (Just for fun, see whether you can read that last sentence in one breath. Why should you? Well, why not?)

As you play the premium games, your America Online account is charged per minute, which is the smallest amount of billable time the America Online computers understand. As I write this book, Game Parlor titles cost 99 cents per hour, and Xtreme Gaming titles are $1.99 per hour, but the prices change periodically, so check the details in each game. The billing is automatic and begins after you pass through the This Costs Money curtain (okay, it's really a window), shown in Figure 15-1, which reminds you, in no uncertain terms, that it costs money to step beyond this point.

For the latest information about premium games, including hourly fees, special offers, and other details of online gaming, go to the Games Guide, at keyword **Games Guide**.

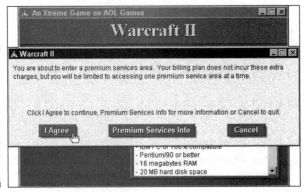

Figure 15-1:
Make no
mistake —
the billing
clock starts
the moment
you click
I Agree.

Opening the door to premium games

By default, only the master screen name (the first screen name you created on America Online) can play the way-cool premium games. All the other screen names on your account start out blocked from the games. If someone signs on with one of those other screen names and tries to play a premium game, a message pops up saying, basically, that America Online would just *love* to let them play, but some heathen scoundrel (namely the keeper of the master screen name) won't let them. After riling the would-be player into a frenzy, the window then suggests that she take up the issue with the account holder.

If you *want* to allow your other screen names to play premium games, you have to tell America Online. To do that, sign on to the system and then use keyword **Parental Controls**. When the window appears, click the Premium Services button. When the Premium Services Controls window appears, clear the Block Premium Services check box for each screen name that gets to play premium games. To clear the check box, just click it. To prevent a screen name from playing the premium games (thus protecting your credit card bill from accidental inflation), make sure that the Block Premium Services check box next to the screen name is checked.

The free games live in Game Shows Online (keyword **Game Shows**), shown in Figure 15-2, and the Gamers Forum (keyword **Gaming**). These games lean more toward the thinking side of life than their premium game counterparts, but it doesn't mean that they aren't just as exciting. Games such as Strike-a-Match (keyword **Strike a Match**), Slingo (keyword **Slingo**), and Out of Order (keyword **Out of Order**) definitely raise your blood pressure, believe me, and the Simming and Role Playing areas in the Gamers Forum stretch your imagination to new lengths. Other free games include a huge variety of trivia titles, online role-playing games, and word puzzles.

Figure 15-2:
The Game
Shows
Online area
fills your
free time
with fun
(and free)
pursuits.

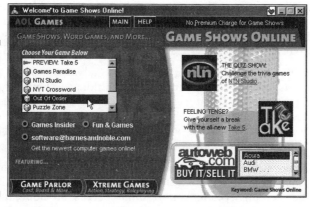

Hopping into the Best Free Games

In our fast-paced society, time is a scarce thing at work and at home. That makes the time you devote to online gaming even rarer! In the hopes of helping you spend most of that precious time actually playing games instead of fruitlessly wandering around looking for them, I've put together the following list of popular (and mostly free) games available on America Online.

Each section includes the name of the game, the keyword for getting there, and a quick description of what the game (or game area) is like. If you have to pay a fee for playing, there's a note about that as well.

So, with no further delay, explanation, or meandering text, here are the America Online games and game areas you don't want to miss:

- ✔ If you love trivia games, the America Online games of trivia (keyword **Trivia**) anxiously await you. This window leads to trivia games in the NTN Studio (keyword **NTN**), Zealot science fiction trivia (keyword **Z),** as well as the resources and community of the Trivia Forum (keyword **Trivia Forum**). For a real challenge, check out the International Trivia area (keyword **Trivia**; then double-click the International Trivia item).

- ✔ To satisfy the word puzzle addict in you (or at your house), turn to the Puzzle Zone (keyword **Puzzle),** as shown in Figure 15-3. This area features four different word puzzle titles, including challenging interactive crossword puzzles in Flexicon, anagram challenges from Elvis-Lives, and Clink, a stream-of-consciousness game that defies rational explanation (makes you immediately want to find out how it works, doesn't it?).

- ✔ Vying for the dual titles of "visually darkest online area" and "most likely to keep you coming back" is Antagonist, Incorporated (keyword **Ant**). Antagonist is a combination game review and online gaming site, with lively discussion and late-breaking stories in the world of both computer and console games (the Nintendos and Segas of the world). Not content to merely talk about the games, the Antagonist also includes several online games in the gothic fantasy realm (several of which cost money to play). They also offer Antagonist Trivia, which you find at keyword **AT.**

- ✔ VGA Planets (keyword **Gaming**; click Strategy/Wargames and then VGA Planets) was one of the first turn-based, multiplayer space strategy games on the market. Its success spawned other similar games, like Stars (keyword **Gaming**; click Strategy/Wargames and then Stars). These games enjoy some of the largest and friendliest game communities on the Net. Check them out for yourself, and join in the fun!

- ✔ Fantasy role-playing games are an extraordinarily popular pastime in the gaming chat rooms of America Online. The Gamers Forum includes several of these creativity-laden entertainment areas, including the Simming Forum, the Role Playing forum, the Red Dragon Inn, and the Stars End

Spaceport. These games are a riot to play, as long as you're up to the challenge. Check the forums for more information about their various games and venues.

✔ For a slightly different (but very fun) approach to online games, try the Urban Legends forum (keyword **Urban Legends**). Among the odd and offbeat diversions in this area are trivia games (using urban legends, of course) and an online theatre troupe that hosts weekly Old West, swashbuckling, and outer space role-playing events.

✔ The folks at BoxerJam Productions supply some of the most delightful game shows in the whole of America Online. Strike-a-Match (keyword **Strike A Match**), Take 5 (keyword **Take 5**), and Out of Order (keyword **Out of Order**) are both fast-playing and challenging, with a high replay factor. Don't blame me if you get hopelessly hooked on them!

✔ Finally, I'd be seriously remiss if I failed to mention the Collectible Cards forum (keyword **Gaming**, and click Collectible Cards). Collectible card games are the hottest new game trend in years. Led by games like the Star Wars Customizable Card Game, Star Trek: The Next Generation, and Magic: The Gathering, collectible card games continue to entrance new players every day with their combination of game play, collectibility, and old-fashioned horse swapping as anxious players trade cards in hopes of collecting a full set. Find out all about the collectible card game world here, and join the fun for chats and live, online tournaments.

✔ There's much more to do in the world of online games than the things on America Online. To dive in to the depths of live, multiplayer action, pick up a copy of *Games Online For Dummies,* by yours truly (IDG Books Worldwide, Inc.). It covers more of the America Online games and opens the door to the games of the Internet.

Keep an eye on the Game Shows Online (keyword **Game Shows**) and Gamers Forum (keyword **Gaming**) areas to watch for new games joining the system. Lots of cool stuff is coming — don't miss it!

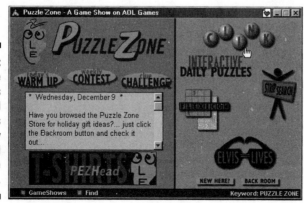

Figure 15-3: The Puzzle Zone offers word puzzles for every skill and patience level.

Chapter 16

Loading Up, Loading Down, and Zipping All Around

● ●

In This Chapter

▶ Finding things to download

▶ Downloading a file

▶ Using the Download Manager

▶ Unzipping, unstuffing, and otherwise decompressing the files that arrive

▶ Uploading your donations

▶ Logging everything you see

● ●

*I*magine a Wal-Mart store where everything is free — you just pick out what you want and carry your selections out to the car. Some items require a small payment directly to the manufacturer, but many don't. Sounds like heaven, right? (Well, heaven probably would be a computer superstore set up this way, but I digress.)

The scenario I just described already exists, except that it's not a Wal-Mart — it's the hundreds of file libraries on America Online. Just find something that interests you, download the file to your computer, and then, if it's a shareware program, pay a small fee to the author because you love the application so much.

Sounds too simple, right? There must be a catch. Well, it *is* simple, and there really *isn't* a catch. This chapter is your guide to getting a share of this digital bonanza. Read on and find out how to find stuff to download, how the download process works, how to share stuff you love by uploading it, and much more.

Welcome to Software Heaven. Come right on in.

Locating Likely Candidates

You're ready to storm the digital gates, eager to get your share of the soft-ware fortunes within. But where do you start? Jeez — hundreds, maybe thousands of places exist for you to look through. Nothing like having too many options to keep your mind spinning in circles, eh?

Start with one or two forums you particularly like. If you're looking for a certain kind of file (such as fonts or clip art), use the software library search feature to see what's available. This section explains both these options.

Forum and service libraries

Almost every forum has a file library. Libraries usually are marked with the disk icon (such as the one shown in Figure 16-1) or, in fancier service areas,, with a big disk button. Both elements ultimately lead to a file list window like the one in Figure 16-2.

Figure 16-1:
A standard
file library,
complete
with all the
trimmings.

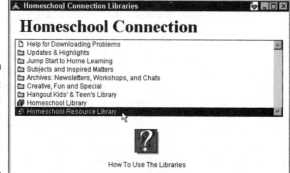

Figure 16-2:
All roads
lead to a file
list window.

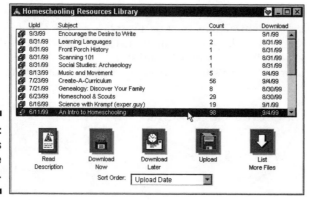

✔ To find out more about a file, double-click its entry in the forum library window (or click the entry and then click the Read Description button). A page of information about the file appears, including its name, size, and author, plus a complete description (or as complete a description as the person contributing it provides). Incidentally, if you're using a session log, all the file descriptions you view are saved there automatically. For more information about session logs, see Chapter 14.

✔ Downloading is a breeze with the Download Now and Download Later buttons (covered in the next section).

✔ Use the Sort Order pull-down menu to see the files by the date they were first uploaded or last downloaded, alphabetically by subject, or by download count (a relative measure of which files are the most popular). Just click the down arrow next to the Sort Order setting, choose your preferred order from the list, and wait a moment while America Online organizes everything for you.

✔ Although most libraries have lots of files, the library's window only displays the first 20. That's why a List More Files button usually appears in the lower-right corner of the forum library window. Click this button to display more files in the window.

For leads on good downloads, read the forum's discussion areas to see what people are talking about, or post a message that describes your interests and asks for recommendations.

Look for files that are popular. The *count* column in the file list window is a good popularity gauge; this column tracks the number of times members downloaded that file.

File library search

If you're looking for something more general or if you just like knowing *all* your options before you start, try the software library search feature. This feature browses through all the libraries in America Online, looking intently for whatever you tell it to look for.

You must be signed on to America Online to use the software library search system. Sorry, but that's just how life goes.

Here's how to do a search:

1. **Get into the file search system by using keyword** Download Center.

   The Download Center window pops up, offering all kinds of software catalogs, plus two places to search for software.

2. **In the Download Center window, click the Shareware button.**

The Software Search window *finally* appears.

The other button in the Download Center window takes you to the *commercial* software area, where the price of admission is your credit card number. That's great if you need a particular program for the office, but it's usually overkill for a home computer. Rather than plunk down the bucks for an overpackaged application, look for a shareware (or even a freeware) program that fills the bill.

For a Macintosh file search, click the Mac Search button along the bottom of the Software Search window.

3. **To limit your search to a particular time period (the past week, the past month, or since time began), select the appropriate radio button in the Select a Timeframe area.**

Barring a specific, burning need to search only the most recent uploads, leave the time frame set to All Dates. The search system displays the file list presorted by category and date with the newest files at the beginning of each category.

4. **Narrow your search if you want to.**

Narrow your search to particular file libraries by clicking one or more of the check boxes in the Category area. To search everywhere, leave all the check boxes clear (the default setting).

When you feel comfortable with the search function, try experimenting with these settings to see if they help you find more of what you want.

5. **Type a few words that describe what you're looking for.**

See Figure 16-3 for an example.

If you know the specific program you want (like WinZip, Paint Shop Pro, or PowerTools), type the program name in this area.

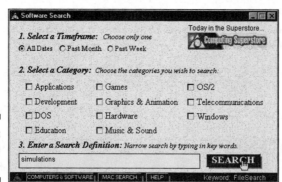

Figure 16-3: The search begins.

6. Click the oversized and relaxingly colored Search button at the bottom of the window (refer to Figure 16-3).

After a moment or two, the File Search Results dialog box appears, looking somewhat akin to Figure 16-4. The File Search Results dialog box is much like the forum's file list window, right down to the buttons along the bottom.

Figure 16-4:
The results
are in!

7. Scroll through the list to see what your search uncovered. Double-click interesting-looking entries to see a full description of the file.

At this point, you're ready to do some downloading, which (surprisingly enough) is covered in the next section.

Incidentally, Paint Shop Pro, PowerTools, and WinZip are *great* shareware applications for everybody who uses Microsoft Windows and America Online. If you don't have them yet, test your new downloading skills on them.

Downloading a File Right Now

You finally found a promising file, checked its description, and decided that you simply *must* have a copy. Cool with me. You're ready to do the dirty deed, then — time to download a file.

Here's the procedure:

1. Click the name of the file you want to download and then click the Download Now button (see Figure 16-5).

If you're in the file list window, Download Now is a square button with a cool graphic of a disk "beaming down," as in *Star Trek*. In the file description window, the button is simply labeled (you guessed it) Download Now.

Clicking the Download Now button accesses the Download Manager's filename dialog box (but not the whole Download Manager itself — that's covered in the next section of this chapter).

The file's name is displayed in the File Name box (see Figure 16-6).

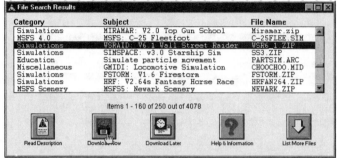

Figure 16-5:
Ready to download your file Captain.

Figure 16-6:
Name the file, and it's on the way.

2. **Change the file's name or its destination directory if you like. When you're satisfied, click OK.**

   Clicking OK starts the download. To keep you updated, America Online displays a progress bar.

   The Download dialog box also has two control buttons: Finish Later and Cancel. If you suddenly need your computer for something more urgent than downloading this file, click Finish Later. America Online remembers that you already received part of the file. When you start to download the file again, the download picks up wherever you stopped the first time. Cancel, on the other hand, is the abort button. Click it if you come to the conclusion that downloading this file is a terrible mistake.

   After the download is complete, a little dialog box pops up to gleefully announce the news.

3. Click OK to make the dialog box go away.

If something goes horribly wrong (for example, the download gets stuck for some reason), try downloading the file again. If it doesn't work that time either, try once more at a different time of day, particularly early in the morning, just before leaving for work or school.

What if you're *not* on the unlimited time plan and you burn up a bunch of online time for a download that doesn't work? It's no problem — just go to keyword **Credit** and ask for a refund. Fill out the form, complete with the time, date, and minutes lost, and click Send Request. The America Online credit elves should reply to you within a few days.

After you get the hang of the America Online file libraries, check out the Internet Connection's FTP (File Transfer Protocol) feature. FTP is your link to millions of files available on the Internet. If instant access to file libraries all over the world already has you salivating, flip to Chapter 17 for details.

How Do You Manage This Many Downloads?

What if you find not 1, not 2, but 47 fascinating files? Well, you can spend much of your copious free time watching the computer draw progress bars (how exciting!). Or you can use the Download Manager to automate the whole sordid process. The Download Manager's main goal in life is to help you download *tons* of stuff from America Online. Really — that's it.

Using the Download Manager is a two-stage process: You mark the files you want to download and then you tell the Download Manager to get them. The best thing is that you don't need to be present for the second step of the process; your computer gleefully sits and catches all the files you want while you're off doing something *really* fun.

Here's how the process works:

1. Click the name of a file you want to download and then click the Download Later button (see Figure 16-7).

The file hops into the Download Manager's queue. By default, the America Online software throws up an annoying little window that *helpfully* explains that you just decided to download this file later (assuming that you mistakenly thought that the Download Later button actually washed your car or something).

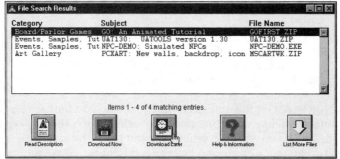

Figure 16-7:
Just leave
it in the
queue; I'll
pick it up
later.

If you plan to use the Download Later feature frequently, turn off the this-is-what-you-just-did dialog box. To do that, open the Download Manager (as described in Step 3) and click the Download Preferences button. When the Download Preferences window appears, deselect the Confirm Additions to My Download List check box and click OK. Finally, close the Preferences window and take a moment to smile smugly in the knowledge that you've silenced yet another silly dialog box.

2. **Repeat Step 1 for all the files you want to download.**

3. **Open the Download Manager by choosing My Files⇨Download Manager from the toolbar.**

   The Download Manager window appears, looking like the one shown in Figure 16-8 (except that your list of files in the middle looks different from mine).

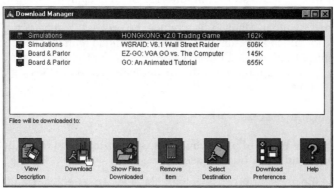

Figure 16-8:
The
Download
Manager is
your digital
shopping
cart, filled
with the
goodies
you've
selected.

To see the file description one more time, double-click the filename in the Download Manager window. The description appears, just as it did in the file list window.

If you have sudden second thoughts about a file and decide that you don't want to download it, click its name on the Download Manager list and then click Remove Item. Repeat the process as many times as you want.

4. **Click the Download button to put the Download Manager to work.**

   Two windows appear on-screen, as shown in Figure 16-9. One window shows the overall status of your massive download. The other window displays a progress bar for the file that's downloading right now.

If you have *lots* of files to get, select the Sign Off after Transfer check box. That option tells the Download Manager to go ahead and sign you off from America Online after the last file arrives. This feature is handy (and makes sure that you don't waste online time if the download finishes before you expect it to).

Remember that Automatic AOL sessions work with the Download Manager. You can mark a bunch of files and download them in the middle of the night, when America Online is the least busy. Chapter 8 explains the basics of Automatic AOL from an e-mail perspective, but you need to check the Help menu for details about scheduling the sessions.

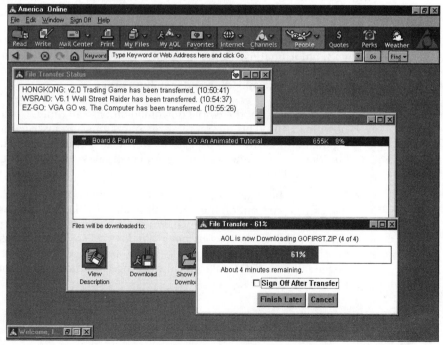

Figure 16-9:
Two windows show you the down-loading status.

The Joys of Stuffing and Zipping

Many files in the various and sundry America Online file libraries end in ZIP, SIT, or ARC. These letters don't mean that they're fast or resting or that they date from the time of Noah; rather, the letters indicate that the files were *compressed* so that they take less time to download (and less space inside the America Online computers). ZIP files come from the PKZip or WinZip programs, and SIT files are created on the Macintosh by StuffIt. ARC files are in an old and rarely used format, but some are still around.

Before using a compressed file, you have to decompress it. To do that, you either need a copy of the right program (as mentioned), or you can let the America Online software handle it by itself.

To simplify your life, the America Online access software automatically unpacks compressed files when you sign off the system. (I tell you, those programmers amaze even me sometimes.) To make sure that this setting is on, choose My AOL⇨Preferences. Click the Download button to open the Download Preferences dialog box. Make sure that the Automatically Decompress Files at Sign-Off check box is selected. Then leave the decompressing to America Online. If you're comfy with a program like WinZip (which, by the way, is one of the most useful programs ever invented for Windows users), leave this setting unchecked and do the unpacking yourself.

Installing programs on your computer involves many little niggling details — too many, unfortunately, for me to go into here. I won't leave you high and dry, though (I'd never do that to you!). Take a look at these resources for more about both downloading and installing programs:

✔ For a great view of the whole download-and-install thing, try keyword **Download 101**. This interactive area offers tips and instructions covering the entire download process as well as lots of links to great file libraries all over America Online. And every now and then, the area offers free, live training chats.

✔ If the mere thought of folders, directories, and software installation makes you pass out on the floor, put some soft blankets down there to cushion your impending arrival. When they're safely in place, pick up a copy of *Windows 98 For Dummies, Windows 95 For Dummies,* 2nd Edition (both by Andy Rathbone), or *Macs For Dummies,* 6th Edition, by David Pogue (all from IDG Books Worldwide, Inc.), hit the blankets, and catch up on your reading.

Well, now it's yours — sort of

Three kinds of programs exist in the world: freeware, shareware, and commercial software. If this sounds like horribly dry, technical drivel, you obviously aren't a lawyer (I knew that I liked you). Please bear with me (and stay awake) while I explain.

Freeware, shareware, and commercial software are the three most common ways in which a program is licensed for use. *Freeware* costs nothing; the author has graciously donated it to the public. *Shareware* is software you can download, try, and pay for if you like it. *Commercial software* is what you buy at the local computer superstore, from companies such as Borland, Lotus, Microsoft, and Novell.

Here are a few basic rules regarding the three kinds of software:

✔ **Freeware:** Download it, use it, give a copy to your friends. Isn't freeware great?

✔ **Shareware:** Download it and give it a try. If you don't like the program, don't pay for it.

If you think it's great, get out your checkbook and send in the registration fee. Whatever you do, don't keep using an unregistered shareware program because you don't think that you should have to pay for something you downloaded from America Online. That would be like stealing a book from the library and then saying that it's okay because the library doesn't charge for books anyway. Shareware is often high-quality work and well worth the minimal registration fee.

✔ **Commercial software:** Never, under *any* circumstances, upload or download something that claims to be a commercial program. If you like WordPerfect, that's fine — just don't show your admiration by giving copies of it to your friends. I won't get on my "pirated software" soapbox, I promise. But I will say this: If you like a program, buy your own copy. Okay?

 Whether or not you plan to download lots of files and programs, I *highly* recommend downloading and registering a copy of WinZip, a Windows-based archiving program. This one program knows how to handle almost any type of compressed file thrown at it. That alone makes WinZip worth the minimal registration fee. But all the other tricks it knows (like making a ZIP file on the fly by dragging and dropping files into it from Windows Explorer) make WinZip truly indispensable.

Donating Your Own Efforts

Most file libraries not only offer files for your downloading pleasure but also accept *uploads* — files donated by other America Online members. After all, the library files had to come from *somewhere*, so why not let members chip in things they like?

To upload a file, you need to know the file's name and location on your computer. You also have to find a potential home for it somewhere on America Online. Look for a place that accepts uploaded files (this step's a must) and has other files like the one you're sending. If you're sending a game, utility, or other program, use your antivirus software to be extra sure that you're not donating a computer virus, too.

✔ Not every file library accepts uploads. If you're looking at a file list and the Upload button is dimmed, it's a good sign that you're browsing a read-only library.

✔ Only public domain, freeware, shareware, or items of your own creation can be uploaded to America Online. If you aren't sure about the appropriateness of something you want to upload, post a message to one of the forum hosts (you can usually find their screen names in a welcome-to-this-forum-type document on the forum's main screen). Describe your file and get the host's opinion about your uploading it. Check out the sidebar "Well, now it's yours — sort of," earlier in this chapter, for a little more information about the whole freeware, shareware, and commercial software issue.

✔ Don't upload something on your first day on America Online. Wait a little while. Get involved in a forum or two, meet some people, post some messages, and generally get a feel for what goes on before you upload anything to a library.

At this point, you're ready to upload the file. Here's what to do:

1. **Display the file list window of the file library to which you want to upload.**

   Get there through whatever combination of keywords, menus, and mouse-clicks works best for you.

2. **Click the Upload button at the bottom of the file list window.**

   The Upload File dialog box appears.

   If the Upload button is dimmed, this file library doesn't accept uploaded files. Sorry, but that's how life goes sometimes. Also, America Online may tell you that the library is full. In that case, post a message on the forum's discussion boards asking whether there's a place for you to upload the file you want to share.

3. **Carefully fill out all the information boxes in the Upload File dialog box.**

   Be as specific as you can. The more that people know about this file, the more likely they are to download it.

4. **Click Select File to display the Attach File dialog box; double-click the name of the file you want to upload; then choose OK to close the dialog box.**

5. **Double-check all the text you typed; after you're happy with it, click Send.**

Don't be surprised if your uploaded file doesn't immediately appear in the file library. Most, if not all, America Online forums check uploaded files for viruses before setting those files free in the library.

Logging Isn't Really Downloading Although It's Close

Sometimes, you want a record of where you were and what you saw. If you didn't, most of the photo film and developing market (as well as a large chunk of camcorder sales) wouldn't exist.

In America Online terminology, what you're looking for is a *session log:* a file that stores the contents of every document you touched during a particular online period. The session log grabs every e-mail, news story, and bulletin board posting and stuffs them into one long text file.

For all the details on the America Online logging features, flip to Chapter 14.

Chapter 17

Cruising the Internet

In This Chapter

▶ Checking out the Internet Connection

▶ Getting started: A brief Internet primer

▶ Skimming the resources

▶ Using Internet e-mail

▶ Trying a mailing list (or two)

▶ Leaping through the World Wide Web

▶ Newsgroups: The Internet's answer to discussion boards

▶ Downloading the world with FTP

*T*urn on the TV news and what do you hear being discussed? The Internet. Go to lunch with some friends and what's bound to either come up at your table or be loudly debated at the one next to you? The Internet. Attend a cocktail party and what's on everyone's mind? Well, if it's boring, they may be thinking about how much better the *last* party was; but to pass the time until they can make a polite departure, they're talking about the Internet. (What's wrong with these people? Don't they have real lives?)

Rising from technoid obscurity to media-star status in just a few short years, the Internet is still a mystery to most people. Frankly, it was a mystery to me until a few years ago. In the hope of sparing you additional moments of fear and anxiety, this chapter explains a little about the Internet (just enough to get you going) and a lot about the powerful America Online Internet Connection. It also unmasks the odd language of the Internet, introducing and explaining terms such as *World Wide Web, FTP,* and *newsgroup.*

A big electronic world is out there, just waiting for you to visit. Grab your modem and get ready to go Internet surfing!

Internet Connection Basics

Like everything else on America Online, the Internet is just a hop, skip, and a click away from wherever you are. In fact, it's even a little closer than that because America Online has a toolbar button for it, too: the cleverly named Internet button.

The Internet Connection (keyword **Internet Connection**) is designed to quickly get you where you want to go. The center of the window displays a Go to AOL NetFind button, which whisks you away to the America Online Web search system. The window also sports a place to enter the address of a Web site you want to visit. On the right side of the window are some buttons leading to interesting stuff, like the Internet newsgroups, the America Online Time Savers list of topical Web sites, and more.

Along the bottom of the window are three featured-area buttons. These buttons take you to various Internet-based areas of interest, such as e-mail finders and lists of Web sites arranged around a particular topic.

So Just What Is This Internet Thing?

Hang on to your seat — I'm about to explain the Internet in four (yes, just *four*) paragraphs. This may get a little hairy at times, but you have nothing to worry about because I'm a trained professional. Kids, don't let your parents try this stuff at home.

The Internet started as a big Department of Defense project somewhere back in the 1960s, slowly expanding through the '70s and '80s and coming into its own in the '90s. It was originally supposed to help university researchers exchange information about supersecret defense projects, thus decreasing the amount of time necessary to find new and ever more fascinating ways to end life on the planet. The government linked computers at colleges, universities, research labs, and large defense contractors. The Internet was born.

At the same time, the seeds of today's digital anarchy were sown. This research network connected lots of bright, intelligent people, and those people started coming up with bright, intelligent ideas about fun, new things to do on the research network. "How about a discussion area where we can swap notes — kinda like a bulletin board?" {Poof!} The network newsgroups were born.

Then anarchy took over. Discussion areas originally intended for deep conversations about megaton yields and armor deflection/implosion ratios carried witty repartee about Buddha, the Rolling Stones, and kite flying. Everyone with an opinion to share was welcome, as long as they could get there in the first place.

Although the Internet continued to slowly bubble and ferment throughout the 1980s, things suddenly changed when the 1990s arrived. In the span of a couple of years, the Internet simply exploded. Thousands of computers and networks around the world joined the fun. Newspaper articles and TV news stories appeared, introducing this electronic Colossus to the normal world. Noncomputer companies linked up to the network as business e-mail use blossomed. Millions of average people began poking around on the Internet through online services such as America Online.

With that brief bit of background under your belt, ponder these important tidbits before venturing out into the online world:

- ✔ No single computer or place is called *the Internet.* The Internet is a collection of millions of computers all over the world.

- ✔ Nobody's really in charge of it all. Nope, nobody. Some committees and groups attempt to keep everything headed in the same direction, but nobody actually leads the parade.

- ✔ No one knows how big the Internet is. Suffice it to say that it's really, *really* big — and still growing.

- ✔ The Internet is not free (even though you and I don't pay extra for it through America Online). It kinda looks like it's free because you just pay for your America Online account — you're not charged for the telecommunications time between the America Online computers in Vienna, Virginia, and the rest of the Internet world. I only bring this up so that you remember that *someone* out there is paying the bill; it's good netiquette to use Internet resources wisely, particularly FTP (covered later in this chapter).

- ✔ Believe it or not, all this anarchy works if everyone's nice about it.

Free speech is the *rule* on the Internet, not the exception. If you see a Web page, read something in a newsgroup, or find a document through gopher that's offensive to you, you have my personal apology. But that's all the sympathy anyone's going to give you. The communications code of the Internet is simple: If something offends you, either ignore it or disagree with it, but *don't* post a message suggesting that "somebody ought to shut those people up." An action such as that is sure to fill your mailbox with angry e-mail questioning your parentage and suggesting that you do some biologically impossible things in the corner.

E-Mail the Internet Way

Perhaps you joined America Online solely to use Internet e-mail. (It wouldn't surprise me at all.) An Internet e-mail account is an absolute must these days, particularly in the business world.

The America Online e-mail system makes Internet e-mail a snap. You don't have to remember any special commands or visit any obscure corner of the service to send an e-mail message through the Internet. Just create the message as you would normally, type in the person's Internet mail address, and click Send. If you need a quick review of the how-tos of America Online e-mail, flip to Chapter 8 or choose <u>M</u>ail Center⇨<u>M</u>ail Center from the toolbar and poke through the information there.

Here are a few notes about e-mail that I just couldn't fit anywhere else:

- ✔ An e-mail message takes anywhere from a few minutes to a few hours to make its way through the Internet and find its destination. If you send a message and it doesn't arrive by the next business day or two, consider the message lost.

- ✔ Yes, Internet mail messages sometimes get lost. No, it's not the Postal Service's fault.

- ✔ Your America Online account can receive mail through the Internet as well as send it. Your Internet e-mail address is your screen name — minus any spaces in it — with @aol.com appended to the end. For example, my Internet mail address on America Online is jkaufeld@aol.com (my screen name first, then the extra Internet stuff tacked on to the end). If my screen name included a space (making it *J Kaufeld*), the Internet e-mail version would still be jkaufeld@aol.com, because the Internet doesn't like spaces in e-mail addresses.

- ✔ The very cool *unsend* feature works only on mail sent *from* an America Online subscriber *to* either an America Online or CompuServe 2000 subscriber. It doesn't work on mail sent through the Internet (so think twice before clicking Send).

- ✔ Look through Chapter 8 for all the particulars about using e-mail both through the Internet and within America Online.

Consider getting an Internet book

If one of the main reasons you joined America Online was for its Internet services, I highly recommend getting a good book about the Internet. I personally suggest *The Internet For Dummies,* 7th Edition (by John R. Levine, Carol Baroudi, and Margaret Levine Young), and *MORE* *Internet For Dummies*, 4th Edition (by John R. Levine and Margaret Levine Young), both from IDG Books Worldwide, Inc. (No, it's not because I *have* to suggest them — I really like them and have them myself.)

Join a Mailing List for Fun and Full Mailboxes

Swapping letters through a mailing list is about the simplest form of information exchange on the Internet. You don't need any special software, you don't have to buy anything, and no salesperson calls. Everything comes straight to your mailbox; you don't even have to go find it. You can find lists for everything and everybody covering hobbies, music groups, religion, mineproofing military vehicles, motorcycle repair, world history — the list goes on and on.

Finding and joining a mailing list

Before enjoying the wonders of discussions that take place in your mailbox, you have to sign up. America Online makes that easy with easy access to *Liszt,* a searchable database of Internet mailing lists. To get there, click in the address box on the navigation bar, and then type www.liszt.com and press Enter. On cue, your Web browser opens and displays the Liszt mailing list directory (as shown in Figure 17-1).

Figure 17-1:
The Liszt mailing list search system makes finding an e-mail discussion easy.

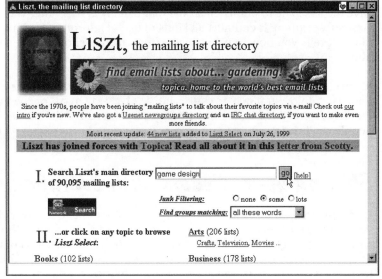

Liszt includes a searchable database (containing nearly 100,000 mailing lists) and a browseable subject-oriented directory named Liszt Select:

- **To search the database:** Type either the list name or subject in the search box and then click Go. Liszt thinks for a moment and then returns a report of what it found. Browse through your results and click anything that looks interesting.

- **For a relaxed browse through the subjects:** Scroll down a little in the Liszt main window until the topic lists appear. When you find a topic that looks interesting, click it to see what Liszt offers there. Remember that the subject listing includes only a small portion of the total Liszt database, so if you don't find something of interest, try the search option mentioned in the first bullet.

When you find an interesting list, follow the subscription instructions to join. Usually, you need to send an e-mail message to either the list moderator or a program that maintains the subscriber list. If the instructions say something about putting the phrase SUBSCRIBE listname your-name in the body of a message, you're dealing with an automated list-keeping program. If you're supposed to send "a politely worded request," a human's doing the work. (Don't sign up for a human-maintained list and then ask to be removed a couple of days later. The poor person on the other end is usually overworked as it is.)

Save the *welcome to our list* message that usually arrives after the list accepts your subscription. It contains all kinds of useful information — most importantly, it tells you how to unsubscribe from the list, should you ever want to quit.

If you can't find the list of your dreams through the Liszt database, try the CataList catalog, at www.listserv.net/catalist.html, or the massive Publicly Accessible Mailing List site (also known as PAML because computer people can't resist a cute acronym), at www.neosoft.com/internet/paml.

Sharing your wisdom with everybody else

Belonging to a list means both reading what others have to say and tossing in your own two cents every now and then. To send a message to the entire list, write your thoughts in an e-mail and send it to the submissions or articles address — *not* to the address you used to subscribe to the list. Your important thoughts find their way out to everybody within a day or so — or at least they may.

Keep your thoughts clear and concise, with emphasis on the word *concise*. People on the Internet appreciate brevity. Remember that some of your readers have to pay for each message they receive; others are charged by the size of the message. Keep your messages short, clear, and to the point, and you will be adored by millions.

Just because your thoughts are lucid and fascinating doesn't guarantee that they'll actually be shared with the rest of the mailing list. Here's a brief guide to help you understand the three basic types of lists and how each affects the chances of sharing your thoughts:

- ✔ **Unmoderated:** Accepts whatever you send; posting is automatic, as long as your contribution makes its way successfully back to the listkeeper (be it machine or otherwise).

- ✔ **Moderated:** Edited and controlled by someone. Everything that goes out to the list's subscribers is okayed by the moderator. If your posting doesn't meet the standards or requirements of the list, it's not distributed. You can ask the moderator why your posting didn't pass the muster, but simply whining doesn't do any good.

- ✔ **Announcement-only:** Doesn't accept submissions from you, the listening audience. They send out information only from a particular source. Writing an article for one of these lists is like trying to convince the recorded weather information to say something else for a while.

Unsubscribing from a list

Yes, the time does come when you must bid adieu to the things of youth and flights of information fancy. And so it is that you may, one day, want to get the heck off that mailing list that fills your mailbox with messages every day.

To unsubscribe from a list, turn back to the information page you so carefully printed or saved when you found the list. Buried among everything else on the page is a notation about "unsubscribing from this list" or something like that. Just follow the instructions, and soon the digital torrents wash through your mailbox no more.

If you lost, erased, or otherwise can't find the information sheet, just search the mailing list database and find it. Send your "I wanna quit" message to the list administration address, not the submission address. You don't want everyone to know that you're quitting, do you?

Topic Hopping in the World Wide Web

It's huge. It's interconnected. It has a funny name. It's the most exciting, promising part of the Internet. It's also the newest addition to the America Online suite of Internet services. It's (electronic drum roll, please!) the *World Wide Web*.

The Web is a most amazing place. Where else can you find newspapers, technical information, company product catalogs, a library of folk song lyrics, far too many personal biographies, and a clock that displays the current time with fish sponges? (Not at the local mall, that's for sure.)

So just what *is* the World Wide Web? Like the Internet, it's not a single, unique "place" out there somewhere. Instead, the *Web* is a collection of interlinked *sites* containing millions of interlinked *pages*). The links between the various sites and pages are what make the Web a truly cool place.

Ever hear of something called hypertext? (You probably know what it is but don't know that it has a name — trust me for now and read on.) Although the term sounds like a book on a sugar high, *hypertext* is a neat way to organize information by *linking* related topics.

Suppose that you're reading an encyclopedia article about wombats and find out that the wombat is an Australian marsupial. Like most rational humans, your next thought is "I wonder what's for lunch." While foraging for food in the wilds of your refrigerator, you casually wonder precisely what a marsupial is. Abandoning your meal in search of knowledge, you pull out the M volume of the encyclopedia and look up marsupials. You discover that kangaroos are also marsupials, a fact that sends you racing for the A volume to determine whether the Australian government is aware that the country is brimming with marsupials.

If this keeps up much longer, you may as well move in with your encyclopedia.

What if you were using a hypertext encyclopedia on the computer? In the wombat article, the words *marsupial* and *Australian* would be highlighted to let you know that they're links to related articles. You click *marsupial* and immediately see the marsupial article. Another click takes you back to the first article so that you can explore the *Australian* link. Talk about fast information — you didn't even have time to eat!

The World Wide Web works just like the hypertext encyclopedia I described. The on-screen page offers information, plus it contains links to other Web pages. Those pages have links to still *other* Web pages. That cloud of links is where the name *Web* comes from — it's a Web of links. It's an information browser's dream come true.

A quick stop at the terminology shop

The Web just wouldn't be a computer thing if didn't have a whole slew of new terms and acronyms to baffle and amaze you. Here are the terms you need in order to make sense of the Web:

- ✔ A *Web page* is the smallest building block of the Web. It's an electronic page with information and links to other places on the Web.

- ✔ A *Web site* is a collection of Web pages. A site may have just a few pages or more than a hundred. It depends on the site's purpose and how much time, energy, and effort the site's builder puts into it.

- ✔ Every Web site has a *home page*. It's usually the first page you see when you visit that site. The term also refers to your own personal Web page (if you created one) or the page that appears when you start your *Web browser* (the software you use to browse the Web — see the next section for more info about the America Online browser).

- ✔ To find something on the Web, you need to know its *Uniform Resource Locator (URL)*. This special code tells the browser software what kind of site you're visiting. All World Wide Web URLs start with `http://`, although `gopher://` and `ftp://` sites are out there, too.

- ✔ *HTTP* is half the magic that makes the Web work. The abbreviation stands for *HyperText Transfer Protocol*. All you need to know about it is that every Web site address starts with `http://`.

- ✔ The other half of the Web's magical underpinnings is *HTML,* the HyperText Markup Language. HTML is the programming language of the World Wide Web. If something has `.html` (or sometimes `.htm`) appended to its name, the odds are that it's a Web page. In everyday conversation, HTML is a spelled abbreviation (such as "I'm working with H-T-M-L").

- ✔ *Links* (or *hyperlinks*) connect Web pages. When you *follow a link,* you click a button or a highlighted word and go careening off to another destination in the online world.

- ✔ Because having only one term for things often fosters understanding and comprehension, the World Wide Web goes by several monikers. It's also referred to as *the Web, WWW,* or *W3.*

For more information about how the Web works, see *The Internet For Dummies,* 7th Edition.

A couple of thoughts about Microsoft Internet Explorer versus Netscape Navigator

The software industry rarely sees a war like the Great Explorer versus Navigator Conflict. Microsoft, the reigning titan of software, stands toe-to-toe with Netscape, rogue challenger and Internet upstart while their respective Web browsers duke it out in head-to-head battle, feature by bloody feature. Suddenly, a new face appears outside the ring — egad, it's America Online!

Yes, in a surprise move, America Online leapt into the Microsoft/Netscape fray by purchasing Netscape lock, stock, and browser code. The pundits fretted, the stock market roared, and the crowd collectively said "Hmmm." It was a glorious day.

What does all this corporate activity mean to you? That's an excellent question. I wish that I had an excellent answer. Here's my insight, for what it's worth:

✔ The America Online 5.0 software relies on Internet Explorer, the Microsoft product, for all your Web-browsing needs. The America Online software and Internet Explorer are so tightly integrated, in fact, that nothing short of high explosives (or a 12-year-old hacker with a free afternoon) could pull them apart.

✔ The odds are good that, even though it owns the competition, America Online will keep Internet Explorer as its primary Web browser. (It's part of the deal to keep America Online prominently displayed in every copy of Windows that Microsoft sells.)

✔ Expect America Online to announce sometime in 2000 that you, the member, can replace Internet Explorer with Netscape Navigator *if you so desire*. Even though the default (Internet Explorer) remains the same, the challenger (Netscape Navigator) can sneak in through the back door.

As with any look into the future, these predictions represent only one nerd's opinion. Other computer people probably harbor different anticipations, but the odds are just as high that they're wrong, too.

Taking the Web browser for a spin

America Online did a great deal of work to integrate the World Wide Web as seamlessly as possible. It was quite a trick, too, because you need special software (called a *browser*) to look at Web pages.

The Web browser shown in Figure 17-2 is built right into the America Online access software. The navigation bar, just underneath the toolbar at the top of the screen, contains all the goodies you need to traverse the Web. Flip to Chapter 3 for all the details about the navigation bar.

✔ Don't be surprised if your America Online home page looks different from the ones in the figures. World Wide Web pages change all the time — it's a natural part of life.

✔ Your World Wide Web browser understands gopher and FTP sites, too. Some pages have links to Internet newsgroups (more about those later in this chapter), which, unfortunately, your browser *can't* understand. If you click a link and the browser displays a window that says something like `Cannot interpret link`, it's a clue that you just clicked something beyond the browser's comprehension. I hope that this difficulty gets fixed, but as long as I'm wishing, I'd like a pony, too.

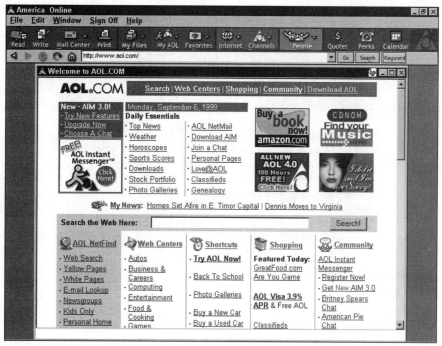

Figure 17-2:
The America Online Web browser, doing its Web browsing thing.

✔ The most common Web-oriented error you see is something to the effect of `Sorry, I can't contact that site` (although the computers don't say it that nicely — they intone more ominous things, such as `Error 404 Requested URL not found`). Double-check the address and try it again. If it *still* doesn't work, either America Online is too busy to be bothered with the Web right now or the Web page you're looking for isn't available at the moment. Either way, try again later.

- ✔ In case you're interested, the foam bath fish clock is at `www.savetz.com/ fishtime`.

- ✔ For some cool (and free) fun, try sending your friends some virtual flowers, an electronic postcard, or even a marvelously smelly goodie you find in a digital Dumpster. For a quick start, send virtual flowers to friends and loved ones from `www.iflowers.com` or `www.InternetFlorist.com` or visit `www.buildacard.com` to create a free online greeting card. When you're ready for more, flip over to Chapter 27 to pick up several other sites (including my favorite, the Digital Dumpster Diver).

- ✔ When you find sites you absolutely love, add them to your Favorite Places window by clicking in the little heart-on-a-page icon in the upper-right corner of the Web browser. For more about the Favorite Places window, see Chapter 7.

Opening a specific page

Even though the America Online home page offers lots of interesting links to explore, sometimes you want to hop directly to a particular page. Maybe you saw the address in a newspaper ad or TV commercial, or perhaps you're champing at the bit to see the fish clock. No matter where a Web address comes from, explaining it to America Online is a piece of cake.

Direct your attention to the new navigation bar (parked just under the tool-bar on your screen). To go directly to a particular page, click in the address area (the big, white box that probably says `Type keyword or Web address here`) of the navigation bar and then type the address of the page you want to see, just like you see in Figure 17-3. You don't need to include the `http://` part in front of the address, but it doesn't hurt if you feel like doing it anyway. When the address is in there, press Enter or click Go. Shortly, the built-in Web browser comes to life, displaying your page in glorious color.

Figure 17-3:
For faster service slide up to the navigation bar and order your Web page there.

Newsgroups Talk about the Craziest Things

The Internet newsgroups are a collection of, oh, about 30,000 discussion topics, from artificial intelligence applications (the `comp.ai` newsgroup) to the latest Kennedy assassination theories (try `alt.conspiracy.jfk` or `alt.assassination.jfk`). Newsgroup discussions get pretty wild sometimes, with ideas flying thick through the network. The language is often fairly (ahem) to the point, so if you're easily offended, you may not want to venture too far into the newsgroups.

I want to be *very* clear on this point because if you can't trust me, who can you trust? When you venture into the Internet newsgroups, you're leaving the friendly, trusting, caring community of America Online and venturing out into the wild, uncontrolled reality of the Internet. It's the difference between the lawns of suburban Indianapolis and the pavement of Manhattan. The Internet has no Terms of Service agreement — anything goes (and usually does).

That's not to say that the Internet has *no* rules, because there definitely are some. They're simple and unwritten, and they apply to almost every newsgroup:

- ✔ You're welcome to join the discussion, as long as you take the time to understand the newsgroup before contributing anything. Read a newsgroup for *at least* a week or two before posting something of your own. Also read the newsgroup's Frequently Asked Questions document (known as the *FAQ*). If you can't find the FAQ anywhere in the current newsgroup postings, post a message asking someone to point you toward it.

- ✔ Stick to the topic of the newsgroup. Posting get-rich-quick schemes and business advertisements to the newsgroups is in very poor taste. People do it, but they're the exception, not the rule.

- ✔ You may agree or disagree with anything that's said. You may agree or disagree as loudly as you want. If you disagree, focus on the point — don't degenerate into personal attacks.

- ✔ You may *not* question a person's right to say whatever comes to mind. Yes, some points of view are, shall we say, distasteful, but some people feel that way about what you and I think, too.

- ✔ If someone disagrees with you rather abusively (known on the Internet as *flaming*), the best thing you can do is ignore the message. If you can reply in a level-headed tone, that's fine, but it probably won't change what the other person thinks. It's best to let the flames die down and just go on with other conversations.

By now, I hope that I've scared you a little about the Internet newsgroups. Well, *scared* really isn't the right term. How about *educated* instead? The newsgroups really aren't as wild and vicious a place as I'm making them out to be, but you need to understand that they also aren't part of America Online — they're completely outside the mores of the America Online world. If you visualize yourself stepping from your neighborhood into a completely foreign environment every time you use the newsgroups, you have the right frame of mind. The newsgroups work much like the America Online discussion areas. They're different from mailing lists, though, because mailing lists come *to* your mailbox; you have to *go* to the newsgroups. Check out *The Internet For Dummies,* 7th Edition for a more complete explanation of newsgroups.

Finding and subscribing to a newsgroup

As I've said, you have literally thousands of newsgroups to choose from — and America Online carries them all. To keep things from getting too out of hand, the newsgroups are organized into categories by topic. Table 17-1 briefly explains the main categories. Other categories certainly exist, but I'll let you explore those on your own. Each category contains a bunch of related newsgroups (or, in the case of the alt and misc categories, a bunch of newsgroups related only because someone said so).

Table 17-1	Newsgroup Category Names
Name	*Description*
alt	Alternative — home of freewheeling discussions on just about any topic
aol	America Online — articles of interest to America Online members
biz	Business — topics generally relating to business on the Internet
comp	Computers and computer science — where the nerds hang out
misc	Miscellaneous — all the stuff that doesn't fit under one of the other hierarchies
news	Network news and information — discussion and information-only groups about the Internet itself
rec	Hobbies and recreation — think sports and hobbies, and you have this one figured out

Name	Description
sci	Science and research — if you thought that nerds were in the comp group, just wait until you look in here
soc	Society and social commentary — focused mainly toward both sociologists in the audience
talk	Talk — talk, talk, talk, talk (get the idea?)

Your search for an interesting newsgroup starts by guessing which hierarchy the topic belongs in and then browsing through that hierarchy's available newsgroups. Simple enough, right? Here's how to do it step by step:

1. **Choose Internet⇨Newsgroups from the toolbar or use keyword** Newsgroups.

   The Newsgroups window pops up.

2. **Click Add Newsgroups.**

   The Add Newsgroups Categories window appears.

3. **Choose a category.**

   Scroll through the list of available categories until you find one that looks interesting. Double-click a hierarchy to see which newsgroups it contains.

   A window listing all the category's newsgroups elbows its way to the screen.

4. **Scroll through all the listed newsgroups, find one that looks interesting, and double-click its entry in the list.**

   Yet another window, which may or may not tell you anything helpful about the newsgroup, appears looking something like Figure 17-4.

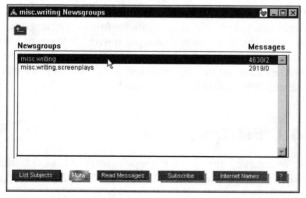

Figure 17-4: Hmm — a writing newsgroup. Sound interesting.

5. **Sample some messages and subscribe to the group if you like what you see.**

For a look at the messages in this newsgroup, click Read Messages. When you're sold, click Subscribe to include the newsgroup on your subscription list. To pretend that you never saw the newsgroup in the first place, just close the window and go about your business.

Subscribing to a newsgroup may take a minute or two to allow the America Online computer to think, ponder, and snicker at its ability to make a human wait for something.

For more about reading messages in a newsgroup, see the next section.

6. **When the confirmation dialog box pops up, click OK to reassure it that you know what you're talking about and that you really want to read that newsgroup. When the "group preferences" dialog box appears, click Save to make it go away, too.**

After a great deal of digital consternation, America Online displays a brief dialog box saying that the newsgroup is now on your list. Click OK to make the confirmation dialog box go away and leave you alone.

Likewise, the "group preferences" dialog offers some advanced tools for simplifying your newsgroup experience. (In one of those odd paradoxes of technology, the tool for making newsgroups easier is itself almost too complex to use.)

For now, don't worry about the "group preferences" settings. You can always get back to the window by clicking on the newsgroup name in the Read My Newsgroups window and then clicking the Preferences button.

7. **Subscribe to more newsgroups if you want.**

To subscribe to more newsgroups, just close the last few windows (click the upper-right corner of the window) until you work your way back to the Add Newsgroups window.

Congratulations — you did it!

If someone describes a marvelous newsgroup and gives you the Internet name of it (which looks like `alt.folklore.urban`), you can use the Expert Add button and skip this whole menu-driven process. However, you must know the exact name, complete with all the required (and occasionally odd) punctuation marks. The Expert Add button is also handy for checking out newsgroups recommended by one of those clever Internet books that I suggest you buy.

Reading messages

Subscribing is, of course, only the first step. Your next task is finding time to read all the stuff you subscribe to. Unlike mailing lists, newsgroup messages don't stack up in your e-mail box — they collect in some mysterious place deep within America Online. To read what's new, you have to pay another visit to the Newsgroups window. Here's what to do:

1. **Choose Internet➪Newsgroup from the toolbar or use keyword** Newsgroups.

   The Newsgroups window pops up.

2. **Click Read My Newsgroups.**

   After a few pensive moments of waiting, the Read My Newsgroups window pops into being. It shows the name of the newsgroup, the number of messages you haven't read, and the total number of messages in that newsgroup.

   Even if you subscribe to only one or two newsgroups, your newsgroups list comes preset with some suggested reading, courtesy of America Online.

3. **Double-click a newsgroup to see what's new.**

   A window that's more a scrolling list than anything else (see Figure 17-5) pops into being. The window shows the article title and the number of responses in the *thread* (that's the newsgroup term for *discussion*).

   To see all the articles in the newsgroup (whether you've read them or not), click the newsgroup name and then click List All Subjects.

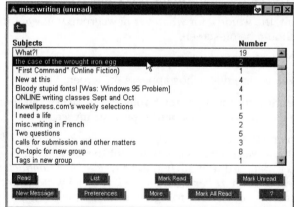

Figure 17-5:
So many
articles, so
little time.

4. **To read an article, double-click its title.**

   A window containing the message text opens. Read to your heart's content and then close the window after you're done.

To reply to a message, click Reply to Group. To see the next message in the thread, click the button labeled Message ->. For the preceding message, click the button labeled <- Message. If you're thirsty, get something to drink.

If you have a specific question for the person who wrote the article, click E-Mail to Author rather than post a reply to the newsgroup.

5. **When nothing else looks interesting enough to read, click Mark All Read.**

   Click OK in the dialog box that wonders whether you really want to do that.

   This last step tells America Online to pretend that you read all the messages in the newsgroup. Therefore, you can quickly tell which messages are new the next time you wander through.

Contributing something

Reading a newsgroup is fun, but soon enough, you decide that it's time to post a few messages of your own. Adding a message to a newsgroup isn't hard, but it does take a couple more steps than your average e-mail message. Here's what to do:

1. **Pretend that you're going to read the messages in a newsgroup, and go through Steps 1, 2, and 3 in the preceding section.**

   At this point, the window for whatever newsgroup you want to post an article to should be on-screen.

2. **Click the New Message button.**

   A Post New Message dialog box appears on-screen.

3. **Type a descriptive subject in the Subject area, press Tab to move down into the Message block, and type your message.**

   A check box marked Use Signature (set in Preferences) sits underneath the Message block. If you want to sign all your newsgroups postings in a standard way, such as *John Doe — Ace Contractor, Incorporated,* or *Sven, Lover of Adventure!,* you can write your signature once and then check the box to sign your name the same way with each posting you send.

   Oh — by the way — although it says that the signature is set in global preferences, you actually find it under the Set Preferences button in the main Newsgroups window.

4. **When the message looks groovy, click Send.**

Click OK when the system asks whether you're serious about posting the article. Click Cancel if you suddenly decide that the world would be a better place without your message in the newsgroup.

When you're writing for a newsgroup, be brief and to the point. Say what you want to say and then stop. Don't go on and on and on. Whatever you do, don't ramble. I used to ramble, but I don't anymore. And it's a good thing, too, what with all the newsgroup postings I write these days.

Unsubscribing from a newsgroup

Getting out of a newsgroup takes a whole lot less time and effort than getting into one. In fact, it's so quick that you'll hardly believe it:

1. **Open the Newsgroups window with either keyword** Newsgroups **or by selecting Internet⇨Newsgroups from the toolbar.**

   The Newsgroups window reports for duty.

2. **Click the Read My Newsgroups button.**

   The now-familiar Read My Newsgroups window appears, which you shouldn't confuse with the George Bush "Read My Lips" window or the William Shatner "Read My Books" window.

3. **Click the name of the newsgroup that you want to kick off your sub-scription list and then click Remove.**

   With only a moment of digital concentration, America Online unsub-scribes you from the selected newsgroup and announces the fact in a little dialog box. Click OK to make the box go away.

Automating your newsgroups

Here's a little piece of advice about getting involved in newsgroups: The words *addictive* and *newsgroups* naturally belong in the same sentence. Although they're not as bad as the People Connection chat rooms, following a newsgroup does rack up your online charges if you use one of the America Online measured billing methods.

Does that mean that you shouldn't do the newsgroup thing? Not at all! You should just do it *smarter* and *quicker* by using an Automatic AOL session — the same familiar technique that prevents your voluminous e-mail traffic from overwhelming your credit card each month. With some careful tweaking, the messages from your favorite newsgroups stream right into your mailbox just like your e-mail does. How could it possibly get better? Actually, I'm glad you asked.

Frankly, it could get better if doing newsgroups through Automatic AOL were slightly easier than disarming a thermonuclear device with a bobby pin and a bag of nacho chips. Unfortunately for you, it seems that the bomb folks moonlighted on the newsgroup Automatic AOL design team.

Before giving this task a try, you must thoroughly understand both the newsgroups you want to keep up with and your America Online Filing Cabinet (having a degree in nuclear engineering doesn't hurt either). Newsgroups are covered in the preceding pages; notes about the Filing Cabinet reside in Chapter 8. The details of making it all work are too complex to attempt here — trust me. If you're still convinced that flashing the newsgroups into your computer sounds like fun, follow these steps for all the details:

1. **Use keyword** Newsgroups **to open the newsgroups window.**

   As expected, the newsgroups window appears.

2. **Click the Read Offline button.**

   The Choose Newsgroups window hops into action.

3. **In the Choose Newsgroups window, click the little question mark button in the lower-right corner.**

   Yet another window piles on the stack. But don't fret — you're done. A text window steps forth, revealing the secrets of this mystic feature.

If merely getting to the instructions sounds like a journey across the Himalayas (with or without a nuclear device), don't attempt to do newsgroups through Automatic AOL. The steps you just scaled were only the foothills — the peak is still waaaaay up there somewhere. Good luck, brave newsgrouper (I'm going back down the mountain for a nap).

A brief word about parental controls

The newsgroups offer a wild array of useful and interesting information, but some of the stuff could send a shipload of sailors into a collective blush. Thanks to the Parental Controls section, you can prevent such a thing from happening at your house (assuming you have a shipload of sailors huddled around your America Online account).

The parental controls for newsgroups are available under the cleverly labeled Parental Controls button in the Newsgroups window. These controls let you do the following:

✔ Block the Expert Add feature, which limits a screen name to only the newsgroups that America Online chooses to list under the Add Newsgroups button.

    ✔ Block access to the newsgroups entirely.

    ✔ Prevent program and file downloads from the newsgroups.

    ✔ Block specific newsgroups you choose.

    ✔ Block newsgroups with "adult" content.

    ✔ Block any newsgroup that contains certain words in its name.

    ✔ Grant a screen name access to the complete list of available newsgroups.

If you have a child using America Online, I *highly* recommend blocking the Expert Add feature for that child's screen name. You may want to go further, but you can worry about that later.

Because little eyes and fingers often get into the darnedest places, America Online offers a strong, flexible group of parental controls. For all the details about your online child-management options, flip to the section "Parental Controls: Taking Away the Online Car Keys" in Chapter 6.

FTP Downloading for the Nerd at Heart

If you think that the file libraries in America Online are a hoot, you haven't seen *anything* yet. Welcome to *File Transfer Protocol,* more commonly known as *FTP.* FTP is the Internet's answer to the Copy command. And let me tell you, it's certainly one answer.

You're about to enter (bring up geeky music in the background) the Technoid Zone, so keep a pocket protector handy. Working with FTP definitely isn't like using gopher or the Internet newsgroups. You're interacting directly with computers all over the world without the benefit of software like gopher to protect you. It's you against the computer. If using the Macintosh Finder or Windows File Manager to track down an errant file on your disk drive makes you queasy, you don't want to try FTP.

You can use the America Online FTP service in two ways: by going to the built-in FTP sites or by typing an address on your own. I suggest using the built-in options at first because you can be relatively sure that they work. After you have some experience under your electronic belt, get brave and flip to Chapter 27 for some other FTP sites to try.

    ✔ I'm deliberately a little vague in my how-to-use-FTP instructions later in this chapter. The reason is simple: FTP really *is* more advanced than the other Internet services. You need to understand a lot of nerdy stuff, such as subdirectories and file compression (including ZIP files and many, many other kinds), before FTP is of much use to you.

✔ If you're absolutely *dying* to discover FTP, check out the Using FTP option in the main FTP window (keyword **FTP**), the FTP help section of Member Services (keyword **Nethelp**), or the Internet help section of the America Online Web site (`www.aol.com/nethelp`).

✔ Trust *nothing* you download from the Internet via FTP. Assume from the start that it's completely virus-infested, like a little digital epidemic just waiting to break loose on your computer. Virus-check absolutely *everything* that comes to roost in your computer from the Internet.

✔ Yes, I'm serious about the virus checks. I do them myself.

✔ Watch out for files with odd extensions like `.Z`, `.gz`, or `.tar.z`. They are compressed files, but they're *not* normal .sit or .zip files. To decompress them requires special software, the patience of Job, and often the rest of your day. If you're intent on trying anyway, get a copy of either GZip or MacGZip from the `/pub/compress` subdirectory of `ftp.aol.com` (which just happens to be on the FTP menu). If that last sentence didn't make *any* sense to you, don't try to mess with these files.

✔ FTP is also called *anonymous FTP* by Those Who Know. That's a fancy way to say that you don't need a special access code or anything to download files. Because the computer sending the files doesn't know who you are, it's an anonymous service. Aren't those computer nerds clever?

All it takes to use FTP is a strong stomach for the technical side of life and these instructions:

1. **Dive into the FTP system by selecting Internet⇨FTP from the toolbar, or with keyword** FTP.

   The FTP (File Transfer Protocol) window opens.

2. **Click the Go To FTP button. The Anonymous FTP window opens.**

   Finally, the File Transfer Protocol window shows its face (see Figure 17-6).

Figure 17-6: The Anonymous FTP window offers to whisk you away to File Transfer Land.

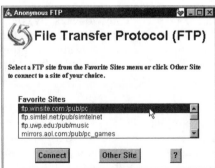

3. Scroll through the Favorite Sites list and double-click one that sounds interesting.

After a moment or two (or perhaps three, if the Internet is having a busy night), another window pops up, explaining where you're about to go. Click OK and proceed directly to the directory listing of whatever computer you just attached yourself to (see Figure 17-7).

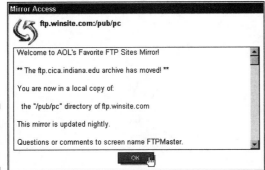

Figure 17-7: Welcome to winsite.

Mirror Access

ftp.winsite.com:/pub/pc

Welcome to AOL's Favorite FTP Sites Mirror!

** The ftp.cica.indiana.edu archive has moved! **

You are now in a local copy of:

the "/pub/pc" directory of ftp.winsite.com

This mirror is updated nightly.

Questions or comments to screen name FTPMaster.

OK

4. If something looks interesting, double-click it.

Different things happen depending on the icon that's next to the item. If the icon is a file folder icon, that entry is a directory; double-clicking it brings up a new window showing you what's in there. If the icon is a document, a dialog box pops up and offers you a View File Now button. To view the document without downloading it, click the button. If the icon is a bunch of disks, you're looking at a program or a compressed file that's available for downloading. Sometimes you also see the funny-looking handshake icon; it stands for a pointer to a particular subdirectory.

5. Keep poking around and have a good time.

Part IV
Going Your Own Way

The 5th Wave   By Rich Tennant

"IT'S ANOTHER DEEP SPACE PROBE FROM EARTH,
SEEKING CONTACT FROM EXTRATERRESTRIALS.
I WISH THEY'D JUST INCLUDE AN E-MAIL ADDRESS."

In this part . . .

With 20 million members (and more joining every day), 19 channels of information, education and entertainment, and hundreds of bulletin boards and chat rooms populated by interesting people from around the world, you never lack options on America Online. Where do you start? What should you see first?

If you have questions like these, you're in the right place. Each chapter in Part IV looks at America Online from a particular point of view, with suggested destinations galore. Everywhere you look, it offers ways to solve problems and actually get things done in your life.

Pretty radical, huh?

Browse through the chapters and see what you can find. They're designed to draw you in, fill your head with ideas, sweep up a little as long as it's in there, and send you on your way with a neat, tidy mind. Use your creativity to take my suggestions and find still better ways to do stuff.

Chapter 18

The Student's Guide to Online Life

*E*ducation is where you find it these days, and you can find a great deal of instructional goodies around America Online. When you're stumped with a problem, digging for facts, or trying to make a perfect (or at least airworthy) kite, plenty of online resources await your call for help, no matter what time of the day or night you yelp.

This chapter, like the others in this part, provides direction rather than answers. It offers some suggestions to get you started but encourages you to think creatively and come up with your own resources as well. I know you can do it — now *do it!*

Places to Start

Even in a digital wonderland such as America Online, you still have to start somewhere. A couple of places stand out as excellent jumping-off points:

  ✔ The hub of any campus is its student center (after all, that's where the food is). It works the same way in online student life, thanks to the Teens channel (keyword **Teens**, as shown in Figure 18-1). As the name implies, this one window offers links and resources for everyone traipsing through the tumultuous teens.

✔ Don't just sit there — Do Something! Find out what Do Something, a national nonprofit youth action and training group, is doing in your area. You've always wanted to change the world. Here's your chance! Find out about the Do Something award winners, share your dreams on the message boards, or read about what others are doing. (The keyword, in case you haven't guessed, is **Do Something**.)

✔ What *can't* you find on the Internet these days? This international network of networks is definitely worth a look. America Online offers lots of Internet services through its Internet Connection (keyword **Internet**). See Chapter 17 for all the details.

Figure 18-1: Celebrate teen life, in full color and at full volume, in the Teens channel (keyword **Teens**).

Getting Help When You Need It

When you're stuck on a homework problem and need some help to get over the hump, fire up the computer and sign on to America Online. Look for your much-needed help in these areas:

✔ When tough homework is on your mind (eww — get it off, get it off!), drop by Ask-A-Teacher (keyword **Ask-A-Teacher**) for help and advice. To reach assistance from the main Ask-A-Teacher window, first choose your grade range (elementary, junior high and high school, or college). Each level's section provides discussion boards and tutoring rooms, plus a database of previously answered questions on nearly any subject. If you need help with a complicated or unusual topic, e-mail a teacher with your question, and in the best of all worlds, a real teacher responds to your query within about 48 hours.

✔ If studying doesn't come naturally, check out the Study Skills service (keyword **Study Skills**). These folks aren't hawking some elixir that unlocks the Secrets of the Ancient Students. Instead, they have a sound, step-by-step approach you can use to recognize your strengths, identify your weaknesses, and build on both to improve your skills. Although the company has some books available for sale, you can use its method without buying anything.

✔ Need a topic for that research paper? Flip to Chapter 13 for direction to the numerous America Online search tools. These doorways lead to an almost endless supply of online information (and almost all of it is free).

✔ The annual science fair looms before you, and you can't think of a great project to save your life. America Online comes to your rescue again, with science fairs (keyword **Science Fair**). Get project ideas, tips for making your project (and its presentation) super, and Web sites where you can begin your research.

✔ Looking at life through another's eyes takes an open mind and an open heart. Of course, it also requires another open-minded person for discussion (after all, unless two of you are in there, it's tough to get a second opinion from yourself on much of anything). Whether you need insight for a creative writing project, a term paper, preparation for a drama course, or simply a desire to expand your personal horizons, gain a taste of life through new eyes in the Ethnicity area (keyword **Ethnicity**).

✔ Stuck trying to understand the *Aeneid?* (Goodness knows I was.) Turn to Barron's Booknotes (keyword **Barron's**) for downloadable study guides and plot synopses. And don't forget the granddaddy of study guides, the indomitable CliffsNotes series, at `www.cliffsnotes.com`.

A Trip to the Virtual Library

Research was never easier. Between the online encyclopedia (keyword **Comptons**), the magazines (keyword **Newsstand**), and the whole Research & Learn channel (keyword **Research**), you may not have to look anywhere else:

✔ Some things in life are free, some cost money, and some tempt you with free stuff in the *hope* of ultimately costing you money. The Electric Library at AOL (keyword **ELP**) lives in this last category. This helpful service includes free searching in an incredibly broad magazine and newspaper database. The search results provide the article title and publication details. (I particularly love the *recurring theme* feature, which automatically picks out topics that consistently appear in your search results.) As you may guess, the *pay* part of the equation begins when you want to read the articles online. America Online offers 30 days of free access when you subscribe. At the time I wrote this book, a one-year subscription cost just under $60, which isn't a bad deal when you factor in all the research trips to the library that you *don't* need to make now.

✔ The University of California Extension Online (keyword **UCAOL**) offers an incredible link collection in its Public Library area (click the Public Library button in the main University of California window). Invest some time (well, a *lot* of time, because this area is big) to check out what's available — it's a gold mine!

✔ An even broader area of the Internet is the World Wide Web (keyword **WWW**). Start out with AOL NetFind (keyword **NetFind**) and then try NetFind's Time Savers Reference Source for links to online encyclopedias, reference desks, and translation dictionaries.

✔ The Internet newsgroups are another great source of information and discussion. Use keyword **Newsgroups** and then try either Add Newsgroups or Search All Newsgroups to see what tweaks your fancy. Chapter 17 covers the Newsgroup beat, so check there for more tips.

✔ When you're looking for obscure information about an even more obscure topic, you need a resource worthy of the search. On America Online, this task calls for a trip to The Straight Dope (`www.straight-dope.com`). Find out whether kosher pickles are really kosher, why ketchup dissolves aluminum foil, and where belly button lint comes from. (Okay — many respectable questions are in there too, but I figure that the odds of your giving the place a try are better if it sounds like more fun than a trip to the local library's Reference Desk and Silence Research Facility.)

Thinking about That Job

If you're over the age of eight, you're probably starting to think about that career at the end of your school years. America Online has some great places that can help you figure out what you want to be when you grow up. (I *still* don't know what I want to be.)

✔ The College Preparation area (keyword **College Prep**) offers all kinds of information and services aimed at the high school and college crowd. The gems of the area include insights into the admissions process, a searchable database of school reviews, and descriptions of the SAT, ACT, GRE, and several other acronym-encrusted tests. If you're headed for college, stop here first.

✔ Here's one I wished for back in college. The RSP Funding Focus (keyword **RSP**) offers searchable information about scholarships, internships, grants, and more. Check out the alluringly-named Money Database button for more details.

✔ If you're considering career options, knowing what the job entails is helpful. Read up on hundreds of different careers in the America Online Career Center's occupational profiles database (keyword **Career Finder**).

✔ Find out what real people do in a particular industry and browse resources designed for full-time workers in Career Center (keyword **Career Center**) and the Professional Forums (keyword **Professional Forums**).

✔ Researching a particular industry or company? Investment Research (keyword **Company Research**) contains stock reports and other financial information for recent years. For up-to-the-moment (or at least *through the past two weeks*) news from Reuters and the Associated Press, use the Search Company News by Ticker system (keyword **Company News**).

As If One School Weren't Enough

If you're one of those people who just wants to *learn, learn, learn,* good for you. The ever-changing technological workplace of today makes constant education (and reeducation) a vital part of every career. Whether your aspirations are for a new degree, some enhanced understanding, or just for the heck of it, America Online has some educational opportunities for you:

✔ For computer know-how (particularly in the programming arena), check out the noncredit (and no-fee) computer classes in the Computing Online Classroom (keyword **Online Classroom**). You can find classes listed for everything from DOS for beginners to programming in Visual Basic 5.0.

✔ The Online Campus (keyword **Online Campus**) offers "personal enrichment" classes in almost any topic for a small fee — usually $20 to $30.

✔ Earn a certificate in computer graphics online from the Corcoran School of Art (keyword **Corcoran**). These courses are less expensive than traditional classroom instruction, but their costs still fall within the ballpark range of college tuition.

✔ Register for college credit courses online. Offered by the University of California (keyword **UCAOL**), the course catalog includes classes in the arts and humanities, business, computer science, hazardous materials management, natural sciences, and social sciences. Choose More Courses to jump to the program's Web site, where various high school courses are also listed. Fees for high school courses hover around $200 per course; college course fees range from $300 to $500 per course.

Time to Relax and Recharge

Remember to have some fun. All work and no play makes you a financially secure, crotchety old nerd (and California's got enough of them already). Take some time to meet people, play games, and enjoy your online life:

✔ Three easy options right off the bat are Lifestyles (keyword **Lifestyles**), Interests (keyword **Interests**) and the People Connection (keyword **People**). Browse around and see what's out there — and who.

✔ The Gamers forum (keyword **Gaming**) is home to all kinds of interesting pursuits, including computer games, board games, role-playing, online simulation games, and collectible card games.

✔ If you love music, theatre, or dance, mark Extreme Culture (keyword **Extreme Culture**, as shown in Figure 18-2) on your Favorite Places list. This area offers a searchable national arts calendar, student discussion boards, scheduled chats with both arts professionals and college arts faculty, and lots more. Take a poll, win a prize, sign up for the newsletter, or just relax with people who share your passion for performance.

✔ Teens who love to program computers find a home at Youth Tech (keyword **YT**). Learn the answer to that sticky coding problem in the chat shack, read computer game reviews, or find some top Web sites — whether you're looking for school help or techy news sites.

✔ If fashion is your thing, curl up with the online edition of *Elle* magazine (keyword **Elle**). Get the scoop on the latest in looking great, feeling good, and emptying your checkbook (sorry — that was a father's perspective).

Figure 18-2:
The arts are where you find them — there's plenty to find in Extreme Culture.

Chapter 19

Parenting Your Offspring (In Diapers, Online, or In Between the Two)

Some days, I think that the sole goal of parenting is to make sure that everybody arrives at the dinner table at roughly the same time. On other days, the incredible size of the job looms over me like a monster in a bad 1950s horror film. And I don't think that I'm alone in my concerns.

Judging by the resources available to parents through America Online, it looks like parents are finally going to get some help. This chapter points out the best of the resources and gives you a gentle push along the way.

All the resources in the world aren't any good unless you take the time to use them.

Keeping Up with the Kids

We parents have to learn about all this parenting stuff the hard way — by trying something, either getting it right or messing it up, and then trying again. America Online gives parents some unique opportunities to simplify this shoddy arrangement and share information and experiences with one another (and to voice opinions about topics of concern):

✔ The Families channel (keyword **Families**) ushers you into the America Online parental information refuge. Start here for links to just about every family-related goodie on America Online (and a bunch of Net-based places, too).

✔ Take some time to find out about the Internet and what it offers. As a parent, you need to understand the wonderful resources on the Net and comprehend the potential dangers as well. The America Online Internet Center (keyword **Internet**) is the place to start. If you're completely new to the Internet, take a stroll through Chapter 17 for a bout with the basics.

✔ Next on the hit list is The National Parenting Center (www.tnpc.com). This area contains some great articles and parents' discussion areas. When you don't know where to ask a question or make a comment, try posting a message here.

✔ If you're a home-schooling family, link up and swap tips with others in the Home Schooling forum (keyword **Homeschooling**. For still more informational wellsprings, search for the term **homeschool** in NetFind (keyword **Netfind**), Yahoo (www.yahoo.com), AltaVista (www.altavista.com), or any of the other Internet search engines mentioned in the Search Engines table (Table 13-1), back in Chapter 13.

Protecting Your Online Kids

This section of the book isn't particularly funny, but it *is* very important. Please take time to read it and then act on what you find.

You already know the bad news: Some sick people are in the online realm, and some of them are trolling for kids. The good news is that you *can* protect your kids — you're not powerless in this frightening mess.

Although it's important that you, as a concerned parent, *do something* to protect your children; knee-jerk reactions are *not* the answer. Remember that America Online and the Internet are much like sprawling digital cities. Just as you don't want the kids visiting certain parts of your own town, you also find areas of the online world that are definitely for adults only. Canceling your account or erasing the access software doesn't protect your kids — doing so just teaches them fear. Instead, you need to interact with your children, help them understand this crazy online world, teach them how to respond appropriately, and take the responsibility that's yours as a parent.

With all this in mind, here are some ideas, tips, and suggestions for keeping your online kids safe; please take them to heart:

✔ **Educate your kids.** Remind them that just because the person they met online sounds like a kid (or even claims to be one) doesn't mean that it's necessarily the truth.

✔ **Teach your kids what not to say online.** Make sure that they never give out their address or phone number. Never.

✔ **Observe what your kids do.** Ask to join them for an evening online. If they know more about how this stuff works than you do, ask them to teach you. If you ask, be ready to take notes and really learn — don't merely nod and comment about how amazingly far technology has come. Think of the online system as a hobby your children enjoy. Your goal is to share that hobby with them.

✔ **Report questionable occurrences.** If your child tells you about being approached in a questionable way, get the user ID of the person your child was interacting with and report it to the online service. Those folks will help you deal with the problem.

✔ **Take the time to find out about the online world.** Reading this book is a great start — congratulations! Beyond that, invest the time to understand America Online's Parental Controls (keyword **Parental Controls**). These controls block kids from various parts of the service, define which America Online software features (like Instant Messages and chat) they can and can't use, and limit World Wide Web access. You choose how much is blocked; they can explore everything else. Look at Chapter 6 for the details of setting and tweaking the Parental Controls.

✔ **Encourage your kids' offline activities and friendships.** Offer to throw a pizza party, game night, or movie extravaganza for your children and their friends. The cost is minimal, but the rewards are many.

✔ **Don't presume that bad things _won't_ happen to your kids.** Denial is a marvelous breeding ground for the worst of problems.

✔ **On the flip side, don't automatically assume that everyone your child meets online is a wacko.** Lots of real kids just like yours populate the online world.

✔ **Don't interrogate your children about their online use.** Be interested, but don't accuse. Show interest, but don't presume guilt. You didn't like it as a child, and neither will they.

Have Some Fun? What's That?

If your kids can have fun on America Online, why shouldn't you? Hmm . . . I can't think of a reason. America Online makes family outings a snap, and offers lots of tips for some parental fun, too. Here's a quick look at great places to start:

✔ I love movies (particularly when they're at the dollar cinema). So much happens behind the scenes, so much money is spent to create the masterpiece, so many people with odd job titles — it almost makes you want to take part in the movie biz yourself. Wander over to Movies (keyword **Movies**) and catch some of the excitement. As Figure 19-1 shows, this area is packed with movie and video information. Read about new flicks, join a movie chat, and catch up on the industry buzz from this window.

✔ For a more parental twist on movies, check out some family movie guides. Start with the Entertainment Asylum Family area (keyword **EA Family**), which reviews movies, home videos, and even TV programs. For a different perspective, visit Parent Soup's Fun and Games area (keyword **PS Fun**, then double-click the Be A Movie Reviewer item in window's list box. On the Internet side of things, browse through the Family Style Web site at www.familystyle.com. This site provides movie and TV reviews, discussion areas, and a lot more.

✔ Despite my love of movies, my top pick for entertainment is still live theatre. To keep up on the latest in Broadway, off-Broadway, regional, and even international professional theatre, check out Playbill Online (keyword **Playbill**). For a more rounded arts experience (including dance, music, art, and theatre), take a peek at CultureFinder (keyword **CultureFinder**).

✔ If you happen to live in Chicago or Florida, you can order tickets to the theater (or any other events you want tickets to) through Ticketmaster Online (keyword **Ticketmaster**). For the rest of us, there's the Ticketmaster Web site (also available through keyword **Ticketmaster**) with its searchable list of all the events that Ticketmaster covers around the country, plus the electronic ticket window at CultureFinder. For Broadway tickets, check out Telecharge (www.telecharge.com).

✔ Few things are more relaxing than a little shopping excursion. Why not wander the online Gifts selection (keyword **Gifts**), Computing Superstore (keyword **CSS**), or any of the other vendors in the America Online Shopping channel (keyword **Shopping**)? Heck, I'm getting relaxed just writing about it.

✔ To unwind after a hard day's work, pick up a new hobby or follow an old one in the Interests areas (keyword **Interests**).

✔ If you're a crossword fan, put down that pencil, throw out the newspaper, and give electronic crosswords a try. For a new puzzle every day, try out the crossword in My News (keyword **My News** and then click the Crossword link in the *Essentials* section).

✔ Want something a little more interactive? Try the People Connection (keyword **People**), the America Online interactive chat area. Also check out the Gamers forum (keyword **Gaming**) for all kinds of online games and game clubs.

Figure 19-1:
Come here
when you
want to
know what's
new at the
movies.

Bringing School Home to Meet the Kids

Who says that you have to leave the house to get a good education? You don't need to leave for entertainment — and there's no reason to take off in the name of learning stuff. Home schooling is growing fast all over the country, as parents look for quality alternatives to the Education-Theory-of-the-Month Club masquerading as the local public school.

America Online offers lots of resources to support and connect home schoolers. Here are some to get you started:

✔ A good general place to start is the Homeschooling forum (keyword **Homeschooling**), although you probably found this one on your own. The area features regularly scheduled chats, a wide variety of lively discussions, and links to education-related areas within America Online (like the Lesson Plan Library and the Academic Assistance Center).

✔ Home schoolers come from all backgrounds and beliefs, as the various education discussion boards around the system definitely show. From the volume of postings, it seems that the Christian home schoolers talk the most (on the Christianity Online message boards, use keyword **COMB**, scroll down the list, click Schools and Jobs, and then click Homeschooling). Also look for education discussions in the Islamic (keyword **Islam**) and Jewish (keyword **Jewish**) forums, plus many of the other ethnic focus areas behind keyword **Ethnicity**.

Doing the Work-at-Home Thing

More and more families have at least one parent working at home. This exciting lifestyle change has lots of positive aspects, but it also brings some, uh, *challenges.*

One of the hard parts of working at home is feeling disconnected from people — missing the impromptu hallway meetings (also known as chats) and unscheduled personal refreshment intervals (or coffee breaks) that often precede them. America Online has some great places to build a group of friends and acquaintances who understand this crazy lifestyle. Here are my top picks (although one is biased, I admit):

- ✔ Check out the home-business discussions in the Business Know-How forum (keyword **Business Know-How**) for freewheeling idea swaps about all aspects of home-work life, including starting, tuning, expanding, and enhancing the business of your dreams. If online business interests you, visit the Workplace channel's Online Business area (keyword **Online Business**).

- ✔ If you're having a sudden attack of the lonelies, jump into the People Connection (keyword **People**) and see who you can see. The rooms are always hopping, even in the middle of the day and night. Honestly, I don't know what all these people do for work, but whatever it is, it pays their America Online bills.

- ✔ Fellow writers, check out a few of the scheduled chats in the Writers Club (keyword **Writers**) and focus on romance, historical, poetry, technical, or the business of writing. Use the keyword to bring up the Writers Club window and then click the Chat button to open the Writers Chat window. Double-click Writers Club Chat Schedule for all the chat and conference information.

Chapter 20

The Well-Connected Teacher

In This Chapter

▶ Finding resources for learning

▶ Tracking down cool artwork

▶ Introducing your class to America Online

▶ Guiding your career

▶ Looking down the road

Creating an interesting, involving, and intellectually stimulating classroom environment isn't easy these days. Arguably, it *never* was easy, but when you're dealing with attention spans measured in seconds, I think that cranks up the old challenge meter a few notches.

Whether you teach at a public or private school or you're leading a home school, America Online has plenty of resources just waiting for you. This chapter points out the highlights, offers you some ideas to start the creativity gears grinding, and sends you off toward other relevant chapters of this book. Keep your mind open as you read through this chapter — you can find a way to use almost *everything* educationally.

The Ultimate Learning Resource Center

As resource centers go, I don't think that you can beat America Online. It's open 24 hours a day, it's stocked with everything from lesson plans to clip art, and it has a friendly face that doesn't yell at you when things go wrong (unlike many resource center keepers I've met in the past).

Here are some ideas to begin your quest for resource material:

> ✔ Take a look at the Research & Learn channel (keyword **Research**) for online forums, reference material, and Web sites that concentrate on content areas, such as history, science, business, health, geography, reading, and writing. Take a look at Figure 20-1 to see your many options.

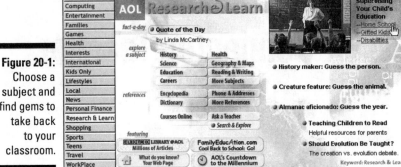

Figure 20-1:
Choose a subject and find gems to take back to your classroom.

✔ Hang out in the Teachers' Lounge (keyword **Teachers Lounge**) for friendly conversation in the Work Room chat. Look on the item list for ideas, resources, and exams organized by subject — for the work-weary teacher, the Teachers' Lounge is truly one of the best resources online.

✔ When looking for children's books, general education titles, or literature, browse through Barnes and Noble @AOL (keyword **BN**) on the Shopping Channel. It's always open — that means easy access for busy teachers.

✔ And then you have the Internet. For a massive infusion of lesson plans and ideas, check out www.lessonstop.org. Play with gopher (keyword **Gopher**) and poke around on the Internet mailing lists (visit www.liszt.com) to find more educational goodies than you can imagine. (See Chapter 17 for more about the Internet in general if you need some help with that.)

✔ Speaking of awesome resource materials, how about picking up electronic copies of classic literature? They're available for downloading from the Palmtop Paperbacks forum (see Figure 20-2) at keyword **Etext** (short for *electronic text*). Because etexts are plain-text files, you can use any word processor to work with them. And they're free. If this area piques your interest, look for even more etexts on the Internet. For starters, try the Etext Archives at www.etext.org and the Online Book Initiative (type **gopher://ftp.std.com/11/obi** into the Navigation bar at the top of the screen).

✔ Covering weather in science this year? Keyword **Weather**provides a great set of current national weather maps that print beautifully on a color ink-jet printer. For weather-related lesson plans, teacher resources, and a host of other goodies, visit the Weather Channel's Web site at www.weather.com/learn_more.

Figure 20-2:
Download a
whole disk
drive full of
books.

✔ Speaking of the Web, don't forget about the mind-boggling sites waiting for you there. For starters, use AOL NetFind (keyword **NetFind**) and try a search for *education* — or any other field of specialty, such as *science* or *special education*. When NetFind returns a list of sites, find one that sounds appealing and click it to go there.

✔ For history, science, and technology, take a trip to keyword **Science**. This area contains links for both America Online-based science stuff and Web sites guaranteed to brighten the eyes of every junior astronaut (or future computer jockey) in your class.

It's an Online Louvre

When you're looking for the perfect addition to a bulletin board, worksheet, or professional presentation, check out these resources and prepare to say "Whoa!"

✔ The pull-down menu in the middle of the Interests channel's Pictures forum (keyword **Interests Pictures**) window links you to photograph libraries all over America Online and the Web. It's a treasure trove of images.

✔ For pictures of the kids' favorite TV stars (and probably more than a few of yours, too), check out the Cartoon Network (keyword **Cartoon Network**), and other media resources.

✔ Of course, no discussion of clip art would possibly be complete without a nod to the Desktop Publishing forum (keyword **Desktop Publishing**). You can also pick up new fonts there to accompany the clip art.

Taking Your Classroom to See the World

If you have a computer in the classroom and access to a phone line, your students' world doesn't end at the walls of the room. Consider the following ideas for field trips without even leaving the school:

✔ Check out today's news (keyword **News**) before class and at lunch. Discuss a current story and follow its development by making "today in the news" a part of your students' day. This idea works well for a unit study (the study of several school subjects around a single item, such as news) because you can concentrate on whatever kind of news you want — sports, business, world, and U.S., for example.

✔ Highlight social studies with information from the Travel area (keyword **Travel**). Students can plan an entire trip with information about airline and train fares, where to eat, weather predictions, and more.

✔ The new America Online international expansions put a wealth of foreign language material at your disposal. Whether you're looking for texts or live interaction with native speakers, it's all waiting for you behind keyword **International**. For all the details, flip to the International channel information in *America Online For Dummies Channels Directory* (the yellow pages in this book), or, to try it right now, sign on and visit the Bistro (keyword **Bistro**).

✔ Combine listening and research skills with supplementary materials in the National Public Radio Outreach (keyword **NPR**).

✔ Study the ins and outs of the federal government through the Congressional Quarterly Online area (keyword **CQ**). Track the latest bills, read the actual text of floor speeches and press announcements, and look up the e-mail addresses and fax numbers for your representatives. It's all here!

✔ For the best in cool Internet stuff for kids, have a look at the Kids Only Top Internet Sites (keyword **Kids Only** and then click the Web button). The Random Surf button takes you to several cool places.

✔ Take advantage of live conferences on America Online. Business leaders, writers (yes, even people like me), media favorites, and all kinds of other people appear in the large conference areas to discuss their areas of expertise and answer questions. What an opportunity for your class! Check out AOL Live (keyword **AOL Live**) for upcoming events. Figure 20-3 shows the AOL Live main screen, where the box office is open 24 hours a day.

✔ Find your own experts in any field and introduce them to the class. Locate a chef through the electronic Gourmet Guide forum (keyword **eGG**), a computer technical wizard through any of the computer forums (keyword **Computing**), and perhaps even a vet through the Pet Care forum (keyword **Pet Care**). Then you can schedule an online chat in a private People Connection room. The possibilities are endless. Look in Chapter 9 for details about the People Connection.

✔ Make history come alive with discussions in SeniorNet Online's Generation to Generation board (use keyword **SeniorNet**, click SeniorNet Forums and then double-click Generation to Generation). This discussion board is specially designed so that seniors and students can learn from and about each other. Classes can post questions and get real-life experience in response.

Figure 20-3:
Welcome to
AOL Live!

The Involved Teacher

There's never enough time for you, the teacher. To make the most of the time you *do* have, check out some of these professional resources:

✔ The National Education Association (NEA) maintains a large forum on America Online that offers services to NEA members and propaganda — er, NEA news — for whomever else wanders in. Use keyword **NEA** to find the details.

✔ Turn to the American Federation of Teachers (AFT) for AFT news, periodicals, and resources. Many of the forum sections are available only to AFT members; keyword **AFT** tells you all about it.

✔ The Internet newsgroups have an entire section of groups called the *K12 hierarchy*. These groups cover all aspects of the kindergarten-through-12th-grade experience, from the points of view of both the teacher and the student. To find these groups, use keyword **Newsgroups** and then click Search All Newsgroups. Search for *K12*. Check out Chapter 17 for more details about where to go from there.

✔ If you need grant money to support a special project, check out the RSP Funding Focus (keyword **RSP**). This service, sponsored by Reference Service Press, tracks money for teachers, students, and non-educators and includes the contact information, requirements, and other information.

Peering into the Future

To keep up on innovations in the classroom, check out the Electronic Schoolhouse (keyword **ESH**). For a peek at how the Internet is already changing education, browse through the Internet Public Library. To get there, click in the address area of the navigation bar and type **www.ipl.org/ref/RR/static/edu0000.html**; then click Go to visit the site.

Chapter 21

Big Help for Small Business

In This Chapter

▶ Starting with the small-business resource
▶ Collecting news of the business world
▶ Promoting and building your business online
▶ Keeping the computer happy
▶ Hopping on the highway

*T*hanks to the wonders of computer technology, your small business can be as "big" as you want. Want inexpensive global e-mail? No problem. How about access to U.S. government contract information? It's a cinch. Sniffing around for product and service ideas? Get ready to find them. This chapter introduces you to the America Online and Internet resources available to build, mold, expand, and promote your small business.

Starting at the Source

The Start-Up Business area (keyword **Startup**) is the America Online official small-business resource. It's home to everything related to small business — and I do mean everything! Figure 21-1 displays your ticket to the best in business seminars, information, magazines, discussion boards, and more. The area is also filled with links to other business-related America Online areas, like *Entrepreneur* magazine (keyword **Entrepreneur Magazine**), the Small Business Administration (keyword **SBA**), and frequent-flyer updates from WebFlyer (keyword **WebFlyer**).

I highly recommend signing up for the *free* "Your Business" electronic newsletter. This weekly report is definitely the best way to keep up with what's new and useful in the burgeoning small business resource area. To sign up, use keyword **Workplace Chat** (don't ask why it's in the Workplace Chat area — it doesn't make sense to me, either), then click the Subscribe to our Free Newsletter link near the bottom of the window.

Figure 21-1:
The small-
business
resources.

Taking the Pulse of Business News

Being in business means staying on top of what's happening in the business world. Information *is* power in business. With America Online, you have access to far more information than your offline competitors do:

- ✔ For general business news and corporate press releases, look to the Business News section of Today's News (keyword **Business News**). Although the window begins with a display of the top news stories, a quick click brings up several other options (see Figure 21-2). I particularly like the Industry section because it narrows your focus to a particular vein of business. If you choose Industry, be sure to use the elevator button on the item list because the window shows only the first half of the industries it covers.

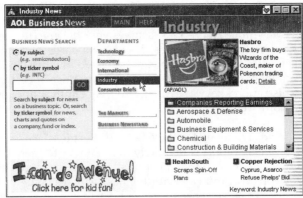

Figure 21-2:
Use this
Department's
buttons to
locate the
business
news you
need.

✔ Newspapers aren't the only source of business information on America Online. Look for the nation's top magazines as well, like *Business Week* (keyword **BW**), *Entrepreneur Magazine* (keyword **EntrepreneurMag**), *Economist Intelligence Unit* (keyword **EIU**) *Investors Business Daily* (www.investors.com), and *Inc.* (www.inc.com).

✔ If you're looking for stories about a particular company in the Business News section, try the Company News area (keyword **Company News**). It scours the recent news archives by the company's ticker symbol.

✔ Regional business highlights are in *The New York Times* on America Online (keyword **Times**), the *Chicago Tribune* (keyword **Chicago Tribune**), and the *Orlando Sentinel* Online (keyword **OSO**).

✔ In small business, you often don't have time to sift through tons of news to find that all-important informational nugget. The America Online News Profiles service (keyword **News Profiles**) solves this problem for you by delivering directly to your mailbox the latest stories about topics you choose. Because this service comes at no extra charge, it's definitely worth a look. One word of caution, though: If you're tracking a popular topic, your mailbox may quickly fill up.

Resources to Relish

When do you sit back, rest on your laurels, and say "Whew! I've done enough! No more working this month (or year)"? If you're a small-business owner, the answer is — never! Just as you never stop thinking, planning, or advancing your business, you also never have enough business resources at your disposal. Who knows what you'll need next? In addition to the areas listed earlier in this chapter, you may utilize some of the following resource areas online:

✔ For reference-oriented material, take a look at the Business section of the Research & Learn channel (keyword **Research**).

✔ Find toll-free numbers, a business directory, and personal phone numbers at the AOL Yellow Pages (keyword **Yellow Pages**).

✔ Research demographics by zip code when you search Neighborhoods, USA (keyword **Neighborhoods**).

✔ Whether you just started your first business or captain an ever-growing enterprise through the reefs of commerce, the business documents, guidebooks, and news in the CCH Business Owner's Toolkit (keyword **CCH**) promise to make your life easier and your business more profitable. (If you're *really* good, you may even get a milkshake and a pony, but no guarantees!)

✔ Relax a few minutes with daily *Dilbert* cartoons (keyword **Dilbert**). Everybody needs a good laugh to keep the doctor away.

Blowing Your Online Bassoon

Now that you and your business are online, advertise your arrival! Be careful because promoting your business online isn't as easy as it sounds. Sure, lots of prospective customers are out there, but you have to approach them appropriately. *Slow* and *subtle* are the keys to your success.

For starters, let your customers know that you're online by printing your company's America Online screen name on business cards and brochures. Depending on how familiar your clientele is with online services and the Internet, you may want to list your address twice. First, identify it as an America Online screen name for your customers who subscribe to America Online. Next, format it as an Internet mailing address by taking out any spaces in your screen name and then adding **@aol.com** to the end of it. For example, my America Online screen name is JKaufeld, so my Internet address is `jkaufeld@aol.com`. Notice that the Internet version is all lowercase — it's a subtle thing, but it shows that you know about the Net.

Here are some other tips to keep you ahead of the game:

- Obey the rules of the digital road. Inside America Online, sending unsolicited (read that as "junk") e-mail messages is a violation of the Terms of Service agreement. Likewise, some discussion areas on the Internet don't appreciate blatant advertising.

- When you're posting a message in a newsgroup or online discussion, pick an area that's relevant to your business *and* accepts business-related postings. If you're promoting financial-planning services, don't post an ad in a cancer-support discussion because you reason that terminally ill people need lots of financial-planning help. If you have to make excuses about why you're posting in a particular area, it's probably not the right place for your message.

Discussion Builds Business

How can your small business even hope to compete with companies that can afford such "luxuries" as extensive market research, product development staff, and customer focus groups? By leveraging your business acumen with the power of America Online, that's how. Here are some ideas to get you started:

- Thinking about taking your company into the wilds of digital space? The Online Business forum (keyword **Online Business**) offers tips, suggestions, links, and discussion boards dedicated to cyberbusiness.

- Want to know what's on your customers' minds? Find the forums they frequent and monitor the discussions.

- If children are part of your market segment, don't forget about the discussion boards in the Kids Only area. Let the kids themselves keep you abreast of new trends and interests.

- Discover new product lines by listening to the complaints and discussions of your customers. No better product idea exists than a customer's hopeful prayer of "Wouldn't it be great if. . . ."

- Conduct live, online meetings in the People Connection area. Use them for brainstorming sessions with other businesspeople from the small-business center, online meetings among your outside sales staff, customer focus groups, or anything else you can imagine.

Self-Help for the Computer

Small businesses, particularly small home-based businesses, often rely heavily on a computer but lack the support resources to haul themselves out of trouble when problems strike.

Take a peek into the Computing channel (keyword **Computing**) for some great places to find the computer help you need. Also, check out the Computing Newsstand (keyword **Computing Newsstand**) for news, features, equipment reviews, Web links, and a buyer's guide. For some good discussion areas, filled with ideas for getting the most from your sometimes-reluctant hardware and software, dive deeply into the Computing channel (keyword **Computing**).

Joining the Information Superhighway

If the 1990s have a certified hot topic, it's the Internet. For a small-business person, the Internet represents an information source you can't afford to pass up. The America Online links to the Internet are quite good. Chapter 17 explores the Internet and explains all those crazy terms, like FTP, WWW, and USENET. Here are some other small-business helps to try on the Internet:

- Join some Internet mailing lists. Visit the Liszt mailing list server, at www.liszt.com, to find the lists you seek. Either enter a word or phrase about your business, your customers, or whatever else interests you or browse through the topical list on their Web page. Either way, you're only moments away from a great mailing list!

- Internet newsgroups are a great place to hear your customers. With well over 30,000 newsgroups out there (and more being added every day), monitoring a few well-chosen newsgroups is almost like target marketing. Look through Chapter 17 for more details.

✔ Put your business in front of millions of potential customers by building a site on the World Wide Web. Many businesses offer their services on the Internet with this graphical, point-and-click system. You're halfway there already because your America Online account includes storage space for a Web site! To find out more about the Web and how to use it in your business, check out Online Business (keyword **Online Business**).

✔ That new Web site comes together pretty easily with America Online's free site development tools. Personal Publisher, the quick and easy America Online Web publishing tool, lives over at keyword **Personal Publisher**. To download a free copy of AOLPress, the full-featured (which is nerd lingo for "infinitely more complex") America Online Web development tool, head to keyword **AOL Press**.

✔ General Web site building programs like Adobe PageMill and Microsoft Front Page work with your America Online Web space through a special area called My FTP Place (keyword **My FTP Place**). Browse through the help files there for all the info you need to connect your software with your Web site area.

Trading on an International Scale

If you've never envisioned your business moving in the realm of international trade, it may be time to think again. World trade is the order of the day, and the Internet can help you join the club. Start with a quick search of the Internet Mailing List database for the International Trade List (see the first bullet in the preceding section to find out how). Subscribe to this list, read it awhile, and get ready to go international.

Part V

Secret Tricks of the AOL Gurus

The 5th Wave
By Rich Tennant

NERD MOMS

Okay young man, it's time to wash your hands, brush your teeth, and defrag your hard disk.

Awwww, Mom.

In this part . . .

*I*n addition to its great content areas, strong Internet links, and dandy little triangular logo, America Online harbors secret powers known only to a select few. In the past, only the Acolytes of the Great Circle–Triangle–Thingie knew the twists and turns of the system's hidden paths — only they were admitted to the powerful inner sanctum of America Online, where customized profiles, Internet software tricks, and personalized menus are part of everyday life.

The chapters in this part tear away this veil of secrecy, exposing the steps that bring these extraordinarily cool extras into your online life, too. With these powerful techniques in hand, you too are ready to join the ranks of the initiated — the ranks of the AOL Gurus.

Chapter 22

Making a Truly Cool Profile

After joining the digital world of America Online, one of your first meet-the-neighbors tasks is filling out your member profile with the My Profile button at keyword **Profile**. Depending on how you fill it out, your online profile may describe who you are and what you do when you're not online (you know — in that *other* world), offer a little peek into your cyberpsyche, or paint a picture of your character in a role-playing game. The space is yours, so use it well!

Unfortunately, the basic member profile offers little flexibility. It's so, well, *basic* — state your name, birthday, occupation, marital status, blah, blah, blah — I feel like I'm filling out a tax form.

To avoid that federal-form feeling, spice up your profile with some custom categories and simple formatting. Thanks to careful research and lengthy undercover investigation (okay, so I accidentally bumped into someone in a chat room and he willingly shared the secret), this chapter reveals the details of the once-clandestine steps to making a perfectly cool profile.

It's All in the Wrists (And the Tabs and Colons)

Customizing your profile involves fooling America Online into doing what you want. (Yes, you're playing tricks on the software — isn't that a wonderful feeling?) When you build a normal profile, it's a fill-in-the-blanks experience. You type some clever thoughts, click Update, and America Online does the rest.

Behind the scenes, America Online adds some extra control characters to your words. When the system displays your profile, it automatically looks for these special characters and uses them to figure out how to display your information.

These special characters are the key to the whole customization process. By typing them in the profile, you can add new categories and generally make your member profile look awesome.

The characters in question are Ctrl+Backspace and Tab. For reasons beyond comprehension (and, frankly, beyond our interest) the America Online programmers chose Ctrl+Backspace to mark the start of a new category and Tab to mark the break between a category heading and its associated text.

Profile Remodeling for the Do-It-Yourselfer

Enough of this dreadful theory — the time has come to haul out the implements of destruction and make a cool, custom profile. Best of all, unlike the folks on those let's-remodel-the-house-in-30-minutes TV shows, you don't need any special equipment, extra software, or even a witty sidekick to accomplish the job. What a deal!

Before signing on to the system and starting profile surgery, take a few minutes to jot down your profile ideas on a handy piece of paper. Just as good blueprints keep a building project on track, knowing precisely what headings and information you want to put in the new profile makes creating the profile much easier.

With your paper-based sample in hand, get ready to join the ranks of Those With Cool Profiles. Here's what to do:

1. **Sign on to America Online.**

   Since the profiles live on the big America Online computers out in Dulles, Virginia, you can't do a thing with the profile before signing on. (Alas!)

2. **Open a blank document window by either selecting File⇨New from the menu or pressing Ctrl+N.**

   This prepares you for capturing a Tab character, a hard to find little creature which plays a vital role in your custom profile. (Yes, these steps really *do* lead to customizing your profile — I didn't forget.)

3. **Press Tab to insert a tab character into the blank document.**

   The blinking toothpick cursor moves over a bit on the screen. That space is really a *Tab* character, just like the ones you get in a word processor by pressing the Tab key. Because pressing Tab in the Edit Your Profile window moves the cursor from one field to another, you have to cheat and find another way to insert a Tab character — and *that* is what you're about to do.

4. **Press Shift+Home to highlight the Tab character, then press Ctrl+C to copy the character for safe keeping (and even safer inserting).**

   This step copies the Tab character into the Windows Clipboard. With the Tab character in hand (or, more specifically, in Clipboard), you're ready to create a masterpiece.

   Follow this step *very* carefully. More than anything else in the instructions, your success with custom profiles depends heavily on catching the Tab character.

5. **Take a deep breath in heady expectation and then choose My AOL⇨My Member Profile from the toolbar.**

   A screen containing your existing profile pops into view.

6. **Pick one of the current entries (Your Name, Hobbies, or one of the others) and click in its text area. When the flashing toothpick cursor appears, press End.**

   The little toothpick cursor moves to the end of the entry.

7. **Press Ctrl+Backspace and then type the name of a new category for your profile. Put a colon (:) after the category name just to make everything look official.**

   If the process worked right, your entry now contains a box (from the Ctrl+Backspace key combo), the category name, and a colon.

   To make a new line without a category heading (it makes long entries look good), insert the Ctrl+Backspace character, but leave out the category and colon. Instead, skip straight to the next step.

8. **With the new category in place, press Ctrl+V or choose Edit⇨Paste from the main menu.**

   The cursor jumps over a bit, thanks to Tab character you borrowed from the blank document window. Despite the screen's increasingly odd look (the screen should look like Figure 22-1 by now), you're doing just fine.

9. **Type the text that goes with your new category.**

   This step works just like it always did — no surprises here.

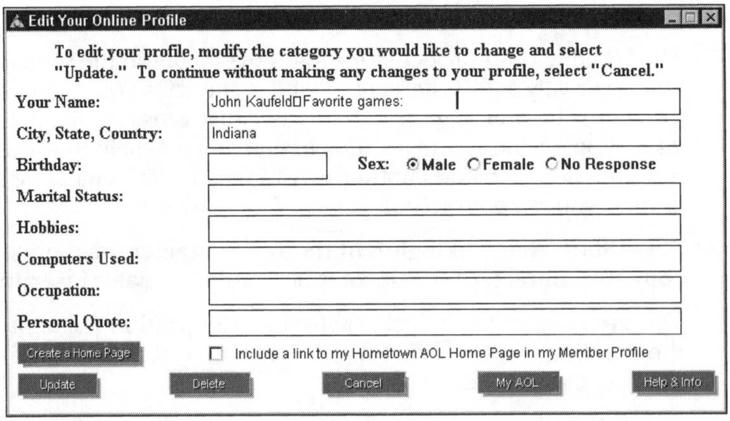

Edit Your Online Profile

To edit your profile, modify the category you would like to change and select "Update." To continue without making any changes to your profile, select "Cancel."

Your Name:	John Kaufeld□Favorite games:
City, State, Country:	Indiana
Birthday:	Sex: ⦿Male ○Female ○No Response
Marital Status:	
Hobbies:	
Computers Used:	
Occupation:	
Personal Quote:	

Create a Home Page   ☐ Include a link to my Hometown AOL Home Page in my Member Profile

Update   Delete   Cancel   My AOL   Help & Info

Figure 22-1:
The Your Name field looks weird as a new category (Favorite Games) takes shape.

10. Repeat Steps 6 through 9 to add more new categories and entries.

Feel free to keep adding new categories and information to your profile.

Although each profile entry holds a limited number of characters (see Table 22-1 for the details), that's not a big problem. When you run out of room in one entry, just go to the next one on the list!

11. After you're done, cross your fingers (this is *very* important) and click Update.

After a moment, America Online acknowledges your request and updates your profile. If all worked well, your new headings and entries tell your story with panache (just like Figure 22-2).

A personal Web page is the ultimate profile

Even though you can add new categories to your member profile, the process still suffers from some frustrating limitations. To escape those restrictions and discover a whole new world of possibilities, check out the America Online Personal Publisher system (keyword **Personal Publisher**) and build your own World Wide Web page.

Want to change fonts? No problem. How about adding a picture? It's a snap. You don't need to know a bunch of technical mumbo jumbo to make it work, either. Personal Publisher puts you in the creativity driver's seat while *it* handles the digital details.

Check the finished profile to make sure that it comes out just as you envisioned. Do that by pressing Ctrl+G and typing your screen name in the dialog box.

Table 22-1	**Category Sizes**
This Category	*Holds This Many Characters*
Your Name	128
City, State, Country	255
Birthday	32
Marital Status	32
Hobbies	255
Computers Used	128
Occupation	128
Personal Quote	255

Figure 22-2:
The finished product, with new headings and extra white space to make the profile informative and pretty.

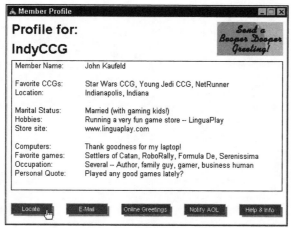

When the time comes to update your cool profile, use the same techniques described above, but with a twist in the process. When you open up the profile for changes (just like Step 5 in this chapter), each category area displays only the *last* set of information you entered — in fact, it looks like the computer ate most of your profile! Don't panic like I did (I positively came unglued the first time I changed my profile because I thought it was gone), because your whole profile is safe and sound.

To see all of the text in each category area, use your cursor keys. Table 22-2 explains how the keystrokes work in the profile window. (And remember to click Update when you finish reworking the masterpiece!)

Table 22-2	Cursor Key Actions in the Profile Window
This Keystroke	*Move the Cursor as Follows*
Home	Puts the cursor at the start of the current custom heading
End	Sends the cursor to the end of the current custom heading
Ctrl+Home	Moves the cursor to the beginning of the category
Ctrl+End	Dispatches the cursor to the end of the category
Right and Left arrows	Move the cursor one character in each direction
Ctrl+Right, Ctrl+Left arrow	Jumps word by word in each direction

Chapter 23

Dressing Up Your Software with Fresh Buttons and a New Menu

In This Chapter

▶ Building a better toolbar

▶ Creating a menu one item at a time

*C*ustomizing means extraordinarily different things to different people. To one person, it means adding a pinstriped dash of color to the exterior of a car; to another, it involves some light-hearted reorganization of the vehicle's body parts with the help of a handy acetylene torch. (Okay, maybe that's *art* rather than customization, but you get the point.)

In the world of software, customer-customizable features started out small ("You want to change the color of your screen? You got it!") and gradually grew to the point where we are today. With many applications on the market, you can adjust almost anything — including the menus and the toolbars.

Both the America Online 4.0 and 5.0 software ride this trend by including those two big customization features. You, the nonprogramming America Online member, can add new buttons to the toolbar and create your own navigational menu system (complete with hot keys). This chapter explores the ins and outs of these two great customizing features. First tackling the toolbar and then illuminating the My Shortcuts menu, this chapter makes both these great tools easy to understand and use.

Although building your own toolbar buttons and menus isn't hard, the task easier if you know about the Favorite Places heart-on-the-paper icon and also understand how keywords work inside America Online. To find out about them both in one easy step, flip to Chapter 7.

Dancing the Toolbar Tango (Or Is That the New Button Bop?)

Until now, the toolbar just sorta hung out at the top of the screen and stared at you. Granted, it's very useful (and colorful), but it wasn't terribly interactive. The America Online programmers put a great deal of thought into precisely which buttons should appear on the toolbar, and they put them there carefully. So, if you didn't like one or another of them (my personal nemesis was the Quotes button — the stock market and I just don't mix), you couldn't do anything about it.

With the America Online 4.0 and 5.0 software, the programmers discovered customization, and now the toolbar (or at least a little corner of it) is your personal navigation playground. Although most of the toolbar is still locked in place — it *has* to be because most of the new menu items migrated from the pull-down menus under the toolbar — the plum-color area on the far-right end of the toolbar (shown in Figure 23-1) belongs to you. Fill it with buttons pointing to your favorite America Online areas, chat rooms, or Web sites.

Figure 23-1:
The three customizable toolbar buttons live on the far right end.

Buttons you're stuck with   Customizable buttons

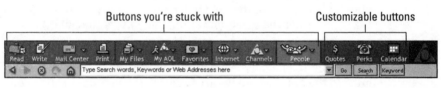

Exactly how many buttons can you put there? The answer depends on your computer. A newer computer probably has space for three to six buttons or maybe even more. On an older computer, you may not see *any* customizable buttons. (Now may be a good time to repeat that reassuring mantra, "Technology is here to help.") For the technical background about the number of buttons on your screen, browse through the Customizable Buttons discussion back in Chapter 3.

If the online area for your prospective toolbar button has a Favorite Places icon in its window, you're only a few moments away from adding that area to your toolbar buttons. Just look at the following steps for all the details. However, if the window *doesn't* have a Favorite Places icon on it, you can't create a toolbar button for the area. Sorry, but that's how it goes. (Even flexibility has limits.)

To put a button of your own on the toolbar (or to replace an existing button with a new one), follow these steps:

1. **If the customizable area of the toolbar is full, decide which of the customizable buttons you don't need anymore.**

   If you have an open space in the toolbar's customizable section, skip ahead to Step 4.

   Granted, it doesn't seem fair that you need to lose a button to gain one, but unless you have open space in the customizable section of your toolbar, that's how things go.

2. **Right-click the button that's going bye-bye.**

   A short pop-up menu (if a menu with only one item can be called a menu) appears next to your cursor.

3. **Click the Remove from Toolbar option on the pop-up menu (it's the only one, as you can see in Figure 23-2) and then click Yes in the Are You Sure dialog box.**

   Quick as a wink, the toolbar button vanishes, leaving an open space on the right side of the screen for your button.

Figure 23-2:
Just one click, and the button is history.

4. **Through whatever way you usually do it (keyword, Favorite Place entry, or menu browsing, for example), view the online area destined for its own toolbar button.**

   Just as it always does, the online area of your heart hops on the screen.

5. **Drag-and-drop the little heart-on-a-page icon into the customizable toolbar area (see Figure 23-3).**

   When you let go of the cursor, the Icon Selector dialog box hops on the screen.

   It doesn't matter where in the customizable section you drop the Favorite Places icon. The America Online software always adds the new button in the last position on the far right side of the toolbar.

Drop area

Figure 23-3:
Drop the
icon on this
end to make
a new
button.

6. **Scroll through the collection of pictures until you find one that looks vaguely like what you want and click it.**

   The picture on the icon list highlights with pride.

   By the way, you can't add your own pictures to the icon list. For now, you simply enjoy the opportunity to use the artwork graciously provided by the America Online developers.

7. **Click in the Label box and then type a 1–8-letter label to go under your new toolbar button. After you're done, click OK.**

   The button proudly takes its place on the toolbar, looking something like Figure 23-4.

New button

Figure 23-4:
The shiny
new toolbar
button.

Each screen name gets its own custom toolbar buttons, so don't be surprised when your new button vanishes the moment you switch to a different screen name. When you change back to the original screen name, the custom button comes back.

To use the button with other screen names on your account, sign on with each of the other names and go through this whole make-a-button process for each one. If you have multiple copies of the America Online software (one on your home computer and one at work, for example), you need to add the buttons in both places. Custom toolbar buttons aren't stored in the America Online computers; they're stored on your computer.

Also, you can't create custom toolbar buttons when you're signed on with the Guest option — it works only on your very own copy of America Online.

A Menu to Call Your Own

My Shortcuts is your very own customizable menu space. Load it with as many as ten of your favorite online destinations. This menu comes preloaded with entries for seven popular parts of America Online (or at least parts America Online *wants* to be popular, like Sign on a Friend), but you can easily change those entries to things *you're* interested in:

✔ Why go to the trouble of putting something in My Shortcuts when it's so easy to add things to your Favorite Places list? Good question — I'm glad you asked. In addition to appearing in My Shortcuts, every item on this special menu gets a *hot key* assigned to it — something that Favorite Places can't do. Rather than work your way through the menu or manually type the area's keyword, you can press a Ctrl-key combination (Ctrl+1 through Ctrl+0, depending on which position the item holds in My Shortcuts) and go there immediately.

✔ You need to keep just one rule in mind: Only services and forums with a keyword can be on the special My Shortcuts menu. If you can't get there with a keyword, you can't get there with the My Shortcuts menu, either.

✔ I probably shouldn't tell you this, but you *can* bend the only-keyword-areas-go-here rule just a bit. In addition to keywords, you can include Internet locations, such as Web sites or gophers. Type the address *exactly* as you do when you're using your Web browser to get there. That means using what the techies call *URL format,* including the http:// part in front of the site's address.

✔ Some of my picks for a starter My Shortcuts menu include *Business Week* magazine (keyword **BW**), the Gamers Forum (keyword **Gaming**), and the multiplayer game shows from BoxerJam games (keyword **BoxerJam**).

Here's how to customize the My Shortcuts menu with *your* Favorite Places:

1. **Find something you want to add to the menu and get its keyword or Internet URL and name.**

   Make sure that the keyword is correct; otherwise, the menu option doesn't work (and the programmers of the world don't need *any* help in developing software that doesn't work).

2. **Choose Favorites➪My Shortcuts➪Edit Shortcuts.**

   This step displays the Edit Shortcut Keys dialog box.

3. **Decide which key you want to use for the new item and click the Shortcut Title box for that key.**

   If the box already has an entry, press Backspace or Delete to remove it (see Figure 23-5).

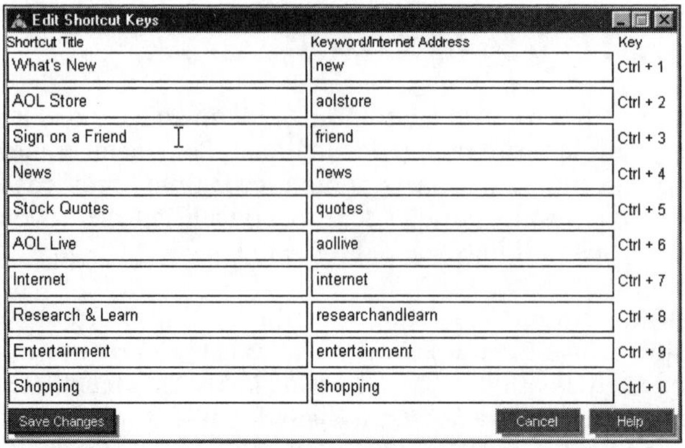

Figure 23-5:
Take out the current entry to make room for your new one.

4. **Type the name of the item in the Menu Entry box.**

   Whatever you type appears on the My Shortcuts menu, so keep it kinda short — one to four words, at most.

5. **Press Tab to move to the Keyword/Internet Address box.**

   If you're replacing an existing entry, press Backspace or Delete to remove it.

6. **Type the keyword or Internet address for your new menu item in the Keyword/Internet Address box (see Figure 23-6).**

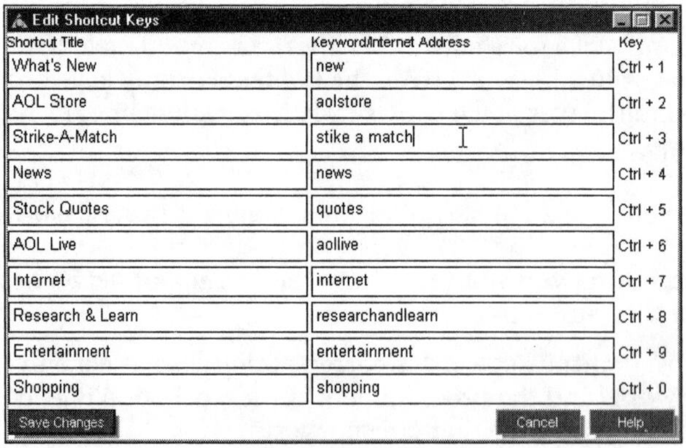

Figure 23-6:
Watch your spelling (after all, nobody else will).

Double-check your typing to make sure that the keyword is correct. If you entered a Web site address, make sure that you include the `http://` part at the beginning!

7. **Click the Save Changes button to make the new entry part of your My Shortcuts menu.**

   Your new menu item is ready to test!

If you have a sudden desire to forget that you ever considered changing the menu, click Cancel in Windows or close the window on a Macintosh.

8. **Choose My A̲OL⇨M̲y Shortcuts and choose your new item from the Favorite Places section (see Figure 23-7).**

If something that looks like the dialog box shown in Figure 23-8 pops up after you try your new menu item, go back to Step 6 and check the entry in the Keyword/Internet Address area. The odds are high that it's a little spelling-challenged.

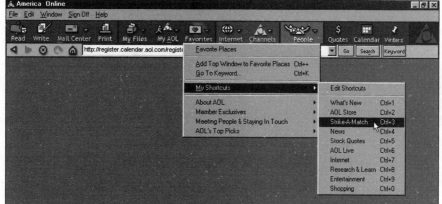

Figure 23-7: Your new entry looks great strutting on the My Shortcuts menu.

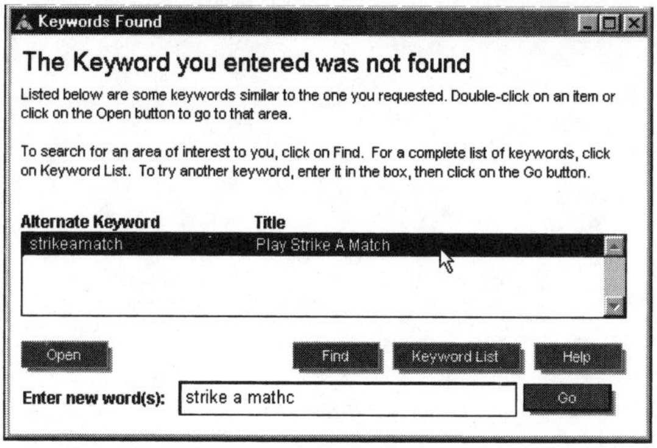

Figure 23-8: Whoops — time to double-check your spelling!

Chapter 24

So You Wanna Go Faster?

In This Chapter

▶ A few words about bandwidth

▶ Touring the technologies at a high rate of speed

*W*hen it comes to technology, we humans have a serious attachment to speed. Fast is good, faster is better, and *really* fast takes our breath away. We expect speed from our cars, our computers, even our cameras (how else do you justify instant-print film and Hello Kitty photo sticker kiosks?).

Online connections live under the same speed demands as every other technical piece of our world (we want information *now,* darn it), and the computer industry has risen to the occasion. Over the last few years, connection speeds have risen steadily while prices have dropped like an old modem thrown from the 53rd floor.

Of course, new technologies bring new terms, concerns, and costs — all of which add up to frustration for people trying to sit on the safe side of the technological cutting edge. This chapter attacks the problem head-on by exploring and explaining the most popular high-speed connection options available on the market today (and a couple coming out tomorrow). Flip through here before plunking down the money for a high-speed Internet connection — you'll be glad that you did!

High Bandwidth Doesn't Mean Oversized Musicians

There's a funky give and take relationship between the speed of your online connection and the things that you do online. Every boost to your connection speed opens up new vistas of online content. America Online slideshows (like the ones in the CBS News area, keyword **CBS News**) play smoothly. Online music with Spinner (www.spinner.com) sounds better than the radio. Files that took an hour or more to download hop onto your hard drive in a matter of minutes. It's pretty close to digital Nirvana.

As you start looking at high-speed connections, the term *bandwidth* pops up over and over. (Once the nerds find a word they like, they use it as much as possible). Bandwidth describes how much data moves through an online connection over a period of time. Modems, for instance, are a low-bandwidth connection, which measure their speed in "bits per second" (the BPS thing again, which I tell you about initially in Chapter 1). High-speed (or high band-width) connections measure speed in KBPS, or *thousand bits per second* (recycling the popular nerd convention of substituting "K" for "thousand" whenever possible).

Browsing the Net Through Rose-Colored Wires

High-bandwidth connections come in all shapes, sizes, costs, and acronyms. The specific connections available where you live depend quite heavily on exactly *where* you live within your city, state, and area of the country. Even though one of the high-speed services might be available in your city, you could discover that it *isn't* in your neighborhood yet.

Don't automatically assume that high-bandwidth connections don't exist in your neck of the woods just because you live far away from a booming metro-politan area. Some of the coolest high-speed projects take place in smaller, more rural cities, because those areas understand the economic importance of the online world better than their big-city brethren.

Cost and ease of installation also vary wildly around the country. (Just because they sell the technology doesn't mean the companies know how to install it yet.)

The following sections look at the most common high-speed technologies for the home and small office/home office market. Big businesses, with their equally big budgets, need more speed than these connections provide, so those folks are on their own (but they can afford a consultant).

Data over Cable: Good speed when it works (but don't tell your friends)

The fist time I heard about "Internet access via cable TV systems" a few years ago, I thought that the person telling me about it was joking. What do the online world and my cable TV company have in common? Sure, they both involve screens, but I hoped for something a little more meaningful than that.

Doesn't bandwidth cost money?

In the world of automobiles, speed costs money. There's no way around it — if you want to go *vroom,* then your budget goes *zoom.* Generally speaking, it works the same way with the wild world of high-speed Internet connections, but the *zoom* factor causes a lot less budgetary stress than in, say, rocket car drag racing.

Although high-speed connections cost more than plain modem connections, the difference isn't exorbitant. In fact, it's probably more inexpensive than you think.

For instance, if you have an extra phone line for your computer (those computers tie up the phone like a caffeinated teenager), you pay about $25 per month. A cable modem connection, which runs 10 to 20 times faster than a regular dial-up modem, costs around $30 per month. Add another $15 per month to rent the cable modem, and you get a total monthly cost of $45 for cable modem service. The *net* cost (because you don't need the extra phone line now) drops to $20.

But the calculation doesn't stop there. High-speed connections usually include their own Internet connection, which drops your America Online fee dramatically. Instead of paying $21.95 per month for America Online, the cost drops to $9.95 per month (using the Bring Your Own Access plan, at keyword **BYOA**). Now the high-bandwidth connection only costs $10 extra. Hmm. . . sounds enticing, doesn't it?

Don't arbitrarily dismiss a high-bandwidth connection without running the numbers yourself and checking the actual costs in your area. Fees vary wildly by region, because every part of the country features a unique collection of competing vendors, a vastly different regulatory structure, and varying infrastructure "challenges" (somewhere out there, a phone company engineer is laughing right now). When you look at the costs, remember to factor in the money that you *already* spend before making your final decision. The outcome may surprise you!

After thinking about it more (and doing some research on my own), the idea made a lot more sense. Moving television signals around a community is a lot like moving data around a network — heck, even some of the wire is the same. It took a few years to get the act together, but the cable TV industry made great strides along the way. Today, cable companies all over the country provide high-speed Internet access over the same cable lines that deliver "Brady Bunch" reruns to your living room. (There's some kind of poetic justice there, but I can't quite nail it down.)

In addition to the cable line itself, cable access requires two special pieces of equipment. First, your computer needs a network card that supports *10baseT Ethernet* connections (which is a fancy way of saying "twisted-pair network wire that looks like overgrown phone cord"). Lots of new machines include a network card as part of the standard configuration, but if yours doesn't, it's not a big deal. Every computer store (and many home electronics places, like Best Buy and The Good Guys) carry the cards. For a small fee, they even install the card for you, too.

The other technical goodie that makes cable communication possible is the *cable modem* itself. This box translates between the cable wire and your computer, moving data back and forth at astonishing speeds. Depending on the whim of your local cable TV company, you might rent the cable modem from them for a minimal monthly fee, or purchase one to have and hold until the warranty doth expire (whereupon the device breaks the next day — at least that's how those things always work for me).

Most, if not all, cable companies bundle their own Internet service (e-mail accounts, newsgroup access, and such) into the price of the high-speed access. Even so, the fee is pretty darned fair considering what you get for the money. When the line works like it should, cable access really screams. It's quite an experience to watch a 12MB file pour into your computer in minutes instead of an hour or more.

A potential down-side of cable access is its "shared resource" concept. Due to the cable system's design, the subscribers in a given area share their Internet access (just like you share the neighborhood roads, particularly during rush hour). If everyone uses the system at once, response time plummets because each person takes their own increasingly small slice of the total bandwidth. If you work at home, your access flies all day, because you aren't sharing bandwidth with anyone (everybody else is at work, so the roads are clear).

Cable's other main issue is reliability. Unfortunately, the key phrase for cable access is "when the line works like it should." The cable companies try hard, but they wrestle with the computer side of their business. Although reports of slow (or *no*) cable connections abound on the Internet newsgroups (check out `comp.dcom.modems.cable` for the latest tidbits), my own experience says that the cable companies see competition on the horizon in the form of DSL (discussed in the next section), and understand that customer service makes or breaks their endeavor. For their sake, I hope they get the message sooner rather than later.

 Since cable connectivity depends entirely on your local cable company, call them first to find out if they do data over cable lines yet. You can also visit the national information site for the biggest cable connectivity system, @Home (`www.home.com`), and search for local cable companies through the site. For more about cable modems in general, visit CableLabs (`www.cablelabs.com`, shown in Figure 24-1).

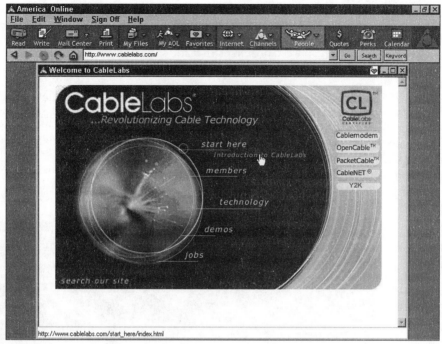

Figure 24-1:
It's a little geeky, but the CableLabs site offers a lot.

DSL: Fastest of the bunch, but not available everywhere

Considering their huge investment in copper wire, it's no wonder that the phone companies looked far and wide for a high-speed solution that leverages all of that old copper wire into a competitive advantage. At first, they thought that the grail carried the name ISDN (covered in the next section), but in mid 1998, they changed the tune to DSL. DSL stands for *Digital Subscriber Line,* a very cool technology that could herald some exciting new dimensions for the online world.

DSL, like ISDN, runs through your existing phone lines. Unlike its slower brother, DSL is only a data link — telephones and fax machines need not darken DSL's doorway. Connecting your computer to the DSL line requires a DSL modem. (It has a more technical name, but most everybody simply calls it a "DSL modem," since that describes what it does.)

Blazing, consistent speed gives DSL a slight advantage in the market. Cable systems claim to run at 10 times the speed of a standard 56K modem. DSL delivers up to five times the cable connection's speed, but without the "shared resource" problems that the cable folks calmly describe as a "feature" of their system.

Like cable connections, vendors usually package an Internet Service Provider plan with the DSL line, which brings the cost to about $50 per month. Compared to ISDN's piecemeal approach (buy the line from one vendor and your Net access from another), DSL shines through as a marvelous bargain.

For more about DSL (including a handy DSL locator system which checks to see if your area offers DSL service yet), visit www.dsl.com (see Figure 24-2).

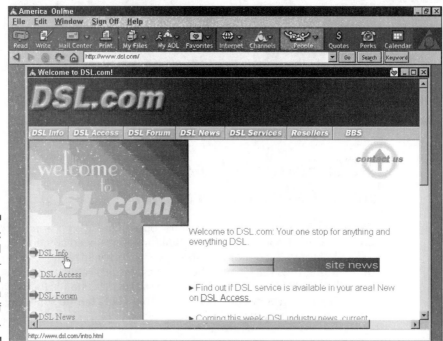

Figure 24-2:
All DSL, all the time — DSL.com offers a wealth of information.

ISDN: Great flexibility, but slower and expensive

ISDN, short for *Integrated Services Digital Network*, arrived on the scene well before either cable access or DSL. It won a dedicated following among small business and advanced home users thanks to its guaranteed connection speed (either 64KBps or 128KBps), and the fact that, for a long time, it was the only high-speed game in town.

Unlike its competitors, ISDN service replaces your existing single phone line with a pair of new, *super* phone lines that operate on the same old piece of wire already installed in your house. Using a special ISDN adapter (an extra piece of gear that you usually purchase from your ISDN provider), connect your computer to directly to the ISDN line for either 64KBps (using one of the two lines) of 128KBps (with both lines) of connectivity to the Internet.

The ISDN line basically takes the place of your old phone line, and its price reflects that idea. ISDN service usually pays for *only* the communication line itself, not your ISP account. Getting an ISDN-capable account from a local Internet Service Provider adds another $20 to $50 per month to the cost of the ISDN line, which stretches its value compared to the other high-speed options.

ISDN wins hands-down in one area: Availability. When I wrote this, all of the "Baby Bells" (Ameritech, Pac Bell, US West, and the others) offered ISDN service throughout their coverage areas, with heavy focus on all of the metropolitan locations. Compared to the limited reach of DSL and cable connections, ISDN truly is everywhere.

Since it only provides a 64KBps or 128KBps data connection, it sits at the very bottom of the speed contest. Considering what DSL and cable can do (and at a much lower price point), it looks like ISDN only makes sense for people who *need* a fast online connection, but don't mind paying an arm, a leg, and half a sideburn for it.

Part VI
The Part of Tens

The 5th Wave — By Rich Tennant

THAT'S RIGHT, THE UPPER CASE BUTTON WORKS ON-SCREEN, BUT THEY'RE NOT COMING OUT ON THE DANG PRINTER! HOLD? SURE, I'LL HOLD.

Poet e.e. cummings makes his last service call.

In this part . . .

As expected, the book closes with The Part of Tens, IDG Books Worldwide's answer to all the silly things you had to memorize as a child in school. Don't memorize them — don't even try. Instead, read them, laugh with them, and put them to work for you.

Chapter 25

Ten Fun Things to Do Online

. . . .

. . . .

*D*epending on whom you ask, the online world and the Internet are either chock-full of the latest information about every topic under the sun or they're factual mirages that look promising from a distance but disappear as you arrive. Why do people hold such radically different views on the subject? Because the first person *found* what she looked for, and the second didn't.

The key to finding stuff, of course, is knowing where to look. In the online world, that's quite a challenge because you have so many places to look. This chapter provides some starting locations as you search for fun people, nifty places, and various online features.

Always watch for new resources — you never know when you may find one. Feel free to jot down the area's keyword or address here in this book, too, so that the address doesn't get accidentally lost in the shuffle. (After all, it *is* your book, so you can write whatever you want.)

Decoding Digital Terminology

The computer industry turns out new technology quicker than you can say "I just bought a new computer." (I suppose the lesson here involves announcing our PC purchases with shorter sentences, but I digress.) But computers are the industry's second most prolific product. More than anything else, the computer nerds make amazing new names for things.

To keep a handle (or at least get a grip) on the wild world of computerese, visit the America Online Webopedia at keyword **Webopedia**. Decipher specific terms by typing them into the Webopedia search box or browse a list of related terms by picking a category. The site also features a Term of the Day, for those days when you need a cool new techo-term to impress the computer folks.

Seeking Out a Chat Room

The People Connection ranks as one of the top America Online destinations. Finding the room that's right for you may take some time, particularly because the area contains hundreds, if not thousands, of active chats all the time.

To simplify your chatting life (and find interesting chats quickly), use Search Featured Chats, the People Connection search feature:

1. **Use keyword** Chat Search **to bring up the Search Featured Chats window.**

   (If that doesn't work, click the People toolbar button, select Find a Chat from the drop-down list, and then click Search Featured Chats on the right side of the window.)

2. **Type a few words to describe the room you're looking for and click Search. Type it carefully — spelling counts!**

   America Online lists rooms matching your description. For rooms that are always open, the list shows only the room name. If the search system finds a special scheduled chat, it shows the name and time of the chat.

3. **Scroll through the list until you find a likely candidate and then double-click the chat room's name.**

   America Online displays a brief description of the chat.

4. **To hop into the chat room, click the big Go Chat button in the description window.**

   If there's space for you (remember that each chat room holds between 23 and 45 people), you immediately pop into the room. If the room is full, the software lets you know.

This set of steps searches all of America Online, looking for interesting chats sponsored by various online areas. It *doesn't* search the general People Connection chats, though. The only way to find a chat in there is by old-fashioned browsing in the Find a Chat window (click the People toolbar button and then choose Find a Chat from the drop-down menu).

After you get into the room, add it to your Favorite Places list by clicking the little heart-on-a-page icon in the chat room's upper-right corner. For more about Favorite Places, see Chapter 7. To delve the depths of chatting, see Chapter 9.

Forget the Scissors — Clip Coupons with Your Computer

I love saving money on things. Offer me a good deal on something that I want, and I'm yours. (Offer me a *really* good deal on just about anything, and we'll at least talk.) But despite my money-saving outlook on life, grocery coupons never torqued my world. Prowling through the pages of the Sunday newspaper, flipping among the many colorful promises of *buy 10 and save* just didn't do a thing for me.

At least they didn't until I found ValuePage (keyword **ValuePage**). This extraordinary online tool turns your printer into a coupon maker, spitting out dollars-off vouchers that are good at your favorite local stores. Just tell the site your zip code, pick a participating store or supermarket, and watch your printer go. *This* is couponing that even a coupon-hater like me could love.

Ferreting Out Long-Lost Friends and Businesses, Wherever They May Be

Want to find your old flame from high school? Interested in seeing your college roommate again? (Maybe he finally has the rent money he owes you!) You've already searched the Member Directory but found nothing. Is there anywhere else to turn? Yes!

Finding a person's e-mail address, street address, and phone number can't get much easier than it is with Switchboard (keyword **Switchboard**) and Four11 (keyword **Four11,** which takes you to the Yahoo! White Pages, at people.yahoo.com). To find a business, use either the AOL Yellow Pages (keyword **Yellow Pages**) or the Yahoo! Yellow Pages (yp.yahoo.com).

Tripping through the Coolest Online Areas

After spending some time on America Online, it's easy to fall into a rut. You find a few areas that match your interests, visit them regularly, and get to know the members there. However, after a while, you may long for something new — a change of pace and scenery, perhaps.

When the urge strikes, answer it with a quick trip to the Find system (keyword **Find**), the What's Hot list (keyword **Hot**), or the Member's Choice selections (keyword **Members Choice**). Each of these resources presents links to both new and popular online areas. It's a never-ending supply of great places to go.

Sending Online Cards, Flowers, and Other Things That Smell

The online world brings people closer in amazing ways. Distance makes no difference on the Internet, so your circle of online friends quickly includes people from everywhere on the globe. Unfortunately, distance *does* make a difference when you want to send greeting cards and other gifts to your buddies. Popping an e-mail over to Guam is one thing, but shipping a batch of Chicago-style pizzas is quite another.

The good news is that programmers love these types of problems and they quickly developed a solution. If your friends exist in the digital world, why shouldn't your cards and gifts live there, too? Thanks to these clever programmers, the Internet is chock-full of digital postcard, greeting card, and flower delivery services. With a few quick clicks, e-mail your sentiments to friends and family. Best of all, most of these services are free!

The following list includes a variety of greeting cards, postcards, and flower bouquets (well, at least *pictures* of flower bouquets — but they don't need any water). I couldn't resist including one off-the-wall delivery service, but I think that you can pick it from the list without further explanation.

To use one of these sites, just type its address in the address area on the navigation bar and then press Enter. America Online automatically starts your Web browser and sends you off to the site. Enjoy!

What It's Called	Web Address
Blue Mountain Arts	www.bluemountain.com
Corbis Picture Experience	pix.corbis.com/postcard
Dumpster Diver	cgi.connect-time.com/cgi-bin/dumpdive
Electronic Postcards	www.electronicpostcards.com
Greet Someone	www.greetsomeone.com
Send A Postcard	www.sendapostcard.com
Virtual Bouquet	www.virtualbouquet.com
Virtual Florist	www.virtualflorist.com
Virtual Flowers	www.virtualflowers.com

For a fancier card that costs a little money, check the American Greetings card center (keyword **American Greetings**). It offers a wide variety of high-quality animated cards for all occasions. They're a hoot!

Hanging Out with Your Favorite Celebrities

Sure, the stars come out at night — but at AOL Live, they shine the rest of the day, too. Some people appear regularly on their own shows (like my *America Online For Dummies* chat at 9:00 p.m. Eastern time on the third Monday of every month), and others drop in for a one-shot event.

To check the schedule for upcoming AOL Live appearances by your favorite entertainment, sports, political, and business personalities, use keyword **Search AOL Live**. When the Search window appears, click Search for Live Events and enter your luminary's name. If that person has an event coming up, a dialog box containing all the details appears on-screen.

To search for transcripts of previous events, click Search Transcripts in the Search window rather than the Search for Live Events button. For the latest info about my monthly AOL Live event, check my online profile (press Ctrl+G, type **JKaufeld**, and press Enter).

Downloading the Best Software

You can't beat a huge, free collection of programs for bringing out the computer person in anyone (it always works for me, but then again, I may not be the best sample population). Let your inner nerd run free in the DOS, Macintosh, and Windows software libraries on America Online. Download some business programs, home-management tools, or even a few games — everything is yours for the taking.

To search the libraries' Windows, Macintosh, or DOS software, use keyword **Filesearch,** click the Shareware button, and follow the prompts. By default, the system searches for Windows and DOS software. To search for Macintosh software, click the tiny Mac Search button at the bottom of the Software Search window.

For more about the perils and pleasures of downloading, see Chapter 16.

Tracking Packages All Over the World

Depending on what you do for a living, following the progress of little boxes as they wing around the world may (or may not) be of particular importance to you. If you ship a number of things, though, or if you work from home, knowing the current location of a much-needed carton or document envelope often makes or breaks your whole day.

Thanks to the Internet, package-tracking information is only moments away. Sign on to America Online, click in the address box on the navigation bar (right next to the Find button, near the top of your screen), and then type the appropriate shipping company address from this list:

Carrier	*Web Site Address*
Airborne Express	www.airborne-express.com
DHL Worldwide Express	www.dhl.com
Federal Express	www.fedex.com
United Parcel Service	www.ups.com
United States Postal Service	www.usps.gov

America Online automatically launches your World Wide Web browser and opens the page. Carefully follow the on-screen instructions to find your package.

Collecting Free Stuff from the Government

I just couldn't resist including this one. You know them from late-night TV and those little ads in the back of your favorite magazines. Now those zany folks from Pueblo, Colorado, are on the Web! Behold: It's the electronic version of the *Consumer Information Catalog.*

Its Web site (`www.pueblo.gsa.gov`) offers hundreds of federal publications for free. Search the site for anything from gardening tips to business loan advice and then either read the documents online or save a copy to peruse later. (I *still* can't believe it's all free — this is just too cool!)

Chapter 26

Ten Common Things That Go Wrong (And How to Fix Them)

1 often think that computers and software were invented by a cabal of psychiatrists and psychologists as a long-term project to ensure that Western civilization would have trouble coping in the 20th century — therefore would need their services for many years to come. With that meaningful observation off my chest, it's time to consider the problem at hand — namely, the one you're having right now. Look for your problem in the following sections. If you find it (or one much like it), read the information in that section and try the solution I suggest.

If you can't find your problem here, try the Doctor Tapedbridge Miracle Elixir: When things start failing for no apparent reason, quit the program, restart your computer, and try again. If that doesn't solve things, check keyword **Help** for more suggestions. If you can't get online at all, call the friendly America Online technical support folks at 800-827-6364.

There's a .MIM File Motioning from My Mailbox

You never know where a mime may show up next. At the amusement park, in the local shopping mall, or perhaps as a wandering entertainer during dinner, you can't beat a mime for hilarious hijinks (particularly when the mime focuses his attention on someone else). But a mime in your online mailbox? Now that's another matter.

I'm not talking about a real mime, of course (although this book may prompt some adventuresome soul to create a routine called *You've Got Mime*). Instead, I mean a MIME file — a file that ends with a `.MIM` extension — attached to an e-mail message in your box.

The MIME tools (short for *Multi-purpose Internet Mail Extensions*) work behind the scenes to send programs, documents, spreadsheets, and other files through the Internet e-mail system. When someone outside America Online sends software, documents, or other files to you, their e-mail program translates the files with the special MIME tools, giving the file that funky .MIM extension in the process. The program then attaches the translated file to an e-mail message, and ships the whole thing off to you.

When the message (and its attached MIME file) arrives at America Online, the e-mail system automatically converts the MIME file back into whatever it was originally (an .EXE, .DOC, .JPG, or such). At least that's how it *should* work.

Unfortunately, America Online's e-mail system gets confused sometimes and can't translate the MIME file back into its original form. Instead, the e-mail system shrugs and simply drops the .MIM file into your mailbox without a single word of condolence, apology, or (worst of all) instruction about what to do next.

When that happens to you, just download the file as you normally do, then use WinZIP to translate the file back to normalcy. Yes, in addition to all the tricks that it does with ZIP files, WinZIP also knows the secrets of unlocking MIME files.

For help with both downloading and the wonders of WinZIP, flip back to Chapter 16.

The Computer Almost Signs On

Your password is in, the modem is singing, and all is well with the world. At least it *was* until you couldn't complete the connection to America Online.

Usually, this happens at Step 6 of the connection process — the one that says `Connecting to America Online`. This problem isn't your fault; the fault belongs to America Online. For some reason, the America Online computers didn't acknowledge your existence. Perhaps the computers have so much going on that they can't spare a moment from their busy schedule for you. Perhaps the computers aren't running. Whatever the reason, wait a while (15 to 20 minutes) and then try again. If this behavior keeps up for more than an hour or two, call the America Online support number (800-827-6364) and find out what's happening.

The Host Isn't Responding to You

This message is nerd lingo for "the computer didn't answer your request," usually expressed in human terms as "Huh? What? Were you talking to me?" You wanted to do something simple (like display the Channels window), but the big computers at America Online weren't paying attention. Isn't that just like computers? Give them a little power, and they walk all over you.

Stuff like this happens when a large number of people are using America Online at the same time. Don't be surprised if you get these errors in the evening, because that's when *everybody* is usually signed on. When this happens to you (and if it hasn't yet, don't feel left out; it will eventually), the first thing to do is try again. This time, it should work. If you're still having problems, sign off, sign on, and try again. Beyond that, throw up your hands in defeat and go have some ice cream. (Sometimes, that's the only thing that helps.)

The System Rudely Kicks You Off (Punted, Part 1)

You're minding your own business, wandering online through this and that, when WHAM! — Dorothy, you're not in Virginia anymore. The technical term for this is being *punted,* as in "Rats, I was punted."

It happens for no particular reason. It could be noise in the phone line; it may be your call-waiting feature kicking in; perhaps the digital gremlins are at work. Whatever the cause, sign on again and continue your pleasurable labors. If this happens frequently (more than about five times a week), call the folks at the phone company, tell them in a confident voice that you "recently lost numerous connections with your online provider" (which is a fancy way of saying that you get punted a lot), and ask them to check your line for interference.

There's usually no charge for checking your phone line, but the phone company only tests your line to the point where it comes into your home or apartment. If they find a problem in the Great Out There, then they fix it for free. If the problem is inside your walls, then someone else (probably you) pays for the repair.

America Online Doesn't Say a Word

Your friends said that America Online would talk to you. They even demonstrated it to really sell you on the point. So you went to the local computer store and spent big bucks on a sound card and speaker system. For that much money, America Online should say "Welcome" or "You've got mail" once in a while, if not perform entire Wagner operas. Instead, the service is mute — nothing changed. This situation quietly bothers you (as well it should).

First, make sure that your speakers are turned on and that the computer's sound system works with other programs. If your favorite game or multimedia program brings forth glorious melodies, the sound card is working just fine. If those programs can't make a peep either, double-check your new sound card to make sure that it's working. (Look for troubleshooting information in the sound card's documentation.)

When you know that the sound card is okay, make sure that the America Online access software knows that it's supposed to use sounds. Sign on and choose My AOL⇨Preferences and click the General button in the Preferences dialog box. Click the Enable Event Sounds and Enable Chat Room Sounds check boxes. Sign off and then sign back on. You should be greeted by a friendly "Welcome" just before the Welcome window appears. If the sound still isn't working, look for assistance in the Member Services area (keyword **Help**).

Your Computer Locks Up While Downloading Files (Punted, Part II)

You started with a simple goal to save some time. You invested in a 56,000-bit-per-second modem, the fastest that America Online supports. You carefully searched the America Online libraries until you found precisely the program you wanted. It's a great plan — except for one tiny little detail: Your computer loses its connection to America Online almost every time you try to download a big file. Whoops.

Don't worry — you're not the target of an electronic conspiracy. Believe it or not, the odds are good that this problem belongs to your America Online software (or maybe your phone line).

When you run the America Online software for the first time, it automatically searches the computer, looking for your modem. After it finds the modem, the software carries on a brief discussion with it. The America Online software wants to know what kind of modem it is, how fast it can communicate, what its favorite color is, and other things like that. Based on what it finds out, the software automatically configures itself.

The problem with this seemingly wonderful process is that modems aren't particularly communicative. In fact, they're pretty stupid. As a result, the America Online software may confuse your modem with another one from the same manufacturer. In the worst cases, it may think that you have a completely different kind of modem than you do!

To fix this problem, you must manually tell the America Online program what kind of modem you have. Luckily, America Online anticipated this problem, so it completely outlined the steps in the program's Offline Help system. Choose Help⇨Offline Help to bring up the Help Topics window and then click the Index tab. (If Windows points out that this is the first time you've ever used the help system, just nod and click whatever button Windows wants you to click to make the dialog box go away.) In the box near the top of the Help window, type **modem**. As you type, the help system locates the modem help files. Near the top of the help window, you should see an entry that says Modem. Just below that should be another entry called configuring manually. Double-click that entry. The help system displays all the steps you need to fix your modem configuration.

File Downloads Take Too Long

When you look at a file description, it displays a statistic labeled DL time, which is the approximate time the file will take to download in a perfect world with whatever speed of modem you're using right now. The most important phrases in that sentence are "approximate time" and "in a perfect world." You see, approximations are rarely correct, and the world is most certainly not perfect. Don't computers make stupid assumptions about real life?

Here's the reality of this download-time thing: The actual time it takes to download something depends on how busy America Online is, how noisy the phone line is, and the current phase of the moon. If your download is *really* big (like multiple megabytes in size), the AOL software may not even try to make an estimate, but instead present you with an approximate download time it picked out of thin air. (No, I'm not making this up.)

If a download seems to take forever, first be patient. If it looks as though the download really *will* take forever, cancel it; then try again or use the Download Manager and an Automatic AOL session to resume the download at a less busy time. See Chapter 16 for more information about that.

Automatic AOL Mail Goes Undercover

Automatic AOL sessions are great things that save you time, money, and effort. Of course, they also kind of hide your incoming mail from you.

Your mail really isn't hidden; you just have to access it through a new menu item (new to those of you who use Windows). To find your "lost" missives, choose MailCenter⇨Read Offline Mail⇨Incoming/Saved Mail.

Your Internet Mail Is Undeliverable

The America Online Internet mail gateway is great if you have friends or business associates on the Internet. Unfortunately, the Internet is a techno-logically wild place. Mail messages that are misaddressed in even the smallest way come screaming back into your mailbox, sent by angry computers with names like MAILER-DAEMON@mail02.mail.aol.com (which sounds like a character from *I Know Who You E-Mailed Last Summer*). The nice thing — if you can really say that about returned mail — is that these computers usually tell you what's wrong with the message.

If your friend's Internet mail address is minstrel@linguaplay.com, minstrel is the *user* part of the address (the person's screen name on that system), and linguaplay.com is the name of the computer, just as aol.com is the system name for America Online.

Such technical drivel is necessary for understanding the two most common mail errors: User Unknown and Host Unknown. Both messages mean that the address you entered has a slight problem. A User Unknown message means that the problem is with something to the left of the @ symbol in the address; Host Unknown means that the problem is to the right of the @ symbol. The error code appears in the subject area of the returned e-mail message.

Whatever is wrong, check and double-check the address to which you're sending mail. Be particularly alert for hostnames ending in something other than .com (such as .org or .net), because more and more of those sites appear on the Internet each year. Also, watch the difference between the number one (1) and the lowercase letter *L* (l), as well as the number zero (0) and the uppercase letter *O*. Computers get all hung up about this stuff.

If the address seems okay but the message still doesn't go through, try having the other person send a message to you. After you get that message, click the Reply button to insert the sender's address automatically. Copy the address (by highlighting it and choosing Edit⇨Copy) and paste it in the Address Book. Now you know that the address is correct.

The New Item on Your Go To Menu Goes to the Wrong Place

In Chapter 23, you skirt the frightening realm of nerddom by creating your own items on the Favorites⇨My Shortcuts menu. Now, however, the item is there in the menu, but it doesn't quite work. Don't let this little setback worry you. It usually takes a professional to make a menu item that doesn't work; you managed to do it with little or no training!

This glitch is relatively easy to fix. The problem is the keyword you entered in the Edit Shortcut Keys box — the odds are high that it suffers from a slight spelling problem. Choose Favorites⇨My Shortcuts⇨Edit Shortcuts from the toolbar and look at the keyword you entered for the nonworking menu item. You'll probably discover that the keyword is just the tiniest bit misspelled.

Use the menus to get back to this favorite of your online places and note the keyword when you arrive. Then go back to the Edit Favorite Places dialog box and type that keyword *very carefully.* Save your changes by clicking Save Changes. Then try your new item. Isn't programming fun?

Chapter 27

Ten Internet Resources Worth Checking Out

• •

In This Chapter

▶ Checking out the coolest newsgroups and mailing lists

▶ Finding fun-filled Gopher, Web, and FTP sites

• •

The Internet is a most amazing place. With connections to most of the countries in the world and a truly daunting array of services and information, the Internet is like a giant library, discussion group, and digital Wal-Mart all rolled into one. (And best of all, nobody hangs over your shoulder reminding you to keep quiet when you visit.)

This chapter gives you the expected ten interesting things to try on the Internet, plus a couple of bonus items. The goal is to pique your interest in the Internet and give you a sample of the incredible range of stuff you can find out there.

To use these Internet services, go to the Internet Connection and click the appropriate service button (World Wide Web, Gopher, Newsgroups, and so on). If you need some help with the Internet Connection itself, see Chapter 17.

alt.folklore.urban (Newsgroup)

Heard the one about the beached whale the Oregon Department of Transportation blew up with dynamite? Or about the Procter & Gamble logo being linked to "forces of evil"? These are *urban legends* — stories that get told and retold until they take on lives of their own. And they have a home on the Internet.

If you like this kind of thing (or if you've heard a legend and want to know whether it's true), check out the `alt.folklore.urban` newsgroup. You find discussion and commentary on all things odd, improbable, and larger than life. Sign up at keyword **Newsgroups**. In the Newsgroups window, click Expert Add, type **alt.folklore.urban**, and then click Add. When the system asks whether you *really* want to subscribe to the newsgroup, click OK.

For an America-Online–based trip through the world of urban legends, check out keyword **Urban Legends**. In addition to a great library of legends, the area includes games, an online theater troupe, and much more. Give it a try!

In case you're wondering, the Procter & Gamble logo is just that — a logo — and nothing more. And yes, the Oregon Department of Transportation really blew up a beached whale with dynamite back in 1970. (Don't worry — the whale was already dead before getting scattered over the landscape.)

rec.food.veg (Newsgroup)

For those of you with an eye for the greener things in food (or you carnivores who'd like to try something a little different for a change), subscribe to the `rec.food.veg` newsgroup. It covers the best in vegetarian food and lifestyles. For help with subscribing, see the preceding section about `alt.folklore.urban`.

If you're looking for recipes, try `rec.food.veg.cooking` — some truly delicious recipes are in there!

The OCF Online Library (Gopher)

A delicate balance keeps the world in order. I don't mean the balance of military power — I'm talking about the Balance of Normality. Some places on earth (like Britain and the Great Plains states) are particularly level-headed. Others, like Berkeley, California, aren't.

So what happens when you give those zanies at Berkeley a bunch of networked computers? They come up with the OCF (Open Computing Facility) Online Library. Who else could (or even would) compile a collection that includes the Declaration of Independence, the CIA World Fact Book, a parody of Edgar Allan Poe's *The Raven* ("Once before a console dreary, while I programmed, weak and weary. . . ."), and a wonderful set of transcripts from *Monty Python* movies and TV shows?

To check out this place for yourself, click in the navigation bar's Address box, and then type **gopher://gopher.ocf.berkeley.edu/11/Library** and press Enter. By the way, capitalization counts in Gopher addresses, so be sure to type *Library* with a capital L.

The Mother of All Gophers (Gopher)

It's the "Big Gophuna" — your link to the Gopher world. With one connection to this service, you can reach almost every Gopher in the whole world. (No, I'm not kidding.) And it's available right from America Online.

To get there, type **gopher://gopher.tc.umn.edu** in the Address box on the navigation bar and press Enter (or Return).

InterText Magazine (Mailing List)

If you like to read, the Internet has plenty to offer — and it comes right to you. If fiction is your interest, subscribe to the *InterText* online magazine, and, every two months, it appears in your America Online mailbox. *InterText* is a moderated collection of subscriber-submitted fiction, which means that it won't necessarily include your story just because you send it in.

Subscribe by e-mailing a request to subscriptions@intertext.com. On the Subject line, type either **ASCII** (to show that you want the magazine e-mailed to you) or **NOTIFY** (you receive an e-mail when a new issue comes out, but you must go to the Web site and pick up a copy on your own). Your subscription starts when the next issue comes out.

NETHUMOR (Mailing List)

The NETHUMOR mailing list offers a daily dose of humorous Web sites, mailing lists, and other Net resources. It includes the site address, general information, and a brief sample of the site's humor. The listing also notes whether the site offers any (ahem) mature jokes that aren't fit for kids (and some accountants).

To add some fun to your life, send an e-mail to majordomo@bapp.com. The subject can be anything, but in the body of the message, type **SUBSCRIBE NETHUMOR** and then your Internet e-mail address (that's your America Online screen name with **@aol.com** after it). Because my screen name is JKaufeld, my subscription request was SUBSCRIBE NETHUMOR jkaufeld@aol.com.

Trojan Room Coffee Machine (World Wide Web)

This entry falls under the heading Technology Run Amok. A bunch of computer people at Cambridge University decided that walking down several flights of stairs for a cup of coffee, only to find out that the pot was empty, was too much trouble, so they devised a clever solution worthy of their time and talents: They put their coffeepot on the Internet.

Yes, from anywhere in the world, you can see a digitized video image of the coffeepot and find out whether those folks are low on java. The address to use is www.cl.cam.ac.uk/coffee/coffee.html.

WimpyPoint Slide Presentations (World Wide Web)

Looking for a quick, easy, and free way to create professional presentations for your next business meeting or Internet chat? Do you need to collaborate with someone across the city or around the world on a presentation? Would you like a simple way to give a presentation using any Internet-connected Web browser on the planet?

If anything in the previous paragraph sounds appealing, take a trip to wimpy.arsdigita.com and try WimpyPoint, the Web-based answer to a laptop presentation system. The service costs nothing to use, requires no special software (other than a Web browser), and takes only a couple of moments to learn. WimpyPoint stores your presentations on its server, which makes working on a presentation with your friends and cohorts easy. In short, WimpyPoint makes a great example of how the Internet puts a new (and highly useful) spin on an old idea.

 Even though the WimpyPoint site doesn't start with the standard www moniker, it's still a Web site. Just feed it to the address box on the America Online navigation bar, press Enter, and watch it appear on your screen.

Net Search Services

After using the World Wide Web and the rest of the Internet a few times, you start wanting more. It's addictive — just like those little candy bars you get in the fall. Luckily, some highly technical people got themselves addicted to the Internet and created a variety of indexes all over the Internet.

To get more of the Net than most television production companies want you to have, check out these indexes:

All search engines (Web)	www.allsearchengines.com
AltaVista (Web)	www.altavista.com
Copernic (Web)	www.copernic.com
DejaNews (Newsgroups)	www.dejanews.com
Excite Netdirectory (Web)	www.excite.com
Gopher Home	gopher://gopher.tc.umn.edu
Infoseek Guide (Web)	www.infoseek.com
Lycos (Web)	www.lycos.com
Mining Company (Web)	www.miningco.com
NetFind (Web)	Keyword **NetFind**
Publicly Accessible Mailing Lists (mailing lists)	www.neosoft.com/internet/paml
Yahoo! (Web)	www.yahoo.com

MS-DOS, Macintosh, and Windows Software Archives (FTP)

These last three entries are software libraries (or *FTP sites*) on the Internet. Each library has a *bunch* of software: business programs, utilities, virus detectors, and (of course) games. Each site specializes in programs for a different platform, so be sure to hook up to the right one for your computer.

MS-DOS	oak.oakland.edu
Macintosh	mirrors.aol.com/pub/info-mac
Windows	ftp.winsite.com
A little of everything	mirrors.aol.com

These are only a few of the most popular FTP sites — you can find plenty more where these came from. Look on the Internet Connection message boards, to find out about other sites. For more about FTP in general, flip to Chapter 17.

Chapter 28

Ten Terms for the Chat-Room-Challenged

In This Chapter

▶ Telling people when you leave, come back, or feel tickled pink

▶ Expressing your heart in four letters or less

No matter where you go in the People Connection area (or any of the other America Online chatting areas), odd abbreviations and wacky terms wait to prey upon you. This chapter unmasks ten (or so) of the most common abbreviations and terms skulking around out there. Read about them, memorize them, and use them — it's for your own safety (and to keep you from ::blushing:: too much in the chats).

Away from the Keyboard (AFK)

You're chatting the night away in the People Connection and suddenly hear the call of nature — or, as so often happens to me, you're assailed by the Call of the Small-Bladdered Dog Who Needs to Go Outside Right Away. It takes too long to type "I have to go let the dog out before she detonates all over the kitchen floor like she did last week when I was in a chat room and ignored her because I was having too good a time." (Besides, nobody really wants to know that much about it.) It's rude to just pop out of the room without saying good-bye to everyone. (Besides, you're having too much fun to leave now.) But the dog's timer is ticking, and the linoleum's looking scared. What to do, oh, what to do?

Here's your solution: Type **AFK**, press Enter (or Return), and then put the pupster on a trajectory for the backyard. *AFK* is the universal chat room notation for Away From the Keyboard — online shorthand for "I'll be right back." Just remember to let everyone know that you're BAK (covered in the next section) when you return!

If someone you're chatting with types a quick AFK, you should reply **K** (short for "okay") so that the person knows that you understand and that you are waiting for him or her to return. Kinda scary that something as wild and frolicsome as a chat room is so darn organized, isn't it?

Back at the Keyboard (BAK)

Telling folks that you're AFK is common courtesy, but it's equally important to let them know when you return from your task, suffused with the glow of a Job Well Done (or a Dog Well Launched, as the case may be). A quick **BAK** is all it takes to announce your reentry into the conversation.

Drinks and Glassware

Nothing soothes the soul (or makes friends faster) than a couple of digital drinks in your favorite chat room. If bartending duties fall to you, be sure that your bar stocks all the best in online glassware. After all, serving coffee in a martini glass certainly won't win you any friends!

c(_)   Coffee cup

c|_| Root beer mug (of course!)

_/   Double old-fashioned or generic bar glass

|_| Water or generic kitchen glass

Y   Martini or stemmed wine glass (yes, it takes some imagination)

As you see other cool glasses wander by online, jot them down here or on the Cheat Sheet in the front of this book. You don't want to drop a good glass!

Emoticons

Sometimes you need to say more than mere words can convey (which explains why we have comic books). But how do you include a picture in a typewritten message? Easy — with *emoticons,* or emotion icons.

Feel free to use these symbols in your e-mail messages, bulletin board postings, and everyday conversation. Emoticons make up for the facial expressions and other kinds of body language that are missing from electronic communication. And they're kinda fun to type, too:

: -)	Smile
; -)	Wink
: - /	Befuddled
: - (	Frown
: - p	Bronx cheer
8 -)	I drew a figure eight on my face (actually, it's a smiley wearing glasses)

For a more complete list of the best emoticons that typing can make, check out the Smileys button behind keyword **Mail Extras**.

Emotion and Action — ::Smiles and Waves::

If you hang out in the People Connection too long or accidentally wander into one of the online simulations (keyword **Gaming**; then click the Simming button), someone may enter the chat room and ::wave to all:: or ::looks bewildered, walks into a wall::. These folks don't love colons that much (only a doctor can muster that much affection for a simple organ). No, they're *doing something* in the chat room. Items encased in double colons usually indicate action (::swinging on the chandelier::), show a facial expression (::looking completely puzzled::), or disclose thoughts (::wondering if I should even answer that question::).

Hugs { } and Kisses*

Have a friend who's feeling glum? There's nothing like a hug or two to keep someone going. You can give someone a little hug { }, lots of little hugs { }{ }{ }{ }, or a great big hug {{{{{ }}}}} — the choice is entirely yours.

These days, the online kiss (*) is one of the best ways to show affection. The kiss can be quick or long — *really* long if need be, and it's safe because it doesn't lead to anything, except perhaps an online hug ({ }).

Laughing Out Loud (LOL)

Although LOL isn't a computer acronym, you certainly see it all over the place these days. *LOL* is Internet shorthand for "I'm laughing out loud!" A variation on this theme is LOLOLOL, which means "That's really, really funny" or "I particularly like consonant-vowel combinations tonight and wanted to share one with you."

Lofting

Conversations flow wild and free in a busy chat room, but sometimes you want to share a private thought with that special someone. Or course, one thought quickly turns to many, and before you know it, the chat room banter leaves you far behind. Focusing on a private, instant-message–based conversation while in a chat room is called *lofting.* Often someone types a message like `Greetings from the loft!` to show that he or she is still around, but not really listening to the chat room right then.

Rolling on the Floor Laughing (ROFL)

Use this abbreviation when someone *seriously* tickles your funny bone. Like its little brother `LOL`, `ROFL` is a communication shortcut that most everybody on America Online understands. Expect to find it in the People Connection and on various message boards.

Swatting IMsects

Instant messages are wonderful things — at least until you get inundated with them, that is. If a swarm of IMs distracts you from the chat room, let everybody know by dropping in a quick comment like `Sorry I'm not paying attention — I'm busy swatting IMsects!` Although it's a small thing, it assures your chat room buddies that you aren't ignoring them (at least not completely).

Index

• *B* •

• C •

• *D* •

• X •

• Y •

• Z •

Notes

Notes

Notes

Notes

Discover Dummies Online!

The Dummies Web Site is your fun and friendly online resource for the latest information about ...For Dummies® books and your favorite topics. The Web site is the place to communicate with us, exchange ideas with other ...For Dummies readers, chat with authors, and have fun!

Ten Fun and Useful Things You Can Do at www.dummies.com

1. Win free ...For Dummies books and more!

2. Register your book and be entered in a prize drawing.

3. Meet your favorite authors through the IDG Books Author Chat Series.

4. Exchange helpful information with other ...For Dummies readers.

5. Discover other great ...For Dummies books you must have!

6. Purchase Dummieswear™ exclusively from our Web site.

7. Buy ...For Dummies books online.

8. Talk to us. Make comments, ask questions, get answers!

9. Download free software.

10. Find additional useful resources from authors.

Link directly to these ten fun and useful things at
http://www.dummies.com/10useful

For other technology titles from IDG Books Worldwide, go to
www.idgbooks.com

Not on the Web yet? It's easy to get started with Dummies 101®: The Internet For Windows® 98 or The Internet For Dummies®, 6th Edition, at local retailers everywhere.

IDG BOOKS WORLDWIDE
BOOK REGISTRATION

We want to hear from you!

Visit **http://my2cents.dummies.com** to register this book and tell us how you liked it!

- Get entered in our monthly prize giveaway.

- Give us feedback about this book — tell us what you like best, what you like least, or maybe what you'd like to ask the author and us to change!

- Let us know any other *...For Dummies*® topics that interest you.

Your feedback helps us determine what books to publish, tells us what coverage to add as we revise our books, and lets us know whether we're meeting your needs as a *...For Dummies* reader. You're our most valuable resource, and what you have to say is important to us!

Not on the Web yet? It's easy to get started with *Dummies 101*®: *The Internet For Windows*® *98* or *The Internet For Dummies*®, 6th Edition, at local retailers everywhere.

Or let us know what you think by sending us a letter at the following address:

...For Dummies Book Registration
Dummies Press
7260 Shadeland Station, Suite 100
Indianapolis, IN 46256-3917
Fax 317-596-5498

BESTSELLING
BOOK SERIES